THE CLAY SANSKRIT LIBRARY
FOUNDED BY JOHN & JENNIFER CLAY

EDITED BY

RICHARD GOMBRICH

WWW.CLAYSANSKRITLIBRARY.ORG
WWW.NYUPRESS.ORG

Artwork by Robert Beer.
Cover design by Isabelle Onians.
Layout & typesetting by Somadeva Vasudeva.
Printed and Bound in Great Britain by
TJ International, Cornwall on acid free paper

MAHĀBHĀRATA
BOOK THREE

THE FOREST
VOLUME FOUR

TRANSLATED BY

W. J. JOHNSON

NEW YORK UNIVERSITY PRESS
JJC FOUNDATION
2005

First Edition 2005

The Clay Sanskrit Library is co-published by
New York University Press
and the JJC Foundation.

Further information about this volume
and the rest of the Clay Sanskrit Library
is available on the following websites:
www.claysanskritlibrary.org
www.nyupress.org

ISBN 978-0-8147-4278-5

Library of Congress Cataloging-in-Publication Data
Mahābhārata. Vanaparva Adhyāya 273–315.
English & Sanskrit.
Mahabharata. Book 3, "The forest." Vol. 4
edited and translated by William Johnson.
p. cm. – (The Clay Sanskrit Library)
In English with Sanskrit parallel text;
includes translation from Sanskrit.
Includes bibliographical references and index.
ISBN 978-0-8147-4278-5
I. Johnson, W.J., 1951–
II. Title. III. Series.
BL1138.242.V36E5 2005
294.5'92304521–dc22 2004020166

CONTENTS

A *sandhi* grid is printed on the inside of the back cover

SANSKRIT ALPHABETICAL ORDER

Vowels:	*a ā i ī u ū ṛ ṝ ḷ ḹ e ai o au ṃ ḥ*
Gutturals:	*k kh g gh ṅ*
Palatals:	*c ch j jh ñ*
Retroflex:	*ṭ ṭh ḍ ḍh ṇ*
Labials:	*p ph b bh m*
Semivowels:	*y r l v*
Spirants:	*ś ṣ s h*

GUIDE TO SANSKRIT PRONUNCIATION

a	b*u*t
ā, â	r*a*ther
i	s*i*t
ī, î	f*ee*
u	p*u*t
ū,û	b*oo*
ṛ	vocalic *r*, American p*ur*dy or English p*re*tty
ṝ	lengthened *ṛ*
ḷ	vocalic *l*, ab*le*
e, ê, ē	m*a*de, esp. in Welsh pronunciation
ai	b*i*te
o, ô, ō	r*o*pe, esp. Welsh pronunciation; Italian s*o*lo
au	s*ou*nd
ṃ	*anusvāra* nasalizes the preceding vowel
ḥ	*visarga*, a voiceless aspiration (resembling English *h*), or like Scottish lo*ch*, or an aspiration with a faint echoing of the preceding vowel so that *taiḥ* is pronounced *taih*^{i}

k	lu*ck*
kh	blo*ckh*ead
g	*g*o
gh	bi*gh*ead
ṅ	a*n*ger
c	*ch*ill
ch	mat*chh*ead
j	*j*og
jh	aspirated *j*, he*dgeh*og
ñ	ca*ny*on
ṭ	retroflex *t*, *t*ry (with the tip of tongue turned up to touch the hard palate)
ṭh	same as the preceding but aspirated
ḍ	retroflex *d* (with the tip of tongue turned up to touch the hard palate)
ḍh	same as the preceding but aspirated
ṇ	retroflex *n* (with the tip of tongue turned up to touch the hard palate)
t	French *t*out
th	ten*t h*ook

d	*d*inner
dh	guil*dh*all
n	*n*ow
p	*p*ill
ph	u*ph*eaval
b	*b*efore
bh	a*bh*orrent
m	*m*ind
y	*y*es
r	trilled, resembling the Italian pronunciation of *r*
l	*l*inger
v	*w*ord
ś	*sh*ore
ṣ	retroflex *sh* (with the tip of the tongue turned up to touch the hard palate)
s	hi*ss*
h	*h*ood

CSL PUNCTUATION OF ENGLISH

The acute accent on Sanskrit words when they occur outside of the Sanskrit text itself, marks stress, e.g. Ramáyana. It is not part of traditional Sanskrit orthography, transliteration or transcription, but we supply it here to guide readers in the pronunciation of these unfamiliar words. Since no Sanskrit word is accented on the last syllable it is not necessary to accent disyllables, e.g. Rama.

The second CSL innovation designed to assist the reader in the pronunciation of lengthy unfamiliar words is to insert an unobtrusive middle dot between semantic word breaks in compound names (provided the word break does not fall on a vowel resulting from the fusion of two vowels), e.g. Maha·bhárata, but Ramáyana (not Rama·áyana). Our dot echoes the punctuating middle dot (·) found in the oldest surviving samples of written Sanskrit, the Ashokan inscriptions of the third century BCE.

The deep layering of Sanskrit narrative has also dictated that we use quotation marks only to announce the beginning and end of every direct speech, and not at the beginning of every paragraph.

CSL PUNCTUATION OF SANSKRIT

The Sanskrit text is also punctuated, in accordance with the punctuation of the English translation. In mid-verse, the punctuation will not alter the *sandhi* or the scansion. Proper names are capitalized, as are the initial words of verses (or paragraphs in prose texts). Most Sanskrit metres have four "feet" *(pāda):* where possible we print the common *śloka* metre on two lines. The capitalization of verse beginnings makes it easy for the reader to recognize longer metres where it is necessary to print the four metrical feet over four or eight lines. In the Sanskrit text, we use French *Guillemets* (e.g. *«kva saṃcicīrṣuḥ?»*) instead of English quotation marks (e.g. "Where are you off to?") to avoid confusion with the apostrophes used for vowel elision in *sandhi*.

Sanskrit presents the learner with a challenge: *sandhi* ("euphonic combination"). *Sandhi* means that when two words are joined in connected speech or writing (which in Sanskrit reflects speech), the last letter (or even letters) of the first word often changes; compare the way we pronounce "the" in "the beginning" and "the end."

In Sanskrit the first letter of the second word may also change; and if both the last letter of the first word and the first letter of the second are vowels, they may fuse. This has a parallel in English: a nasal consonant is inserted between two vowels that would otherwise coalesce: "a pear" and "an apple." Sanskrit vowel fusion may produce ambiguity. The chart at the back of each book gives the full *sandhi* system.

Fortunately it is not necessary to know these changes in order to start reading Sanskrit. For that, what is important is to know the form of the second word without *sandhi* (pre-*sandhi*), so that it can be recognized or looked up in a dictionary. Therefore we are printing Sanskrit with a system of punctuation that will indicate, unambiguously, the original form of the second word, i.e., the form without *sandhi*. Such *sandhi* mostly concerns the fusion of two vowels.

In Sanskrit, vowels may be short or long and are written differently accordingly. We follow the general convention that a vowel with no mark above it is short. Other books mark a long vowel either with a bar called a macron (*ā*) or with a circumflex (*â*). Our system uses the macron, except that for initial vowels in *sandhi* we use a circumflex to indicate that originally the vowel was short, or the shorter of two possibilities (*e* rather than *ai*, *o* rather than *au*).

When we print initial	*â*, before *sandhi* that vowel was	*a*
	î or *ê*,	*i*
	û or *ô*,	*u*
	âi,	*e*

âu,	*o*
ā,	*ā* (i.e., the same)
ī,	*ī* (i.e., the same)
ū,	*ū* (i.e., the same)
ē,	*ī*
ō,	*ū*
āi,	*ai*
āu,	*au*

', before *sandhi* there was a vowel *a*

FURTHER HELP WITH VOWEL SANDHI

When a final short vowel (*a*, *i* or *u*) has merged into a following vowel, we print ' at the end of the word, and when a final long vowel (*ā*, *ī* or *ū*) has merged into a following vowel we print " at the end of the word. The vast majority of these cases will concern a final *a* or *ā*.

Examples:

What before *sandhi* was *atra asti* is represented as *atr' âsti*

atra āste	*atr' āste*
kanyā asti	*kany" âsti*
kanyā āste	*kany" āste*
atra iti	*atr' êti*
kanyā iti	*kany" êti*
kanyā īpsitā	*kany" ēpsitā*

Finally, three other points concerning the initial letter of the second word:

(1) A word that before *sandhi* begins with *ṛ* (vowel), after *sandhi* begins with *r* followed by a consonant: *yatha" rtu* represents pre-*sandhi* *yathā ṛtu*.

(2) When before *sandhi* the previous word ends in *t* and the following word begins with *ś*, after *sandhi* the last letter of the previous word is *c* and the following word begins with *ch*: *syāc chāstravit* represents pre-*sandhi* *syāt śāstravit*.

(3) Where a word begins with *h* and the previous word ends with a double consonant, this is our simplified spelling to show the pre-*sandhi*

form: *tad hasati* is commonly written as *tad dhasati*, but we write *tadd hasati* so that the original initial letter is obvious.

COMPOUNDS

We also punctuate the division of compounds (*samāsa*), simply by inserting a thin vertical line between words. There are words where the decision whether to regard them as compounds is arbitrary. Our principle has been to try to guide readers to the correct dictionary entries.

EXAMPLE

Where the Deva·nágari script reads:

कुम्भस्थली रक्षतु वो विकीर्णसिन्दूररेणुर्द्विरदाननस्य।
प्रशान्तये विघ्नतमश्छटानां निष्ठ्यूतबालातपपल्लवेव॥

Others would print:

kumbhasthalī rakṣatu vo vikīrṇasindūrareṇur dviradānanasya /
praśāntaye vighnatamaśchaṭānāṃ niṣṭhyūtabālātapapallaveva //

We print:

Kumbha|sthalī rakṣatu vo vikīrṇa|sindūra|reṇur dvirad'|ānanasya
praśāntaye vighna|tamaś|chaṭānāṃ niṣṭhyūta|bāl'|ātapa|pallav" êva.

And in English:

"May Ganésha's domed forehead protect you! Streaked with vermilion dust, it seems to be emitting the spreading rays of the rising sun to pacify the teeming darkness of obstructions."

"Nava·sáhasanka and the Serpent Princess" I.3 by Padma·gupta

INTRODUCTION

"The Forest Book" *(Vana/parvan)** is the third book of the great Indian epic, the Maha·bhárata. The central narrative of the Maha·bhárata deals with the conflict between two sets of cousins, the Káuravas and the Pándavas (who are both the descendants of a ruler called Bharata), for the lordship of what is now an area of northwest India. In terms of this narrative, "The Forest Book" covers the twelve years of the Pándavas' exile in the forest, a penalty imposed upon them by the Káuravas because they have lost a rigged dicing match.

Much of the material presented in the *Vana/parvan* is, however, tangential to that account, and the book has been described as a "storehouse of myths, legends and instructions of all sorts, told to relieve the tedium of life in the forest."* If that was the intention, then it must be counted successful beyond the frame of the narrative, since a number of these stories are now among the best known in Indian literature.*

The present volume consists of the concluding four episodes of "The Forest Book":* "The Story of Rama" *(Rām'/ôpākhyāna)*, "The Glorification of the Faithful Wife" *(Pati/vratā/māhātmya)*,* "The Robbing of the Earrings" *(Kuṇḍa-l'/āharaṇa/parvan)* and "About the Drilling Sticks" *(Āraṇe-ya/parvan)*.

Although consecutive in the text, these episodes differ considerably from one another in character, and as a result they give some indication of the range, preoccupations and style of the Maha·bhárata as a whole. The first two episodes are stories told by the brahmin sage Markandéya to the exiled Pándava king Yudhi·shthira, who is feeling sorry for himself, especially after the events surrounding the abduction of Dráupadi (*Kṛṣṇā*), the Pándavas' wife. The stories of Rama and Sávitri are therefore presented as morale-raising instances of, respectively, a hero overcoming even greater odds, and a virtuous wife who rescues her whole family. The third episode tells of how one of the Pándavas' main opponents (and unbeknownst to them, their older half brother),* Karna, is tricked, and thereby weakened, by the god Indra acting on their behalf. "The Forest Book" concludes with a near-fatal encounter between the Pándavas and a personification of Dharma, the Law. This takes the form of a verbal contest, which is eventually won by Dharma's son, Yudhi·shthira—a victory that secures the Pándavas' ability to remain incognito during their thirteenth year in exile, an additional condition imposed by the Káuravas after the dicing match. This marks a major transition in the epic story and provides a bridge to the next book of the Maha·bhárata, "The Book of Viráta" *(Virāṭa/parvan)*, in which the events of that final year are narrated.

The Story of Rama
Rām'/ôpākhyāna (3.273–292)

The basic narrative tells how Rama, having been dubiously exiled from his kingdom to the forest, suffers the abduction of his wife Sita at the hands of the demon Rávana. With the aid of his brother Lákshmana and an army of monkeys, Rama rescues her from her imprisonment in Lanka, kills Rávana and eventually regains his kingdom. There has been considerable debate about the relation of this condensed account of the story of Rama to that presented at length in Valmíki's epic Ramáyana. Most current scholarship accepts the view that "the source of the *Rām'/ôpākhyāna* was a memorized version of the Ramáyana," probably drawn from the Northern recension of the latter prior to the completion of the Ramáyana as we now have it.* Indeed, BROCKINGTON suggests that the completed version itself depends on the *Rām'/ôpākhyāna*, with each epic having been, by turns, the source of the other.* It is not surprising, therefore, that there are instances where the two narratives diverge, where material is rearranged, and where differences in detail and emphasis are evident.

One difference in emphasis between the *Rām'/ôpākhyāna* and the finalized Ramáyana concerns the depiction of Rama.* With the exception of a brief episode where he is apparently presented as an incarnation of Vishnu (276.5), the Maha·bhárata's version of the story portrays Rama as a heroic, human figure. Indeed, the fact that Rama can, as a human, overcome his misfortune is precisely the point that Markandéya is trying to make when he tells the story to Yudhi·shthira, in an attempt to encourage similar resilience in the Pándava hero.

Other differences of emphasis concern the comparatively greater interest shown by the *Rām'/ôpākhyāna* in the details of the battle, and in the treatment of Sita. Because the *Rām'/ôpākhyāna* is not aware of the *Uttara/kāṇḍa* of the Ramáyana,* the contentious episodes of Rama's banishment of his wife after their return to Ayódhya, at the prompting of public opinion, and her subsequent final disappearance into the earth, are both absent from the Maha·bhárata's version of the story.

What is present, however, is a scene in which Rama, comparing Sita to an "oblation licked by a dog" (291.13), rejects her on the ground that she has, willy-nilly, been polluted by Rávana's touch. At this point, Sita, supported by the gods, offers a spirited defense of herself, and Rama agrees to take her back, but without the ordeal by fire that is required of her in the Ramáyana. In due course husband and wife proceed together to Ayódhya. As SCHARF has pointed out,* the parallel that the Maha·bhárata apparently intends to draw between Yudhi·shthira and Rama on the one hand, and *Kṛṣṇā* (alias Dráupadi) and Sita on the other, is therefore hardly exact,* since Yudhi·shthira harbors no doubts at all about *Kṛṣṇā*'s purity, and is full of regret for her abduction and distress. In fact, while he is clearly supposed to draw strength from the example of Rama, Yudhi·shthira evidently imagines no such inspiring correspondence between his own wife and Sita,* since he goes on to ask if there has ever been a wife so pure and devoted as *Kṛṣṇā* (293.3). And in response, it is not to Sita that Markandéya turns as an exemplar, but to Sávitri.

THE GLORIFICATION OF THE FAITHFUL WIFE
Pativratā/māhātmya (293–299)

This section of the "The Forest Book," otherwise known after its heroine as "The Story of Sávitri," is one of the best-known episodes in the epic, and has been widely admired both in India and beyond.

Gustav Holst, for instance, composed a chamber opera on the theme of the devoted wife Sávitri, who proves herself a match for death and brings her husband Sátyavat back to life. Holst omitted what, in the Indian context, is perhaps as significant: Sávitri causes her father-in-law's eyesight to be restored, and ensures that her father has a hundred sons to continue the lineage.

Whereas the Western (and Christian) tradition is concerned with the redemptive power of love, the Indian is as much, or more, preoccupied with Dharma, "the Law." It is Sávitri's demonstrable knowledge of Dharma—right behavior in the right context, in accordance with universal principles—that convinces Yama (Death) to release Sátyavat and to grant her other requests. Dharma, in Sávitri's own words, "is the essential thing,"* "the eternal duty,"* known and acted upon by "the wise."

Clearly, Sávitri herself is one of the wise, but it is the nature of her dharma as a woman that, without a husband, she is incomplete, effectively "dead."* By saving her husband she thereby saves herself. It is this double peril (more than double, if the wider effect on parents and parents-in-law is to be taken into account) which makes Sávitri's encounter with Yama so crucial and so dramatically compelling.

While the parallel with Dráupadi as savior of the Pándavas frames "The Glorification of the Faithful Wife" and accounts for its inclusion in the Maha·bhárata as a whole, it needs no special justification when it comes to its own merits. In contrast to the compressed and sometimes breathless narrative of "The Story of Rama," the story of Sávitri unfolds with considerable charm and attention to detail, effortlessly evoking familial relationships and the life of various ascetic and exiled groups in the forest. Its reputation as a distinctive work of literature is fully deserved.

The Robbing of the Earrings
Kuṇḍal'|āharaṇa|parvan (300–310)

The earrings referred to in the title of this section belong to Karna, a major ally of Duryódhana and the Káuravas, although, as is shown in this episode (and as later becomes clear to the protagonists themselves), he is actually the Pándavas' older half brother.* Yudhi·shthira is concerned that, by virtue of his earrings and armor, Karna cannot be killed in battle. Indra (Shakra) undertakes to benefit the Pándavas by disguising himself as a brahmin and begging the earrings. Karna's father, the Sun (Surya), tries to preempt the "robbery" by warning his son of Indra's intention (300–302). Karna, however, cannot refuse a mendicant brahmin or break his vow to give alms, and he exchanges his immortality-conferring earrings for the single use of an infallible spear (310).

In this way he weakens himself and ensures his eventual death at the hands of his archrival, the Pándava hero Árjuna, who is also Indra's son.

Karna is presented here as conforming to the duty *(dharma)* of a perfect warrior *(kṣatriya)* in his devotion to brahmins, and in being the donor par excellence.* Given that he is supposed to come from a *sūta* family—i.e., one of mixed, and therefore inferior, caste—this warrior behavior is seemingly ironic. However, embedded at the heart of the tale of the robbing of the earrings, there is the story of Karna's true parentage, and of his adoption after his real mother, Kunti (Pritha), has had to cast him adrift (303–309). This provides what, in literary terms, is probably the most striking passage in the entire episode, Kunti's lament for her baby son as she launches him, Moses-like, onto the waters of the Ashva River (308.10–21).

About the Drilling Sticks
Āraṇeya/parvan (311–315)

The drilling sticks in question are the two sticks used by a brahmin to light his ritual fires in the forest. After the sticks are carried off on the antlers of a deer, the brahmin asks the five Pándava brothers to retrieve them and thereby save the ritual. The brothers set off, but are thwarted. Tired and thirsty, each in turn approaches a pond to drink. There they are challenged by the voice of a yaksha (a tree spirit) to answer its questions before they drink, on pain of death. All the brothers, except for Yudhi·shthira, ignore the yaksha, drink from the pond, and fall down dead. Yudhi·shthira, however, allows himself to be questioned at length by the yaksha about the nature of the world and its denizens. Knowing all the answers, precisely because he is so well versed in dharma (the way things are), he is rewarded with his brothers' resurrection. The yaksha then reveals itself to be Yudhi·shthira's father, the personification of the Law (Dharma). He returns the drilling sticks to the brahmin, and guarantees the Pándavas' anonymity during their forthcoming yearlong stay in the court of King Viráta. With brahmin blessings ringing in their ears, the brothers and their wife, *Kṛṣṇā* (Dráupadi), prepare to quit the forest and start their thirteenth year in exile.

The yaksha's questions, which occupy the bulk of this episode, almost all belong to a category of verbal puzzle known as *praśna*. In this they link themselves to a lengthy speculative tradition that reaches back through the Upanishads. As SHULMAN puts it:*

> *Both questions and answers tend to the metaphysical, with the latent center of meaning—the ultimate reality that is the true object of the quest—usually present only as a suggested power situated somewhere between the two explicit poles of the contest.*

The exchanges between the yaksha and Yudhi·shthira culminate in a well-known set of questions and responses (313.114–118) about the nature of worldly existence.* The yaksha asks:

> *Who is happy? What is quite extraordinary? What is the path? And what is the news?*

Ever-present are the twin powers of time and death. Dharma may seem opaque, but that is because our experience is opaque. The highest dharma in such circumstances is, in Yudhi·shthira's view, compassion (313.129). His father approves, and returns his brothers to life. Like Sávitri, the Pándava king has used his knowledge and wisdom—his mastery of Dharma—to gain a reprieve. Beyond this, Yudhi·shthira's answers demonstrate that beguiling mixture of the universal and the particular which exemplifies the Maha·bhárata's underlying poetic power—a power that has the potential to speak to common human concerns across cultures and centuries. It is the aim of this translation to realize at least some of that potential.

NOTES

1 Referred to as the *Āraṇyaka/parvan* in the Critical Edition.

2 BROCKINGTON, J. *The Sanskrit Epics* (Leiden: Brill, 1998), p. 30.

3 Which is not to say that they may not have existed in other forms before the Maha·bhárata was compiled.

4 *Adhyāyas* 273–315 of the edition of the Maha·bhárata used as the basis for this volume: *The Mahābhāratam with the Bharata Bhawadeepa Commentary of Nīlakaṇṭha*, RAMACHANDRASHASTRI KINJAWADEKAR, ed. (Poona: Chitrashala Press, 1929–36; repr. New Delhi: Oriental Book Reprint Corporation, 1978; 2nd ed. 1979). Vol. 3 *Vana Parva.* The differences between this text and that constituting the Critical Edition are mostly trivial. The most notable variance is the retention by KINJAWADEKAR of some verses that the editors of the Critical Edition relegate to the critical apparatus or the Appendix, most extensively in the Aranéya·parvan ("About the Drilling Sticks").

5 Referred to as "The Story of Sávitri" *(Sāvitry/upākhyāna)* in the Critical Edition.

6 To be precise, he is the older half brother of the three eldest Pándavas, viz. Yudhi·shthira, Bhima and Árjuna, since, in Kunti, they share the same mother.

7 BROCKINGTON, JOHN *The Sanskrit Epics* (Leiden: Brill, 1998), p. 474.

8 Ibid. p. 477. See BROCKINGTON pp. 473–77 for a summary of views about the relationship of the two accounts, and some treatment of the principal divergences.

9 The difference between the two versions on this point is, however, perhaps not as great as is sometimes suggested, given that the core story in the Ramáyana shows little interest itself in a significant equation of Rama and Vishnu, as, for instance, pointed out by PETER SCHARF, *Rāmopākhyāna—The Story of Rāma in the Mahābhārata* (London: Routledge Curzon, 2003), pp. 5–6.

10 Clearly a late addition to the text as we now have it.

11 SCHARF, p. 15.

12 No doubt as a result of the interplay between the two epics.

13 Perhaps, as MADELEINE BIARDEAU suggests, Yudhi·shthira finds Sita too passive in comparison to the woman who has saved them all *(Le Mahābhārata* Tome 1 (Éditions du Seuil: Paris, 2002), p. 727.)

14 297.24, 25: *dharmam... pradhānam.*

15 297.35: *dharmaḥ sanātanaḥ.*

16 297.52.

17 See note 6, above.

18 As Madeleine Biardeau points out *(Le Mahābhārata* Tome 1 (Éditions du Seuil: Paris, 2002), p. 751).

19 DAVID SHULMAN, *The Wisdom of Poets: Studies in Tamil, Telugu, and Sanskrit* (Oxford University Press: New Delhi, 2001), p. 43. In a chapter entitled "The Yakṣa's Questions" (pp. 40–62), SHULMAN discusses at length the formulation of the *yaksha*'s puzzles, and what may underlie them.

20 These verses provide another example of a well-known passage that has been omitted from the main text of the Critical Edition of the Maha·bhárata (although it is recorded in the Appendix). Consequently, VAN BUITENEN did not translate it.

BIBLIOGRAPHY

THE MAHA·BHÁRATA IN SANSKRIT

Text used for this edition:

The Mahābhāratam with the Bharata Bhawadeepa Commentary of Nīlakaṇṭha, RAMACHANDRASHASTRI KINJAWADEKAR, ed. (Poona: Chitrashala Press, 1929–36; repr. New Delhi: Oriental Books Reprint Corporation, 1978; 2nd ed. 1979). Vol. 3 *Vana Parva.*

The Mahābhārata, for the first time critically edited, V. S. SUKTHANKAR, S. K. BELVALKAR, P. L. VAIDYA, et al., eds., 19 vols. plus 6 vols. of indexes (Poona Bhandarkar Oriental Research Institute 1933–72). Vol. 4 *The Āraṇyakaparvan* (Part 2), 1942.

TRANSLATIONS

GANGULI, KISARI MOHAN (trans.) [early edns. ascribed to the publisher, P. C. Roy], *The Mahabharata of Krishna-Dwaipayana Vyasa*, 12 vols. (1884–99; 2nd edn. Calcutta, 1970; repr. New Delhi: Munshiram Manoharlal, 1970 (5th edn. 1990)).

SCHARF, PETER (trans. and ed.), *Rāmopākhyāna—The Story of Rāma in the Mahābhārata: An Independent-study Reader in Sanskrit* (London: Routledge Curzon, 2003).

VAN BUITENEN, J. A. B. (trans. and ed.), *The Mahābhārata, Books 1–5*, 3 vols. (Chicago: University of Chicago Press, 1973–78).

OTHER WORKS

(Either used in the Introduction and Notes, or works that contribute to understanding this part of the Maha·bhárata)

BIARDEAU, MADELEINE, *Le Mahābhārata* 2 vols.(Éditions du Seuil: Paris, 2002).

BROCKINGTON, JOHN, *The Sanskrit Epics* (Leiden: Brill, 1998).

SHULMAN, DAVID, *The Wisdom of Poets: Studies in Tamil, Telugu, and Sanskrit* (Oxford University Press: New Delhi, 2001).

MAHA·BHÁRATA BOOK 3
THE STORY OF RAMA

JANAMEJAYA uvāca:

273.1 EVAṂ HṚTĀYĀṂ KṚṢṆĀYĀṂ prāpya kleśam anuttamam
ata ūrdhvaṃ nara|vyāghrāḥ kim akurvata Pāṇḍavāḥ?

VAIŚAṂPĀYANA uvāca:

Evaṃ Kṛṣṇāṃ mokṣayitvā vinirjitya Jayadratham
āsāṃ cakre muni|gaṇair dharma|rājo Yudhiṣṭhiraḥ.
Teṣāṃ madhye maha"|rṣīṇāṃ śṛṇvatām anuśocatām
Mārkaṇḍeyam idaṃ vākyam abravīt Pāṇḍu|nandanaḥ:

YUDHIṢṬHIRA uvāca:

Bhagavan deva'|rṣīṇāṃ tvaṃ khyāto bhūta|bhaviṣya|vit
saṃśayaṃ paripṛcchāmi chindhi me hṛdi saṃsthitam.
5 Drupadasya sutā hy eṣā vedi|madhyāt samutthitā
ayonijā mahā|bhāgā snuṣā Pāṇḍor mah"|ātmanaḥ.
Manye kālaś ca balavān* daivaṃ ca vidhi|nirmitam
bhavitavyaṃ ca bhūtānāṃ yasya n' âsti vyatikramaḥ,
Imāṃ hi patnīm asmākaṃ dharma|jñāṃ dharma|cāriṇīm
saṃspṛśed īdṛśo bhāvaḥ śuciṃ stainyam iv' ânṛtam.
Na hi pāpaṃ kṛtaṃ kiṃ cit karma vā ninditaṃ kva cit
Draupadyā brāhmaṇeṣv eva dharmaḥ su|carito mahān.

Janam·ejaya said:

So, after the unparalleled trouble that came with Krishná's* abduction, what did those tigerish men, the Pándavas, do next? 273.1

Vaisham·páyana said:

When, in this fashion, he had freed Krishná, and conquered Jayad·ratha, Yudhi·shthira, the Law-king, sat down with a company of sages. In the midst of those attentive and sympathetic seers, Pandu's son said this to Markandéya:

Yudhi·shthira said:

Lord, among the gods and the seers you are celebrated for your knowledge of the past and the future—I implore you to slice through a doubt stuck in my heart:

This is Drúpada's daughter: she wasn't born from a womb, 5
she sprang from the middle of the sacrificial altar. She is the virtuous daughter-in-law of great-souled Pandu. I believe that time is powerful and destiny is subject to rules, and that, for human beings, what has to be cannot be sidestepped, since such an event could touch this wife of ours, who knows the Law and acts in accordance with it. It is like a false charge of theft brought against a pure man. For Drúpada's daughter has performed no evil at all, and has nowhere done anything for which she could be blamed. Indeed, she has well carried out the great Law in respect of brahmins.

Tāṃ jahāra balād rājā mūḍha|buddhir Jayadrathaḥ.
tasyāḥ saṃharaṇāt pāpaḥ śirasaḥ keśa|pātanam
Parājayaṃ ca saṃgrāme sa|sahāyaḥ samāptavān.
pratyāhṛtā tath" âsmābhir hatvā tat Saindhavaṃ balam.
Tad dāra|haraṇaṃ prāptam asmābhir avitarkitam -
duḥkhaś c' âyaṃ vane vāso mṛgayāyāṃ ca jīvikā
Hiṃsā ca mṛga|jātīnāṃ van'|âukobhir van'|âukasām,
jñātibhir vipravāsaś ca mithyā|vyavasitair ayam.*
Asti nūnaṃ mayā kaś cid alpa|bhāgyataro naraḥ?
bhavatā dṛṣṭa|pūrvo vā śruta|pūrvo 'pi vā bhavet?

MĀRKAṆḌEYA uvāca:

274.1 Prāptam apratimaṃ duḥkhaṃ Rāmeṇa Bharata'|rṣabha
rakṣasā Jānakī tasya hṛtā bhāryā balīyasā.
Āśramād rākṣas'|êndreṇa Rāvaṇena dur|ātmanā
māyām āsthāya tarasā hatvā gṛdhraṃ Jaṭāyuṣam.
Pratyājahāra tāṃ Rāmaḥ Sugrīva|balam āśritaḥ
baddhvā setuṃ samudrasya dagdhvā Laṅkāṃ śitaiḥ śaraiḥ.

YUDHIṢṬHIRA uvāca:

Kasmin Rāmaḥ kule jātaḥ? kiṃ|vīryaḥ? kiṃ|parākramaḥ?
Rāvaṇaḥ kasya putro vā? kiṃ vairaṃ tasya tena ha?
Etan me bhagavan sarvaṃ samyag ākhyātum arhasi.
śrotum icchāmi caritaṃ Rāmasy' âkliṣṭa|karmaṇaḥ.

MĀRKAṆḌEYA uvāca:

Ajo nām" âbhavad rājā mahān Ikṣvāku|vaṃśa|jaḥ,
tasya putro Daśarathaḥ śaśvat svādhyāyavāñ śuciḥ.
Abhavaṃs tasya catvāraḥ putrā dharm'|ârtha|kovidāḥ
Rāma|Lakṣmaṇa|Śatrughnā Bharataś ca mahā|balaḥ.

The muddy-minded king, Jayad·ratha, abducted her by
force; and because of her abduction the wicked man had
his hair lopped from his head, and with his fellows was 10
defeated in battle. With the slaughter of the Sáindhava army
we have recovered her; the abduction of our wife happened
without warning. This life in the forest is a misery; we live
by hunting—violence by forest-dwellers to forest-dwelling
species. And this exile is at the hands of relatives determined
to be false. Is there really anyone more wretched than I? Has
your lordship seen, or even heard of, such a man before?

MARKANDÉYA said:

Bull of the Bharatas, Rama suffered immeasurably. His 274.1
wife, the daughter of Jánaka, was forcibly abducted from
the hermitage by a powerful demon—the evil-minded Rá-
vana, lord of demons—who used his magical power, and
killed the vulture Jatáyu. Relying on Sugríva's army, Rama
took her back by building a bridge across the ocean and,
with his keen arrows, burning Lanka.

YUDHI·SHTHIRA said:

Into which family was Rama born? What kind of hero
was he? How bold? Whose son was Rávana? What was his
quarrel with him? Tell me all of this properly, lord. I want to 5
hear about the deeds of Rama, whose actions were tireless.

MARKANDÉYA said:

There was a great king called Aja, born into Ikshváku's line. His son, Dasha·ratha, was pure, and always reciting the Veda. He had four sons, experts in the Law and the way of the world: Rama, Lákshmana, Shatru·ghna and Bharata the mighty. Rama's mother was Kausálya, but Kaikéyi was

Rāmasya mātā Kausalyā Kaikeyī Bharatasya tu
sutau Lakṣmaṇa|Śatrughnau Sumitrāyāḥ param|tapau.
Videha|rājo Janakaḥ Sītā tasy' ātma|jā vibho
yāṃ cakāra svayaṃ tvaṣṭā Rāmasya mahiṣīṃ priyām.
10 Etad Rāmasya te janma Sītāyāś ca prakīrtitam.
Rāvaṇasy' âpi te janma vyākhyāsyāmi jan'|ēśvara.
Pitā|maho Rāvaṇasya sākṣād devaḥ Prajāpatiḥ
svayaṃ|bhūḥ sarva|lokānāṃ prabhuḥ sraṣṭā mahā|tapāḥ.
Pulastyo nāma tasy' āsīn mānaso dayitaḥ sutaḥ
tasya Vaiśravaṇo nāma gavi putro 'bhavat prabhuḥ.
Pitaraṃ sa samutsṛjya pitā|maham upasthitaḥ.
tasya kopāt pitā rājan sasarj' ātmānam ātmanā.
Sa jajñe Viśravā nāma tasy' ātm'|ârdhena vai dvijaḥ
pratīkārāya sa|krodhas tato Vaiśravaṇasya vai.
15 Pitā|mahas tu prīt'|ātmā dadau Vaiśravaṇasya ha
amaratvaṃ dhan'|ēśatvaṃ loka|pālatvam eva ca
Īśānena tathā sakhyaṃ putraṃ ca Nalakūbaram
rāja|dhānī|niveśaṃ ca Laṅkāṃ rakṣo|gaṇ'|ânvitām.
Vimānaṃ Puṣpakaṃ nāma kāma|gaṃ ca dadau prabhuḥ
yakṣāṇām ādhipatyaṃ ca rāja|rājatvam eva ca.

MĀRKAṆḌEYA uvāca:

275.1 Pulastyasya tu yaḥ krodhād ardha|deho 'bhavan muniḥ
Viśravā nāma sa|krodhaḥ sa Vaiśravaṇam aikṣata.
Bubudhe taṃ tu sa|krodhaṃ pitaraṃ rākṣas'|ēśvaraḥ
Kuberas tat|prasād'|ârthaṃ yatate sma sadā nṛpa.

Bharata's. Lákshmana and Shatru·ghna were the enemy-incinerating sons of Sumítra. Jánaka was the king of Vidéha. His daughter, my lord, was Sita, whom the creator himself made to be Rama's beloved queen. I have told you of the birth of Rama and Sita; I shall tell you about Rávana's birth too, lord of the people.

Rávana's grandfather was the god Praja·pati himself, the self-existent, the great ascetic lord and creator of all the worlds. His beloved son, born from his mind, was called Pulástya. He in turn had a mighty son, Vaishrávana, born from a cow, who, abandoning his father, looked after his grandfather. Angry, his father created a self from himself, my king. Out of half of the self he was born, in fury, as the twice-born called Víshravas to revenge himself on Vaishrávana. But, pleased with Vaishrávana, his grandfather gave him immortality, lordship of wealth, protectorship of a quarter, friendship with Isháana, a son, Nala·kúbara, and the royal seat and dwelling place of Lanka, full of troops of demons; he also gave a vehicle called Púshpaka, lord, which would go anywhere he wished, and the lordship of the *yakshas*, and sovereignty over kings.

Markandéya said:

The sage called Víshravas, who came in fury from half 275.1
of Pulástya's body, looked angrily on Vaishrávana. But the king of demons, Kubéra, knew that his father was angry, and ever tried to calm him, King.

Sa rāja|rājo Laṅkāyāṃ nyavasan nara|vāhanaḥ
rākṣasīḥ pradadau tisraḥ pitur vai paricārikāḥ.
Tās tadā taṃ mah"|ātmānaṃ saṃtoṣayitum udyatāḥ
ṛṣiṃ Bharata|śārdūla nṛtya|gīta|viśāradāḥ.
5 Puṣpotkaṭā ca Rākā ca Mālinī ca viśāṃ pate
anyonya|spardhayā rājañ śreyas|kāmāḥ sumadhyamāḥ.
Sa tāsāṃ bhagavāṃs tuṣṭo mah"|ātmā pradadau varān
loka|pāl'|ôpamān putrān ek'|âikasyā yath"|ēpsitān.
Puṣpotkaṭāyāṃ jajñāte dvau putrau rākṣas'|ēśvarau
Kumbhakarṇa|daśa|grīvau balen' âpratimau bhuvi.
Mālinī janayām āsa putram ekaṃ Vibhīṣaṇam,
Rākāyāṃ mithunaṃ jajñe Kharaḥ Śūrpaṇakhā tathā.
Vibhīṣaṇas tu rūpeṇa sarvebhyo 'bhyadhiko 'bhavat
sa babhūva mahā|bhāgo dharma|goptā kriyā|ratiḥ.
10 Daśa|grīvas tu sarveṣāṃ śreṣṭho rākṣasa|puṃgavaḥ
mah"|ôtsāho mahā|vīryo mahā|sattva|parākramaḥ.
Kumbhakarṇo balen' āsīt sarvebhyo 'bhyadhiko yudhi
māyāvī raṇa|śauṇḍaś ca raudraś ca rajanī|caraḥ.
Kharo dhanuṣi vikrānto Brahma|dviṭ piśit'|âśanaḥ,
siddha|vighna|karī c' âpi raudrī Śūrpaṇakhā tadā.
Sarve Veda|vidaḥ śūrāḥ sarve sucarita|vratāḥ
ūṣuḥ pitrā saha ratā Gandhamādana|parvate.

Tato Vaiśravaṇaṃ tatra dadṛśur nara|vāhanam
pitrā sārdhaṃ samāsīnam ṛddhyā paramayā yutam.
15 Jāt'|āmarṣās tatas te tu tapase dhṛta|niścayāḥ
Brahmāṇaṃ toṣayām āsur ghoreṇa tapasā tadā.
Atiṣṭhad eka|pādena sahasraṃ parivatsarān
vāyu|bhakṣo daśa|grīvaḥ pañc'|âgniḥ susamāhitaḥ.

This king of kings, his vehicle a man, lived in Lanka; he gave three demonesses as servants to his father. Then, Bharata tiger, skilled in song and dance, they took pains to
satisfy that great-souled seer—slender-waisted Pushpótka- 5
ta, Raka and Málini, competing with each other, lord of the people, wanting the best. Pleased, the great-souled lord gave them gifts: sons like world-guardians, as each desired. Two sons were born to Pushpótkata: lords of the demons, Kumbha·karna and ten-necked Rávana, unequalled on earth in their strength. Málini bore one son, Vibhíshana; Raka bore the twins, Khara and the girl Shurpa·nakha. Now Vibhíshana exceeded them all in beauty. He was most fortunate,
a protector of the Law, who delighted in ritual. But the ten- 10
necked one was the best of them all—a bull of a demon, full of energy, virility, courage and character. Kumbha·karna surpassed all with his strength in a fight; he had magical powers, he was drunk on battle—a wild night-ranger. Khara was good with the bow, a flesh-eating brahmin-hater; and Shurpa·nakha was a wild balk to ascetics. They were all Veda-knowing warriors who performed their vows well. Devoted to him, they lived with their father on Mount Gandha·mádana.

Then they saw Vaishrávana, who has a man as his vehicle, at one with stupendous prosperity, sitting there with their father.

15 Indignant, they thereupon made a definite resolve to practice asceticism. And so they satisfied Brahma with their terrible austerities. The ten-necked Rávana stood on one foot for a thousand years, eating nothing but the wind,

Adhaḥ|śāyī Kumbhakarṇo yat'|āhāro yata|vrataḥ.
Vibhīṣaṇaḥ śīrṇa|parṇam ekam abhyavahārayan
Upavāsa|ratir dhīmān sadā japya|parāyaṇaḥ
tam eva kālam ātiṣṭhat tīvraṃ tapa udāra|dhīḥ.
Kharaḥ Śūrpaṇakhā c' âiva teṣāṃ vai tapyatāṃ tapaḥ
paricaryāṃ ca rakṣāṃ ca cakratur hṛṣṭa|mānasau.
20 Pūrṇe varṣa|sahasre tu śiraś chittvā daś'|ānanaḥ
juhoty agnau durādharṣas, ten' âtuṣyaj jagat|prabhuḥ.
Tato Brahmā svayaṃ gatvā tapasas tān nyavārayat
pralobhya vara|dānena sarvān eva pṛthak pṛthak.

BRAHM" ÔVĀCA

«Prīto 'smi vo nivartadhvaṃ varān vṛṇuta putrakāḥ.
yad yad iṣṭam ṛte tv ekam amaratvaṃ tath" âstu tat.
Yad yad agnau hutaṃ sarvaṃ śiras te mahad|īpsayā
tath" âiva tāni te dehe bhaviṣyanti yathā purā.
Vairūpyaṃ ca na te dehe kāma|rūpa|dharas tathā
bhaviṣyasi raṇe 'rīṇāṃ vijetā na ca saṃśayaḥ.»

RĀVAṆA uvāca:

25 «Gandharva|dev'|âsurato yakṣa|rākṣasatas tathā
sarpa|kiṃnara|bhūtebhyo na me bhūyāt parābhavaḥ.»

in the middle of five fires, completely concentrated. Kumbha·karna lay on the ground, limiting his food, stringent in his vows. Vibhíshana subsisted on just the one mangled leaf—delighting in fasting, wise, noble-minded, focussed on muttered recitations, he was intent at that time on the most exacting asceticism. With happy hearts, Khara and Shurpa·nakha served and protected them as they performed their ascetic practices.

But after a thousand years, the ten-headed Rávana, so 20
hard to attack, struck off his head and offered it to the fire. This pleased the lord of the universe. So Brahma himself arrived and made them stop their asceticism, tempting them all with individual gifts.

BRAHMA said:

"I am pleased with you, my little sons. Stop now, and choose some gifts. With the single exception of immortality, whatever you want shall be yours. If heads of yours have been fully offered into the fire out of a desire for something great, thanks to that desire, they shall be rejoined to your body, as before. Your body shall not be misshapen, and you shall assume any shape you wish. And you will conquer your enemies in battle—be in no doubt about that."

RÁVANA said:

"May *gandhárva*s, gods, anti-gods, *yaksha*s, demons, ser- 25
pents, *kim·nara*s and ghosts not defeat me."

BRAHM" ÔVĀCA

«Ya ete kīrtitāḥ sarve na tebhyo 'sti bhayaṃ tava
ṛte manuṣyād bhadraṃ te tathā tad vihitaṃ mayā.»

MĀRKAṆḌEYA uvāca:

Evam ukto daśa|grīvas tuṣṭaḥ samabhavat tadā,
avamene hi durbuddhir manuṣyān puruṣ'|âdakaḥ.
Kumbhakarṇam ath' ôvāca tath" âiva prapitā|mahaḥ
sa vavre mahatīṃ nidrāṃ tamasā grasta|cetanaḥ.
«Tathā bhaviṣyat' îty» uktvā Vibhīṣaṇam uvāca ha
«varaṃ vṛṇīṣva putra tvaṃ prīto 'sm' îti» punaḥ punaḥ.

VIBHĪṢAṆA uvāca:

30 «Param'|āpad|gatasy' âpi n' âdharme me matir bhavet
aśikṣitaṃ ca bhagavan Brahm'|âstraṃ pratibhātu me.»

BRAHM" ÔVĀCA

«Yasmād rākṣasa|yonau te jātasy' âmitra|karśana
n' âdharme dhīyate buddhir amaratvaṃ dadāmi te.»

MĀRKAṆḌEYA UVĀCA:

Rākṣasas tu varaṃ labdhvā daśa|grīvo viśāṃ pate
Laṅkāyāś cyāvayām āsa yudhi jitvā dhan'|īśvaram.
Hitvā sa bhagavāl̄ Laṅkām āviśad Gandhamādanam
gandharva|yakṣ'|ânugato rakṣaḥ|kiṃpuruṣaiḥ saha.

BRAHMA said:

"None of those you have named shall endanger you—only a man. Honor to you! I have ordained it so."

MARKANDÉYA said:

Addressed in this way, the ten-necked Rávana was satisfied. For the bad-minded man-eater despised human beings.

Then the great-grandfather addressed Kumbha·karna in a similar way. His consciousness was enveloped in darkness—he chose a deep sleep.

"Let it be so!" he said. To Vibhíshana he said repeatedly: "I am pleased, my son. Choose a gift."

VIBHÍSHANA said:

"Even in the most extreme adversity, may my thought not 30
contravene the Law, and may the Brahma weapon appear to me without the need for instruction, my lord."

BRAHMA said:

"Thinner of enemies, although you were born in a demon's womb, because your mind is not engrossed in Lawlessness, I give you immortality!"

MARKANDÉYA said:

But lord of the people, once the ten-headed demon had obtained his gift, he beat the lord of wealth in battle and toppled him from Lanka. The lord left Lanka and went to Gandha·mádana, accompanied by *gandhárvas*, *yakshas*, demons and *kim·púrushas*.

Vimānaṃ Puṣpakaṃ tasya jahār' ākramya Rāvaṇaḥ.
śaśāpa taṃ Vaiśravaṇo: «na tvām etad vahiṣyati.
35 Yas tu tvāṃ samare hantā tam ev' âitad vahiṣyati
avamanya guruṃ māṃ ca kṣipraṃ tvaṃ na bhaviṣyasi.»
Vibhīṣaṇas tu dharm'|ātmā satāṃ dharmam anusmaran
anvagacchan mahā|rāja śriyā paramayā yutaḥ.
Tasmai sa bhagavāṃs tuṣṭo bhrātā bhrātre dhan'|ēśvaraḥ
sainā|patyaṃ dadau dhīmān yakṣa|rākṣasa|senayoḥ.
Rākṣasāḥ puruṣ'|âdāś ca piśācāś ca mahā|balāḥ
sarve sametya rājānam abhyaṣiñcan daś'|ānanam.
Daśa|grīvaś ca daityānāṃ devānāṃ ca bal'|ôtkaṭaḥ
ākramya ratnāny aharat kāma|rūpī vihaṃ|gamaḥ.
40 Rāvayām āsa lokān yat tasmād Rāvaṇa ucyate.
daśa|grīvaḥ kāma|balo devānāṃ bhayam ādadhat.

MĀRKAṆḌEYA uvāca:

276.1 Tato Brahma'|rṣayaḥ sarve Siddhā deva|rāja'|rṣayas tathā
havya|vāhaṃ puras|kṛtya Brahmāṇaṃ śaraṇaṃ gatāḥ.

AGNIR uvāca:

«Yo 'sau Viśravasaḥ putro daśa|grīvo mahā|balaḥ
avadhyo vara|dānena kṛto bhagavatā purā.
Sa bādhate prajāḥ sarvā viprakārair mahā|balaḥ,
tato nas trātu bhagavan n' ânyas trātā hi vidyate.»

Rávana attacked, and captured his aerial vehicle Púshpa-
ka. Vaishrávana cursed him: "It won't carry you! The man 35
who shall kill you in battle is the only one it will carry. And since you have slighted me, an elder, you shall soon be dead!"

But supremely radiant Vibhíshana, the soul of the Law, remembering the Law of the good, followed Vaishrávana, great king. Pleased, his thoughtful brother, the lordly king of wealth, gave his brother the generalship of the *yaksha* and demon armies. The man-eating demons and mighty *pisháchas* all gathered together and consecrated ten-headed Rávana as king. And bursting with strength, assuming whatever shape he willed, roaming the skies, the ten-necked one attacked the *daityas* and the gods, and took their wealth.

He was called Rávana because he made the worlds cry 40
out.* Ten-necked and headstrong, he spread terror among the gods.

MARKANDÉYA said:

Then the brahmin seers, the Siddhas, the gods and royal 276.1
seers, placed the oblation-bearer (Fire) in front of them, and went to Brahma for refuge.

FIRE said:

"That mighty ten-necked son of Víshravas cannot be killed because, earlier, your lordship gave him a gift. That powerhouse is subjugating all creatures through his hostile actions. So save us, lord, we can find no other savior."

Brahm” ôvāca

«Na sa dev’|âsuraiḥ śakyo yuddhe jetuṃ vibhāvaso
vihitaṃ tatra yat kāryam abhitas tasya nigrahe.
5 Tad|artham avatīrṇo ’sau man|niyogāc catur|bhujaḥ
Viṣṇuḥ praharatāṃ śreṣṭhaḥ, sa tat karma kariṣyati.»

Mārkaṇḍeya uvāca:

Pitā|mahas tatas teṣāṃ saṃnidhau Śakram abravīt:
«sarvair deva|gaṇaiḥ sārdhaṃ saṃbhavadhvaṃ mahī|tale.
Viṣṇoḥ sahāyān ṛkṣīṣu vānarīṣu ca sarvaśaḥ
janayadhvaṃ sutān vīrān kāma|rūpa|bal’|ânvitān.»
Tato bhāg’|ânubhāgena deva|gandharva|dānavāḥ
avatartuṃ mahīṃ sarve mantrayām āsur añjasā.
Teṣāṃ samakṣaṃ gandharvīṃ Dundubhīṃ nāma nāmataḥ
śaśāsa varado devo «gaccha deva|kāry’|ârtha|siddhaye.»
10 Pitā|maha|vacaḥ śrutvā gandharvī Dundubhī tataḥ
Mantharā mānuṣe loke kubjā samabhavat tadā.
Śakra|prabhṛtayaś c’ âiva sarve te sura|sattamāḥ
vānara’|rkṣa|vara|strīṣu janayām āsur ātmajān.
Te ’nvavartan pitṝn sarve yaśasā ca balena ca
bhettāro giri|śṛṅgāṇāṃ śāla|tāla|śil”|āyudhāḥ
Vajra|saṃhananāḥ sarve sarve c’ âugha|balās tathā
kāma|vīrya|balāś c’ âiva sarve yuddha|viśāradāḥ
Nāg’|âyuta|sama|prāṇā vāyu|vega|samā jave
yatr’|êcchaka|nivāsāś ca ke cid atra van’|âukasaḥ.

BRAHMA said:

"O Fire, gods and anti-gods cannot defeat him in battle. This is a case where what has to be done to subdue him
has been ordained. It is for that purpose that four-armed 5
Vishnu, the best assailant, has descended at my request. He shall do the deed."

MARKANDÉYA said:

Then, in their presence, the grandfather* said to Shakra: "Take birth on the face of the earth with all the hosts of the gods. On female bears and monkeys all of you must generate heroic sons to be Vishnu's companions, able to assume any shape at will." Then the gods, *gandhárvas* and *dánavas* all determined how to descend quickly to the earth with various fractions of themselves.

In their presence, the gift-giving god instructed a *Gandhárvi* called Dúndubhi to set out for the successful execu-
tion of the gods' purpose. Then, having heard the grandfa- 10
ther's word, the *Gandhárvi* Dúndubhi became the hunchback Mánthara in the world of men. And all those fine gods, from Shakra down, generated offspring on the foremost female monkeys and bears. They all took after their fathers in fame and strength, splitters of mountain peaks, armed with *shala* trees, palms and stones; all were as hard as diamonds, as strong as torrents, all were deft in battle, with the power and strength they desired. Their life-force was equal to that of ten thousand elephants, they had the speed of the wind; some lived where they liked, some dwelt here in the forest.

15 Evaṃ vidhāya tat sarvaṃ bhagavāl̃ loka|bhāvanaḥ
Mantharāṃ bodhayām āsa yad yat kāryaṃ yathā yathā.
Sā tad|vacaḥ samājñāya tathā cakre mano|javā
itaś c' êtaś ca gacchantī vaira|saṃdhukṣaṇe ratā.

Yudhiṣṭhira uvāca:

277.1 Uktaṃ bhagavatā janma Rām'|ādīnāṃ pṛthak pṛthak
prasthāna|kāraṇaṃ Brahman śrotum icchāmi kathyatām.
Kathaṃ Dāśarathī vīrau bhrātarau Rāma|Lakṣmaṇau
samprasthitau vane Brahma Maithilī ca yaśasvinī?

Mārkaṇḍeya uvāca:

Jāta|putro Daśarathaḥ prītimān abhavan nṛpa
kriyā|ratir dharma|rataḥ satataṃ vṛddha|sevitā.
Krameṇa c' âsya te putrā vyavardhanta mah"|âujasaḥ
Vedeṣu sarahasyeṣu dhanur|vedeṣu pāragāḥ.
5 Carita|brahmacaryās te kṛta|dārāś ca pārthiva
yadā tadā Daśarathaḥ prītimān abhavat sukhī.
Jyeṣṭho Rāmo 'bhavat teṣāṃ ramayām āsa hi prajāḥ
mano|haratayā dhīmān pitur hṛdaya|nandanaḥ.

Tataḥ sa rājā matimān matv" ātmānaṃ vayo 'dhikam
mantrayām āsa sacivair dharma|jñaiś ca purohitaiḥ.
Abhiṣekāya Rāmasya yauva|rājyena Bhārata
prāpta|kālaṃ ca te sarve menire mantri|sattamāḥ.
Lohit'|âkṣaṃ mahā|bāhuṃ matta|mātaṅga|gāminam
dīrgha|bāhuṃ mah"|ôraskaṃ nīla|kuñcita|mūrdhajam

With all that ordered, the lordly creator of the world 15
made clear to Mánthara what kinds of things she was to do and in what kinds of ways. Then, understanding his command, she acted quick as thought, going hither and thither, intent on stoking up hostility.

YUDHI·SHTHIRA said:

Your lordship has related the birth of Rama and the others 277.1
individually. I should like, brahmin, to hear the reason for their departure. Tell me, brahmin, how were Rama and Lákshmana, the heroic sons of Dasha·ratha, banished to the forest with the radiant princess of Míthila?

MARKANDÉYA said:

Dasha·ratha, delighting in ritual, devoted to the Law, ever the servant of his elders, was pleased, my king, with the birth of his sons. And over time these sons of his grew very energetic; they were well versed in the Vedas and their mysteries, and in the treatises on archery. And when, my 5
king, their period of Vedic study was complete, and they had taken wives, Dasha·ratha was pleased and happy. The eldest of them was called Rama, because he delighted the people; intelligent, he gladdened his father's heart with his charm.

Then the wise king, realizing that he was growing old, consulted his ministers and Law-knowing priests. And all those excellent advisers thought, Bhárata, that the time had come to consecrate Rama as crown prince. Red-eyed, great-armed, striding like a rutting elephant, long-armed, broad-chested, with dark curling hair, shining in splendor, a hero, 10
not to be outdone by Shakra in battle, fully conversant with every law, Brihas·pati's equal in thought, his subjects

10 Dīpyamānaṃ śriyā vīraṃ Śakrād anavaraṃ raṇe
pāragaṃ sarva|dharmāṇāṃ Bṛhaspati|samaṃ matau
Sarv'|ânurakta|prakṛtiṃ sarva|vidyā|viśāradam
jit'|êndriyam amitrāṇām api dṛṣṭi|mano|haram
Niyantāram asādhūnāṃ goptāraṃ dharma|cāriṇām
dhṛtimantam anādhṛṣyaṃ jetāram aparājitam
Putraṃ rājā Daśarathaḥ Kausaly"|ānanda|vardhanam
saṃdṛśya paramāṃ prītim agacchat Kuru|nandana.
Cintayaṃś ca mahā|tejā guṇān Rāmasya vīryavān
abhyabhāṣata «bhadraṃ te!» prīyamāṇaḥ purohitam:
15 «Adya Puṣyo niśi brahman
puṇyaṃ yogam upaiṣyati
saṃbhārāḥ saṃbhriyantāṃ me
Rāmaś c' ôpanimantryatām.»
Iti tad rāja|vacanaṃ pratiśruty' âtha Mantharā
Kaikeyīm abhigamy' êdaṃ kāle vacanam abravīt.
«Adya Kaikeyi daurbhāgyaṃ rājñā te khyāpitaṃ mahat.
āśīviṣas tvāṃ saṃkruddhaś caṇḍo daśatu durbhage.
Subhagā khalu Kausalyā yasyāḥ putro 'bhiṣekṣyate
kuto hi tava saubhāgyaṃ yasyāḥ putro na rājya|bhāk?»
Sā tad vacanam ājñāya sarv'|ābharaṇa|bhūṣitā
vedī|vilagna|madhy" êva bibhratī rūpam uttamam
20 Vivikte patim āsādya hasant" îva śuci|smitā
praṇayaṃ vyañjayant" îva madhuraṃ vākyam abravīt:
«Satya|pratijña yan me tvaṃ kāmam ekaṃ nisṛṣṭavān
upākuruṣva tad rājaṃs tasmān mucyasva saṃkaṭāt!»

were completely devoted to him. He was skilled in every branch of knowledge, he was in control of his senses, even his enemies were pleased to see him. He was a check on the wicked, a protector of the Law-abiding, firm, unassailable, a conqueror, unconquered—beholding such a son, adding to Kausálya's joy, King Dasha·ratha became very happy, delight of the Kurus.

Dwelling on Rama's qualities, the most lustrous and heroic king was pleased, and addressed his priest: "Be blessed! Tonight, brahmin, the Pushya asterism enters an auspicious conjunction. Prepare my equipment, and invite Rama."

Hearing the king's words, Mánthara went to Kaikéyi and said this in due time: "Kaikéyi, today the king has revealed your great misfortune! Miserable woman, may you be bitten by a cruel and enraged venomous snake! Fortunate indeed is Kausálya, whose son will be consecrated. Where is your good fortune when your son has no share in the kingdom?" Understanding what she meant, she dressed herself in all her jewelry—her figure so wonderful, her waist as slender as the curved center of the sacrificial altar—and approached her husband in private, as though amused, smiling sweetly. Seeming affectionate, she spoke the honied words:

"King, true to your word, grant the one wish you gave me. Free yourself from that obligation!"

RĀJ" ôvāca

«Varaṃ dadāni te hanta tad gṛhāṇa yad icchasi
avadhyo vadhyatāṃ ko 'dya? vadhyaḥ ko 'dya vimucyatām?
Dhanaṃ dadāni kasy' âdya? hriyatāṃ kasya vā punaḥ?
brāhmaṇa|svād ih' ânyatra yat kiṃ cid vittam asti me.
Pṛthivyāṃ rāja|rājo 'smi cātur|varṇyasya rakṣitā.
yas te 'bhilaṣitaḥ kāmo brūhi kalyāṇi mā ciram»

25 Sā tad vacanam ājñāya parigṛhya nar'|âdhipam
ātmano balam ājñāya tata enam uvāca ha:
«Ābhiṣecanikaṃ yat te Rām'|ârtham upakalpitam
Bharatas tad avāpnotu, vanaṃ gacchatu Rāghavaḥ.»
Sa tad rājā vacaḥ śrutvā vipriyaṃ dāruṇ'|ôdayam
duḥkh'|ārto Bharata|śreṣṭha na kiṃ cid vyājahāra ha.
Tatas tath" ôktaṃ pitaraṃ Rāmo vijñāya vīryavān
vanaṃ pratasthe dharm'|ātmā, rājā satyo bhavatv iti.
Tam anvagacchal lakṣmīvān dhanuṣmāl̃ Lakṣmaṇas tadā
Sītā ca bhāryā bhadraṃ te Vaidehī Janak'|ātmajā.
30 Tato vanaṃ gate Rāme rājā Daśarathas tadā
samayujyata dehasya kāla|paryāya|dharmaṇā.
Rāmaṃ tu gatam ājñāya rājānaṃ ca tathā gatam
ānāyya Bharataṃ devī Kaikeyī vākyam abravīt:
«Gato Daśarathaḥ svargaṃ, vana|sthau Rāma|Lakṣmaṇau.
gṛhāṇa rājyaṃ vipulaṃ kṣemaṃ nihata|kaṇṭakam.»

The KING said:

"I shall give you your gift, indeed! Whatever you wish, you shall receive. What innocent shall be executed today? What criminal shall now be freed? To whom shall I grant wealth today? Or from whom shall I remove it? All the riches on earth are mine—apart from the property of the brahmins. I am the king of kings on earth, the guardian of the four classes. Don't hesitate, beautiful woman, tell me: what pleasure is your desire?"

Taking in that speech, she embraced the lord of men; 25
then, realizing her power, she said to him:

"Let Bhárata receive the consecration prepared for Rama, and let Rághava* go to the forest."

On hearing that disagreeable, depressing request, the king was overcome with misery, best of Bharatas, and said nothing at all. But then, understanding what his father had been asked, heroic Rama, the soul of the Law, set out for the forest, so that the king might be true to his word.

Then the majestic bowman Lákshmana followed him,
as did, bless her, his wife Sita, princess of Vidéha, daughter
of Jánaka. After Rama had gone to the forest, King Da- 30
sha·ratha was subject to the law of the body—the passage
of time.

So perceiving that Rama had gone and that the king had passed away, Queen Kaikéyi sent for Bhárata and said this:

"Dasha·ratha has gone to heaven. Rama and Lákshmana are in the forest. Seize the vast kingdom; it has been secured, the sting has been removed!"

Tām uvāca sa dharm'|ātmā: «nṛśaṃsaṃ bata te kṛtam
patiṃ hatvā kulaṃ c' êdam utsādya dhana|lubdhayā.
Ayaśaḥ pātayitvā me mūrdhni tvaṃ kula|pāṃsane
sakāmā bhava me mātar!» ity uktvā praruroda ha.

35 Sa cāritraṃ viśodhy' âtha sarva|prakṛti|saṃnidhau
anvayād bhrātaraṃ Rāmaṃ vinivartana|lālasaḥ.
Kausalyāṃ ca Sumitrāṃ ca Kaikeyīṃ ca suduḥkhitaḥ
agre prasthāpya yānaiḥ sa Śatrughna|sahito yayau.
Vasiṣṭha|Vāmadevābhyāṃ vipraiś c' ânyaiḥ sahasraśaḥ
paura|jānapadaiḥ sārdhaṃ Rām'|ānayana|kāṅkṣayā.

Dadarśa Citrakūṭa|sthaṃ sa Rāmaṃ saha|Lakṣmaṇam
tāpasānām alaṃkāraṃ dhārayantaṃ dhanur|dharam.

Visarjitaḥ sa Rāmeṇa pitur vacana|kāriṇā
Nandigrāme 'karod rājyaṃ puras|kṛty' âsya pāduke.
40 Rāmas tu punar āśaṅkya paura|jānapad'|āgamam
praviveśa mah"|âraṇyaṃ Śarabhaṅg'|āśramaṃ prati.
Satkṛtya Śarabhaṅgaṃ sa Daṇḍak'|âraṇyam āśritaḥ.
nadīṃ Godāvarīṃ ramyām āśritya nyavasat tadā.

Vasatas tasya Rāmasya tataḥ Śūrpaṇakhā|kṛtam
Khareṇ' āsīn mahad vairaṃ Janasthāna|nivāsinā.
Rakṣ"|ârthaṃ tāpasānāṃ ca Rāghavo dharma|vatsalaḥ
caturdaśa|sahasrāṇi jaghāna bhuvi rākṣasān.
Dūṣaṇaṃ ca Kharaṃ c' âiva nihatya sumahā|balau
cakre kṣemaṃ punar dhīmān dharm'|âraṇyaṃ sa Rāghavaḥ.

That soul of the Law said to her: "Alas, you have done a cruel thing! Because of your lust for wealth, you have killed your husband and ruined this family. You have brought down disgrace on my head, family-wrecker. I hope you're satisfied, mother!" So saying, he wept.

Then, before all the subjects, he cleared his conduct of 35
suspicion, and went after his brother Rama, hoping to make him return. Sending Kausálya, Sumítra and Kaikéyi in front with vehicles, he went along, most sorrowfully, with Shatru·ghna, Vasíshtha, Vama·deva and thousands of other brahmins, and with townsmen and countryfolk as well, in the hope of bringing Rama back.

He saw Rama with Lákshmana on Mount Chitra·kuta, carrying his bow, and wearing the insignia of ascetics.

Sent away by Rama, who was honoring his father's pledge, he made his kingdom in Nandi·grama, placing his sandals*
in front of him. But Rama, fearing that the townsmen and 40
countryfolk would come again, entered the great forest near to Shara·bhanga's hermitage. After honoring Shara·bhanga, he continued to the Dándaka forest and the beautiful Godávari River, where he settled down.

Then, while Rama was living there, he fell into a great conflict, brought about by Shurpa·nakha, with Khara, who lived in Jana·sthana. Then Rághava,* who cared for the Law, killed fourteen thousand demons on earth to protect the ascetics. And by killing the exceptionally powerful Dúshana and Khara, the wise Rághava made the forest of the Law secure again.

45 Hateṣu teṣu rakṣaḥsu tataḥ Śūrpaṇakhā punaḥ
yayau nikṛtta|nās"|âuṣṭhī Laṅkāṃ bhrātur niveśanam.
Tato Rāvaṇam abhyetya rākṣasī duḥkha|mūrchitā
papāta pādayor bhrātuḥ saṃśuṣka|rudhir"|ānanā.

Tāṃ tathā vikṛtāṃ dṛṣṭvā Rāvaṇaḥ krodha|mūrchitaḥ
utpapāt' āsanāt kruddho dantair dantān upaspṛśan.
Svān amātyān visṛjy' âtha vivikte tām uvāca saḥ:

«ken' âsy evaṃ kṛtā bhadre mām acinty' âvamanya ca?
Kaḥ śūlaṃ tīkṣṇam āsādya sarva|gātrair niṣevate?
kaḥ śirasy agnim ādāya viśvastaḥ svapate sukham?
50 Āśīviṣaṃ ghorataraṃ pādena spṛśat' îha kaḥ?
siṃhaṃ kesariṇaṃ kaś ca daṃṣṭrāyāṃ spṛśya tiṣṭhati?»
Ity evaṃ bruvatas tasya srotobhyas tejaso 'rciṣaḥ
niścerur dahyato rātrau vṛkṣasy' êva sva|randhrataḥ.

Tasya tat sarvam ācakhyau bhaginī Rāma|vikramam
Khara|Dūṣaṇa|saṃyuktaṃ rākṣasānāṃ parābhavam.
Sa niścitya tataḥ kṛtyaṃ svasāram upasāntvya ca
ūrdhvam ācakrame rājā vidhāya nagare vidhim.
Trikūṭaṃ samatikramya Kāla|parvatam eva ca
dadarśa makar'|āvāsaṃ gambhīr'|ôdaṃ mah"|ôdadhim.
55 Tam atīty' âtha Gokarṇam abhyagacchad daś'|ānanaḥ
dayitaṃ sthānam avyagraṃ śūla|pāṇer mah"|ātmanaḥ.
Tatr' âbhyagacchan Mārīcaṃ pūrv'|âmātyaṃ daś'|ānanaḥ
purā Rāma|bhayād eva tāpasyaṃ samupāśritam.

And when those demons had been slain, Shurpa·na- 45
kha, her nose and lips sliced, went to Lanka, the home
of her brother. Weighed down with grief, the demoness
approached Rávana and fell at her brother's feet, her face
covered in dry blood.

Seeing her so mutilated, Rávana, blinded by rage, leaped
from his seat, incensed and grinding his teeth. Dismissing
his ministers, he asked her in private:

"Who, without remembering or regarding me, did this
to you, dear sister? Who, getting hold of a sharp spike,
uses it on all his limbs? Who lights a fire on his head, and
then relaxes and sleeps easy? Who among us pokes a terrible 50
venomous snake with his foot? Who, having touched the
tooth of the maned lion, stands still?" As he spoke, brilliant
flames shot from his pores as from a hollow tree burning
at night.

His sister told him the whole tale of Rama's valor—the
defeat of the demons, and of Khara and Dúshana. Then the
king resolved what had to be done: he consoled his sister, set
up the rule of law in the city, and stepped up into the sky.
He stepped beyond Mount Tri·kuta and Mount Kala, and
saw the great deep ocean, where the sea monsters live. Then 55
ten-headed Rávana crossed it and went toward Go·karna,
the beloved, safe haven of the great-souled trident-bearer.*
There, ten-headed Rávana approached Marícha, who had
once been his minister, but had since resorted to a life of
asceticism from fear of Rama.

MĀRKAṆḌEYA uvāca:

278.1 Mārīcas tv atha saṃbhrānto dṛṣṭvā Rāvaṇam āgatam
pūjayām āsa sat|kāraiḥ phala|mūl'|ādibhis tataḥ.
Viśrāntaṃ c' âinam āsīnam anvāsīnaḥ sa rākṣasaḥ
uvāca prasṛtaṃ vākyaṃ vākya|jño vākya|kovidam:
«Na te prakṛtimān varṇaḥ. kaccit kṣemaṃ pure tava?
kaccit prakṛtayaḥ sarvā bhajante tvāṃ yathā purā?
Kim ih' āgamane c' âpi kāryaṃ te rākṣas'|ēśvara?
kṛtam ity eva tad viddhi yady api syāt su|duṣkaram.»
5 Śaśaṃsa Rāvaṇas tasmai tat sarvaṃ Rāma|ceṣṭitam
samāsen' âiva kāryāṇi krodh'|âmarṣa|samanvitaḥ.
Mārīcas tv abravīc chrutvā samāsen' âiva Rāvaṇam:
«alaṃ te Rāmam āsādya vīrya|jño hy asmi tasya vai.
Bāṇa|vegaṃ hi kas tasya śaktaḥ soḍhuṃ mah"|ātmanaḥ?
pravrajyāyāṃ hi me hetuḥ sa eva puruṣa'|rṣabhaḥ.
Vināśa|mukham etat te ken' ākhyātaṃ durātmanā?»
tam uvāc' âtha sakrodho Rāvaṇaḥ paribhartsayan:
«Akurvato 'smad|vacanaṃ syān mṛtyur api te dhruvam!»
Mārīcaś cintayām āsa: «viśiṣṭān maraṇaṃ varam.
10 Avaśyaṃ maraṇe prāpte kariṣyāmy asya yan matam.»
tatas taṃ pratyuvāc' âtha Mārīco rākṣasāṃ varam:
«Kiṃ te sāhyaṃ mayā kāryaṃ kariṣyāmy avaśo 'pi tat.»
tam abravīd daśa|grīvo: «gaccha Sītāṃ pralobhaya
Ratna|śṛṅgo mṛgo bhūtvā ratna|citra|tanū|ruhaḥ.
dhruvaṃ Sītā samālakṣya tvāṃ Rāmaṃ codayiṣyati.
Apakrānte ca Kākutsthe Sītā vaśyā bhaviṣyati.
tām ādāy' âpaneṣyāmi. tataḥ sa na bhaviṣyati,
Bhāryā|viyogād durbuddhir. etat sāhyaṃ kuruṣva me!»

MARKANDÉYA said:

So Marícha, when he saw Rávana arriving, was agitated, 278.1
and greeted him with offerings, such as fruit and edible roots. Sitting next to his resting guest, the demon knew how to talk, and he spoke eloquently to the other skilled orator:

"This is not your normal color. Is your city safe? Do all your subjects love you as before? And what, lord of demons, is your purpose in coming here? Whatever the difficulty,
consider it done." Rávana, filled with frustration and anger, 5
told him all that Rama had accomplished and, summarily, what needed to be done.

But, on hearing this, Marícha said tersely to Rávana: "Give up attacking Rama—I am one who knows his power. Who can withstand the impact of that great-souled man's arrows? That bull of a man is the reason I became an ascetic. What evil soul has shown you this gateway to destruction?"

Then Rávana answered him in an angry and threatening manner: "Refusing to do what I ask will certainly mean death for you!"

Marícha thought: "It's better to die at the hands of a su-
perior being. Since death is certain, I shall do as he wishes." 10
So Marícha answered the greatest of demons: "I shall do whatever I can to help you, albeit unwillingly."

The ten-necked Rávana said to him: "Go and tempt Sita. Become a deer with bejewelled antlers, its hide covered in dazzling gems. When Sita has seen you, she will certainly incite Rama. And when Kakútstha* has departed, Sita will be in my power. Then, when I have captured her and carried her away, he shall be no more, the fool, because he's separated from his wife. Assist me in this way!"

ity evam ukto Mārīcaḥ kṛtv" ôdakam ath' ātmanaḥ.
15 Rāvaṇaṃ purato yāntam anvagacchat su|duḥkhitaḥ.
tatas tasy' āśramaṃ gatvā Rāmasy' âkliṣṭa|karmaṇaḥ
Cakratus tad yathā sarvam ubhau yat pūrva|mantritam.
Rāvaṇas tu yatir bhūtvā muṇḍaḥ kuṇḍī tri|daṇḍa|dhṛk
Mṛgaś ca bhūtvā Mārīcas taṃ deśam upajagmatuḥ.
darśayām āsa Mārīco Vaidehīṃ mṛga|rūpa|dhṛk.
Codayām āsa tasy' ârthe sā Rāmaṃ vidhi|coditā.
Rāmas tasyāḥ priyaṃ kurvan dhanur ādāya satvaraḥ
Rakṣ"|ârthe Lakṣmaṇaṃ nyasya prayayau mṛga|lipsayā.
sa dhanvī baddha|tūṇīraḥ khaḍga|godh'|âṅguli|travān.
20 Anvadhāvan mṛgaṃ Rāmo Rudras tārā|mṛgaṃ yathā.

so 'ntarhitaḥ punas tasya darśanaṃ rākṣaso vrajan
Cakarṣa mahad adhvānaṃ. Rāmas taṃ bubudhe tataḥ.
niśā|caraṃ viditvā taṃ Rāghavaḥ pratibhānavān.
Amoghaṃ śaram ādāya jaghāna mṛga|rūpiṇam.

sa Rāma|bāṇ'|âbhihataḥ kṛtvā Rāma|svaraṃ tadā:
«Hā Sīte Lakṣmaṇ' êty!» evaṃ cukroś' ārta|svareṇa ha.
śuśrāva tasya Vaidehī tatas tāṃ karuṇāṃ giram.
Sā prādravad yataḥ śabdas, tām uvāc' âtha Lakṣmaṇaḥ:
«alaṃ te śaṅkayā bhīru ko Rāmaṃ prahariṣyati?
25 Muhūrtād drakṣyase Rāmam bhartāraṃ tvaṃ śuci|smite!»
ity uktvā sā prarudatī paryaśaṅkata Lakṣmaṇam.
Hatā vai strī|svabhāvena śukla|cāritra|bhūṣaṇam
sā taṃ paruṣam ārabdhā vaktuṃ sādhvī pati|vratā:

So addressed, Marícha performed the water offering for himself,* and followed sorrowfully after Rávana. Arriving at the hermitage belonging to Rama, the man whose actions are unblemished, the two of them then did everything as previously planned. So, Rávana, having become a shaven-headed renouncer, complete with a water pot and three staves, and Marícha, having turned himself into a deer, they approached that place. Marícha, in the deer's form, showed himself to the princess of Vidéha.* Driven by precept, she incited Rama to follow it. To do as she desired, Rama quickly took his bow, and, installing Lákshmana as her protector, set out to catch the deer. Like Rudra after the stellar deer,* so Rama, a bowman equipped with quiver, sword, arm-guards and finger-guards, pursued the beast.

The demon disappeared, then showed himself again. Shifting about, he led him a long way. Then Rama recognized him. Knowing him to be a creature of the night, quick-witted Rághava took an infallible arrow and felled the one who had disguised himself as a deer.

Then, hit by Rama's arrow, he put on Rama's voice, crying, "Oh, Sita, Lákshmana!," in a pained tone. Hearing his heartbreaking cry, the princess of Vidéha rushed in the direction of the sound. Then Lákshmana said to her: "Don't be afraid, timid woman. Who shall strike Rama? Shortly, you shall see Rama, your husband, sweet-smiling woman!" Spoken to in this way, she started crying: overtaken by her woman's nature, she suspected Lákshmana, the paragon of pure conduct. That good, devoted wife began to abuse him:

«N' âiṣa kāmo bhaven mūḍha yaṃ tvaṃ prārthayase hṛdā.
apy ahaṃ śastram ādāya hanyām ātmānam ātmanā.
Pateyaṃ giri|śṛṅgād vā viśeyaṃ vā hut'|âśanam,
Rāmaṃ bhartāram utsṛjya na tv ahaṃ tvāṃ kathaṃ cana
Nihīnam upatiṣṭheyaṃ śārdūlī kroṣṭukaṃ yathā.»
etādṛśaṃ vacaḥ śrutvā Lakṣmaṇaḥ priya|Rāghavaḥ.
30 Pidhāya karṇau sad|vṛttaḥ prasthito yena Rāghavaḥ.
sa Rāmasya padaṃ gṛhya prasasāra dhanur|dharaḥ.
Avīlakṣmaṇo bimb'|oṣṭīṃ prayayau Lakṣmaṇas tadā.
etasminn antare rakṣo Rāvaṇaḥ pratyadṛśyata
Abhavyo bhavya|rūpeṇa bhasmac|channa iv' ânalaḥ
yati|veṣa|praticchanno jihīrṣus tām aninditām.
Sā tam ālakṣya saṃprāptaṃ dharma|jñā Janak'|ātma|jā
nimantrayām āsa tadā phala|mūl'|âśan'|ādibhiḥ.
Avamanya tataḥ sarvaṃ sva|rūpaṃ pratipadyata
sāntvayām āsa Vaidehīm iti rākṣasa|puṃgavaḥ:
35 «Sīte rākṣasa|rājo 'haṃ Rāvaṇo nāma viśrutaḥ.
mama Laṅkā purī nāmnā ramyā pāre mah"|ôdadheḥ.
Tatra tvaṃ nara|nārīṣu śobhiṣyasi mayā saha
bhāryā me bhava suśroṇi! tāpasaṃ tyaja Rāghavam!»
Evam|ādīni vākyāni śrutvā tasy' âtha Jānakī
pidhāya karṇau suśroṇī «m" âivam ity» abravīd vacaḥ:
«Prapated dyauḥ sa|nakṣatrā pṛthivī śakalī|bhavet
śaityam agnir iyān n' âhaṃ tyajeyaṃ Raghu|nandanam.
Kathaṃ hi bhinna|karaṭaṃ padminaṃ vana|gocaram
upasthāya mahā|nāgaṃ kareṇuḥ sūkaraṃ spṛśet?

"This desire locked in your heart cannot happen, fool! I would rather take a sword and kill myself, I would rather throw myself from a mountain peak, or walk into the fire, than ever give up my husband, Rama, and attend on you, low man, like a tigress on a jackal." Hearing this speech, Lákshmana, who was devoted to Rághava,* shut his ears, and set out, the virtuous man, as Rághava had; in Rama's footsteps, he ran with his bow in hand.

So Lákshmana went, without glancing at the woman whose lips were like the *bimba* fruit. At the same time, the demon Rávana appeared—the impious in a pious form, hidden beneath an ascetic's apparel, like a fire covered in ashes, hoping to abduct that blameless woman. Seeing him arrive, Jánaka's Law-knowing daughter invited him to a meal of roots and fruits, and other things.

But despising all that, the bullish demon reverted to his own form, and made up to the princess of Vidéha: "Sita, I am the famed king of the demons, Rávana. My delightful city, called Lanka, is on the far shore of the great ocean. There, among the most beautiful men and women, you shall shine alongside me. Be my wife, fair-hipped woman! Abandon Rághava the ascetic!"

Hearing these and similar words from him, fair-hipped Jánaki shut her ears, and said: "Don't say such a thing! May the sky and the stars fall down, the earth shatter to pieces, may fire burn cold—I would not abandon the delight of Raghu.* For having attended on the great, forest-ranging, mottled, split-templed bull elephant, how can the elephant cow touch a pig? How I wonder, could any woman

40 Kathaṃ hi pītvā mādhvīkaṃ pītvā ca madhu|mādhavīm
lobhaṃ sauvīrake kuryān nārī kā cid? iti smare.*»
Iti sā taṃ samābhāṣya praviveś' āśramaṃ tataḥ
krodhāt prasphuramāṇ' âuṣṭī vighunvānā karau muhuḥ.
Tām abhidrutya suśroṇīṃ Rāvaṇaḥ pratyaṣedhayat,
bhartsayitvā tu rūkṣeṇa svareṇa gata|cetanām
Mūrdha|jeṣu nijagrāha ūrdhvam ācakrame tataḥ.
tāṃ dadarśa tadā gṛdhro Jaṭāyur giri|gocaraḥ
rudatīṃ «Rāma Rām' êti» hriyamāṇāṃ tapasvinīm.

Mārkaṇḍeya uvāca:

279.1 Sakhā Daśarathasy' āsīj Jaṭāyur Aruṇ'|ātma|jaḥ
gṛdhra|rājo mahā|vīraḥ Saṃpātir yasya sodaraḥ.
Sa dadarśa tadā Sītāṃ Rāvaṇ' âṅka|gatāṃ snuṣām
sa|krodho 'bhyadravat pakṣī Rāvaṇaṃ rākṣas'|ēśvaram.
Ath' âinam abravīd gṛdhro: «muñca muñcasva Maithilīm!
dhriyamāṇe mayi kathaṃ hariṣyasi niśā|cara?
Na hi me mokṣyase jīvan yadi n' ôtsṛjase vadhūm!»
uktv" âivaṃ rākṣas'|êndraṃ taṃ cakarta nakharair bhṛśam.
5 Pakṣa|tuṇḍa|prahāraiś ca śataśo jarjarī|kṛtaḥ
cakṣāra rudhiraṃ bhūri giriḥ prasravaṇair iva.
Sa vadhyamāno gṛdhreṇa Rāma|priya|hit'|âiṣiṇā
khaḍgam ādāya ciccheda bhujau tasya patatriṇaḥ.
Nihatya gṛdhra|rājaṃ sa chinn'|âbhra|śikhar'|ôpamam
ūrdhvam ācakrame Sītāṃ gṛhītv" âṅkena rākṣasaḥ.
Yatra yatra tu Vaidehī paśyaty āśrama|maṇḍalam
saro vā sarito v" âpi tatra muñcati bhūṣaṇam.
Sā dadarśa giri|prasthe pañca vānara|puṃgavān
tatra vāso mahad divyam utsasarja manasvinī.

have a desire for sour jujube juice after drinking mead and sweet liquor?"

With these words she entered the hermitage, her lip trembling in anger, her arms flapping with emotion. Rávana ran after the fair-hipped woman and blocked her way. And having threatened her in a harsh voice, he grasped her, unconscious, by the hair, and ascended. Then Jatáyu, the vulture that roams the mountains, saw that female ascetic being carried away, crying, "Rama, Rama!"

MARKANDÉYA said:

The king of vultures, the great hero Jatáyu, son of Áruna, 279.1
brother of Sampáti, was a friend of Dasha·ratha. Seeing his daughter-in-law at Rávana's side, the bird angrily rushed at Rávana, lord of demons. Then the vulture said to him: "Let go! Release the princess of Míthila! While I live, how shall you abduct her, night stalker? For I won't release you alive, unless you let go of my daughter-in-law!"

So addressing the demon-king, he slashed at him vi-
ciously with his talons. Torn a hundred times by hits from 5
his wings and beak, he shed plentiful blood like a mountain covered in torrents. Hit by the vulture, who was trying to help those to whom Rama was dear, he took his sword and cut off the bird's wings. Having stricken the vulture king, who was like a mountain peak with tattered clouds, the demon took Sita on his hip and went upward.

Now wherever the princess of Vidéha saw a ring of hermitages, a lake or a river, she let fall an ornament. On a tabletop mountain she saw five bullish monkeys. There
the clever woman let fall her great celestial garment. Lifted 10

10 Tat teṣāṃ vānar'|êndrāṇāṃ papāta pavan'|ôddhatam
madhye supītaṃ pañcānāṃ vidyun megh'|ântare yathā.
Acireṇ' âticakrāma khe|caraḥ khe carann iva.
dadarś' âtha purīṃ ramyāṃ bahu|dvārāṃ mano|ramāṃ
Prākāra|vapra|saṃbādhāṃ nirmitāṃ Viśvakarmaṇā,
praviveśa purīṃ Laṅkāṃ sa|Sīto rākṣas'|ēśvaraḥ.
Evaṃ hṛtāyāṃ Vaidehyāṃ Rāmo hatvā mahā|mṛgam
nivṛtto dadṛśe dhīmān bhrātaraṃ Lakṣmaṇaṃ tadā.
«Katham utsṛjya Vaidehīṃ vane rākṣasa|sevite?»
ity taṃ bhrātaraṃ dṛṣṭvā «prāpto 's'» îti vyagarhayat.
15 Mṛga|rūpa|dhareṇ' âtha rakṣasā so 'pakarṣaṇam
bhrātur āgamanaṃ c' âiva cintayan paryatapyata.
Garhayann eva Rāmas tu tvaritas taṃ samāsadat:
«api jīvati Vaidehī? n' êti* paśyāmi Lakṣmaṇa.»
Tasya tat sarvam ācakhyau Sītāyā Lakṣmaṇo vacaḥ
yad uktavaty asadṛśaṃ Vaidehī paścimaṃ vacaḥ.
Dahyamānena tu hṛdā Rāmo 'bhyapatad āśramam.
sa dadarśa tadā gṛdhraṃ nihataṃ parvat'|ôpamam.
Rākṣasaṃ śaṅkamānas tu vikṛṣya balavad dhanuḥ
abhyadhāvata Kākutsthas tatas taṃ sahaLakṣmaṇaḥ.
20 Sa tāv uvāca tejasvī sahitau Rāma|Lakṣmaṇau:
«gṛdhra|rājo 'smi bhadraṃ vāṃ sakhā Daśarathasya vai.»
Tasya tad vacanaṃ śrutvā saṃgṛhya dhanuṣī śubhe:
«ko 'yaṃ pitaram asmākaṃ nāmn" āh' êty?» ūcatuś ca tau.
Tato dadṛśatus tau taṃ chinna|pakṣa|dvayaṃ khagaṃ,
tayoḥ śaśaṃsa gṛdhras tu Sīt"|ârthe Rāvaṇād vadham.
Apṛcchad Rāghavo gṛdhraṃ: «Rāvaṇaḥ kāṃ diśaṃ gataḥ?»
tasya gṛdhraḥ śiraḥ|kampair ācacakṣe mamāra ca.

by the wind, that bright yellow cloth fell among the five monkey-lords, like lightning among clouds. Like a bird in the sky, he* quickly went a long way. Then he saw his beautiful, pleasant city with its many gates; The demon-lord, together with Sita, entered the city of Lanka, bounded by ramparts and walls, the work of Vishva·karman.

While the Vidéha princess was being abducted in this way, wise Rama, who had killed the great deer, turned back and saw Lákshmana. Seeing his brother, he rebuked him: "Why have you come here, leaving the princess of Vidéha in a forest haunted by demons?" Then, thinking of how he had been drawn away by a demon in the form of a deer, and of his brother's arrival, he was consumed with worry.

Reproaching him, Rama hurried up to him: "Is the Vidéha princess still alive? I don't see her, Lákshmana." Lákshmana reported all Sita's words to him—the final unbalanced words the Vidéha princess had spoken. With a burning heart Rama rushed to the hermitage. So he saw the fallen vulture, looking like a mountain. Suspecting a demon, Kakútstha, his powerful bow drawn, ran with Lákshmana toward it.

The lustrous bird addressed Rama and Lákshmana: "I am king of the vultures, bless you—a friend of Dasha·ratha." Hearing this, they relaxed their bright bows and said: "Who is this who calls our father by name?" Then they saw that bird with both his wings cut off, and the vulture told them how, for Sita's sake, he had been stricken by Rávana. Rághava asked the vulture: "Which direction did Rávana go in?" With head movements the vulture told them, and died.

Dakṣiṇām iti Kākutstho viditv" âsya tad iṅgitam
sat|kāraṃ lambhayām āsa sakhāyaṃ pūjayan pituḥ.
25 Tato dṛṣṭv" āśrama|padaṃ vyapaviddha|bṛsī|maṭam
vidhvasta|kalaśaṃ śūnyaṃ gomāyu|śata|saṃkulam
Duḥkha|śoka|samāviṣṭau Vaidehī|haraṇ'|ârditau
jagmatur Daṇḍak'|āraṇyaṃ dakṣiṇena paraṃtapau.
Vane mahati tasmiṃs tu Rāmaḥ Saumitriṇā saha
dadarśa mṛga|yūthāni dravamāṇāni sarvaśaḥ,
Śabdaṃ ca ghoraṃ sattvānāṃ dāv'|âgner iva vardhataḥ.
apaśyetāṃ muhūrtāc ca Kabandhaṃ ghora|darśanam
Megha|parvata|saṃkāśaṃ śāla|skandhaṃ mahā|bhujam
uro|gata|viśāl'|âkṣaṃ mah"|ôdara|mahā|mukham.
30 Yadṛcchay" âtha tad rakṣaḥ kare jagrāha Lakṣmaṇam
viṣādam agamat sadyaḥ Saumitrir atha Bhārata.
Sa Rāmam abhisaṃprekṣya kṛṣyate yena tan|mukham
viṣaṇṇaś c' âbravīd Rāmaṃ: «paśy' âvasthām imāṃ mama.
Haraṇaṃ c' âiva Vaidehyā mama c' âyam upaplavaḥ
rājya|bhraṃśaś ca bhavatas tātasya maraṇaṃ tathā.
N' âhaṃ tvāṃ saha Vaidehyā sametaṃ Kosalā|gatam
drakṣyāmi pṛthivī|rājye pitṛ|paitā|mahe sthitam.
Drakṣyanty āryasya dhanyā ye kuśa|lāja|śamī|lavaiḥ
abhiṣiktasya vadanaṃ somaṃ śānta|ghanaṃ yathā.»
35 Evaṃ bahu|vidhaṃ dhīmān vilalāpa sa Lakṣmaṇaḥ.
tam uvāc' âtha Kākutsthaḥ saṃbhrameṣv apy asaṃbhramaḥ:
«Mā viṣīda nara|vyāghra! n' âiṣa kaś cin mayi sthite.
chindhy asya dakṣiṇaṃ bāhuṃ chinnaḥ savyo mayā bhujaḥ!»

Kakútstha, understanding his gesture to point to the south, accorded him reverence, honoring his father's friend.
25 Seeing the site of the empty hermitage, where seats had been thrown about, and jars smashed, thronging with hundreds of jackals, the incinerators of their foes, overcome by grief and sorrow, tormented by the Vidéha princess's abduction, took the southern path through the Dándaka forest. But in that great forest Rama and Sumítra's son Lákshmana saw herds of deer running in all directions, and heard the terrible sound of the creatures, like a spreading forest fire. And shortly they saw the loathsome looking *kabándha*, who appeared like a mountain of clouds, broad-shouldered as a *shala* tree, mighty-armed, with huge eyes in his chest, and a great mouth in his great belly.

30 Suddenly that demon grasped Lákshmana in his hand, and, instantly, Sumítra's son was filled with despair, O Bhárata. As he was drawn toward his mouth, he looked at Rama and said, despairingly: "See my plight—the Vidéha princess abducted, my current calamity, your fall from the kingdom, and our father's death. I shall not see you reunited with the Vidéha princess, or returned to Kósala and established again in the kingdom of your fathers and grandfathers on earth. Fortunate are they who shall see your lordship's face consecrated with grass, parched rice and *shami* logs, like the moon when its clouds have been dispelled."

35 Such was the manifold lament of Lákshmana the wise. Then, unmoved among the confusion, Kakútstha said to him: "Tigerish man, don't despair! While I am here, he is nothing. Cut off his right arm*—I have severed his left!" With these words, Rama lopped off his arm, sliced with

Ity evaṃ vadatā tasya bhujo Rāmeṇa pātitaḥ
khaḍgena bhṛśa|tīkṣṇena nikṛttas tila|kāṇḍavat.
Tato 'sya dakṣiṇaṃ bāhuṃ khaḍgen' ājaghnivān balī
saumitrir api saṃprekṣya bhrātaraṃ Rāghavaṃ sthitam.
Punar jaghāna pārśve vai tad rakṣo Lakṣmaṇo bhṛśam.
gatāsur apatad bhūmau Kabandhaḥ sumahāṃs tataḥ.
40 Tasya dehād viniḥsṛtya puruṣo divya|darśanaḥ
dadṛśe divam āsthāya divi sūrya iva jvalan.
Papraccha Rāmas taṃ vāgmī: «kas tvaṃ? prabrūhi pṛcchā
kāmayā kim idaṃ citram? āścaryaṃ pratibhāti me!»
Tasy' ācacakṣe: «gandharvo Viśvāvasur ahaṃ nṛpa
prāpto brahm'|ânuśāpena yoniṃ rākṣasa|sevitām.
Rāvaṇena hṛtā Sītā rājñā Laṅk"|âdhivāsinā.
Sugrīvam abhigacchasva sa te sāhyaṃ kariṣyati.
Eṣā Pampā śiva|jalā haṃsa|kāraṇḍav'|āyutā
Ṛṣyamūkasya śailasya saṃnikarṣe taṭākinī.
45 Vasate tatra Sugrīvaś caturbhiḥ sacivaiḥ saha
bhrātā vānara|rājasya Vālino hema|mālinaḥ.
Tena tvaṃ saha saṃgamya duḥkha|mūlaṃ nivedaya,
samāna|śīlo bhavataḥ sāhāyyaṃ sa kariṣyati.
Etāvac chakyam asmābhir vaktuṃ: draṣṭāsi Jānakīm.
dhruvaṃ vānara|rājasya vidito Rāvaṇ'|ālayaḥ.»
Ity uktv" ântarhito divyaḥ puruṣaḥ sa mahā|prabhaḥ
vismayaṃ jagmatuś c' ôbhau pravīrau Rāma|Lakṣmaṇau.

Mārkaṇḍeya uvāca:

280.1 Tato 'vidūre nalinīṃ prabhūta|kamal'|ôtpalām
Sītā|haraṇa|duḥkh'|ārtaḥ Pampāṃ Rāmaḥ samāsadat.
Mārutena suśītena sukhen' âmṛta|gandhinā
sevyamāno vane tasmiñ jagāma manasā priyām.

his super-sharp sword, like a sesame stalk. Then Sumít-
ra's powerful son, seeing his brother Rághava holding fast,
struck off his right arm with his sword. Again Lákshmana
struck the demon powerfully on the side. Then the gigantic
Kabándha fell lifeless to the ground. From his body there 40
emerged a godlike person; it was seen to mount into the
sky, blazing like a sun in the heavens.

Eloquently, Rama asked him: "Who are you? Answer me, I need to know. What is this strange event? To me, it's a wonder!"

He told him: "King, I am the *gandhárva* Vishva·vasu.
Through a brahmin curse I was born in a womb which
was serviced by a demon. Sita was abducted by Rávana,
the king who lives in Lanka. Go to Sugríva—he will help
you. Here near Mount Rishya·muka there are the beneficent
waters of Lake Pampa, full of geese and ducks. Sugríva, the 45
brother of the golden-garlanded monkey-king Valin, lives
there with four counsellors. Go to him, and tell him the
root of your sorrow. His case is similar to yours—he will
help you. We can tell you this much: you will see Jánaka's
daughter. The monkey-king definitely knows where Rávana
lives." With these words, the super-radiant, godlike person
disappeared, to the astonishment of the the two heroes,
Rama and Lákshmana.

MARKANDÉYA said:

Then Rama, full of grief at the abduction of Sita, reached 280.1
nearby Lake Pampa, covered in red and blue lotuses. Escor-
ted through that forest by a gentle cooling wind, fragrant
with the elixir of immortality, his thoughts turned to his

Vilalāpa sa rāj'|êndras tatra kāntām anusmaran
kāma|bāṇ'|âbhisaṃtaptaḥ. Saumitris tam ath' âbravīt:
«Na tvām evaṃ|vidho bhāvaḥ spraṣṭum arhati māna|da
ātmavantam iva vyādhiḥ puruṣaṃ vṛddha|śīlinam.
5 Pravṛttir upalabdhā te Vaidehyā Rāvaṇasya ca,
tāṃ tvaṃ puruṣa|kāreṇa buddhyā c' âiv' ôpapādaya.
Abhigacchāva Sugrīvaṃ śaila|sthaṃ hari|puṃgavam
mayi śiṣye ca bhṛtye ca sahāye ca samāśvasa.»
Evaṃ bahu|vidhair vākyair Lakṣmaṇena sa Rāghavaḥ
uktaḥ prakṛtim āpede kārye c' ânantaro 'bhavat.
Niṣevya vāri Pampāyās tarpayitvā pitṝn api
pratasthatur ubhau vīrau bhrātarau Rāma|Lakṣmaṇau.
Tāv Ṛṣyamūkam abhyetya bahu|mūla|phala|drumam
giry|agre vānarān pañca vīrau dadṛśatus tadā.
10 Sugrīvaḥ preṣayām āsa sacivaṃ vānaraṃ tayoḥ
buddhimantaṃ Hanūmantaṃ himavantam iva sthitam.
Tena saṃbhāṣya pūrvaṃ tau Sugrīvam abhijagmatuḥ
sakhyaṃ vānara|rājena cakre Rāmas tadā nṛpa.
Tad vāso darśayām āsus tasya kārye nivedite
vānarāṇāṃ tu yat Sītā hriyamāṇā vyapāsṛjat.
Tat pratyaya|karaṃ labdhvā Sugrīvaṃ plava|g'|âdhipam
pṛthivyāṃ vānar'|āiśvarye svayaṃ Rāmo 'bhyaṣecayat.
Pratijajñe ca Kākutsthaḥ samare Vālino vadham
Sugrīvaś c' âpi Vaidehyāḥ punar ānayanaṃ nṛpa.
15 Ity uktvā samayaṃ kṛtvā viśvāsya ca paras|param
abhyetya sarve Kiṣkindhāṃ tasthur yuddh'|âbhikāṅkṣiṇaḥ.

beloved. And there, remembering his beloved, the lord of kings lamented, scorched by love's arrow. Then Sumítra's son said to him:

"Honor-giver, this kind of feeling can no more touch you than a disease a self-possessed man whose habits are healthy. You've been given news of the Vidéha princess and Rávana. Use human effort and intelligence to rescue her. Let's go to Sugríva, the bullish monkey on the mountain. You can be confident in me, your pupil, servant and companion."

Addressed in this way, with many kinds of words, by Lákshmana, Rághava became himself again, and concentrated on what had to be done. They worshipped the Pampa's water, and also made the water offering to their ancestors; then the two heroic brothers, Rama and Lákshmana, set out. They arrived at Rishya·muka, full of roots, fruit and trees; then the heroes saw five monkeys on the mountaintop. Sugríva sent them his monkey counsellor, wise Hanúmat, steady as the Himálayas. Speaking with him first, they then approached Sugríva. So, my lord, Rama made friends with the monkey-king.

When he had told them what he had to do, they showed him the garment that Sita had dropped on the monkeys while she was being abducted. Receiving that proof from Sugríva, the monkey-lord, Rama himself consecrated him to lordhip of earthly monkeys. And Kakútstha promised to kill Valin in battle, and Sugríva to recover the Vidéha princess, my king. So saying, they made an agreement, encouraged one another, and all went to Kishkíndha, where they waited, eager for battle.

Sugrīvaḥ prāpya Kiṣkindhāṃ nanād' âugha|nibha|svanaḥ
n' âsya tan mamṛṣe Vālī. Tārā taṃ pratyaṣedhayat:
«Yathā nadati Sugrīvo balavān eṣa vānaraḥ
manye c' āśrayavān prāpto. na tvaṃ niṣkrāntum arhasi!»

Hema|mālī tato Vālī Tārāṃ tār'|âdhip'|ānanām
provāca vacanaṃ vāgmī tāṃ vānara|patiḥ patiḥ:
«Sarva|bhūta|ruta|jñā tvaṃ paśya! buddhyā samanvitā
kena c' āśrayavān prāpto mam' âiṣa bhrātṛ|gandhikaḥ?»

20 Cintayitvā muhūrtaṃ tu Tārā tār'|âdhipa|prabhā
patim ity abravīt prājñā: «śṛṇu sarvaṃ kap'|īśvara!
Hṛta|dāro mahā|sattvo Rāmo Daśarath'|ātmajaḥ
tuly'|âri|mitratāṃ prāptaḥ Sugrīveṇa dhanur|dharaḥ.
Bhrātā c' âsya mahā|bāhuḥ Saumitrir aparājitaḥ
Lakṣmaṇo nāma medhāvī sthitaḥ kāry'|ārtha|siddhaye.
Maindaś ca Dvividaś c' âpi Hanūmāṃś c' ânil'|ātmajaḥ
Jāmbavān ṛkṣa|rājaś ca Sugrīva|sacivāḥ sthitāḥ.
Sarva ete mah"|ātmāno buddhimanto mahā|balāḥ
alaṃ tava vināśāya Rāma|vīrya|bal'|āśrayāt.»
25 Tasyās tad ākṣipya vaco hitam uktaṃ kap'|īśvaraḥ
paryaśaṅkata tām īrṣuḥ Sugrīva|gata|mānasām.

Tārāṃ paruṣam uktvā sa nirjagāma guhā|mukhāt
sthitaṃ Mālyavato 'bhyāśe Sugrīvaṃ so 'bhyabhāṣata:
«Asakṛt tvaṃ mayā pūrve nirjito jīvita|priyaḥ
mukto jñātir iti jñātvā. kā tvarā maraṇe punaḥ?»

Reaching Kishkíndha, Sugríva roared with a noise like a flood. Coming from him, Valin could not tolerate it. Tará stopped him: "According to his roaring, Sugríva is a powerful monkey, and I think he's arrived with support. Don't go out!"

Then her husband, the eloquent, golden-garlanded Valin, the monkey-lord, made this speech to Tará, whose face was as beautiful as the moon: "You know the sound that every creature makes; you have intelligence. Look! With whose support has this seeming brother of mine turned up?"

Having thought for a moment, intelligent Tará, who 20
shone like the moon, said to her husband: "Listen to all this, monkey-lord! The great being Rama, Dasha·ratha's son, a great bowman, whose wife has been abducted, has contracted an alliance with Sugríva in which they share the same friends and foes. And his brother, the mighty-armed, unconquered and intelligent son of Sumítra, known as Lákshmana, stands ready to succeed in attaining the goal. And Sugríva's counsellors, Mainda, Dvi·vida, Hanúmat, the son of the Wind, and the bear-king Jámbavat stand ready. Great-souled, intelligent, super-strong—by depending on Rama's power and might, all these are sufficient to destroy
you." Ignoring her speech, which had been uttered to help 25
him, the monkey-lord jealously suspected her of thinking of Sugríva.

Speaking harshly to Tará, he came out from the mouth of the cave, and said to Sugríva, who was standing near to Mount Mályavat: "I have defeated you many times before—you who are as dear as life to me—and released you know-

Ity uktaḥ prāha Sugrīvo bhrātaraṃ hetumad vacaḥ
prāpta|kālam amitra|ghno Rāmaṃ saṃbodhayann iva:
«Hṛta|rājyasya me rājan hṛta|dārasya ca tvayā
kiṃ me jīvita|sāmarthyam? iti viddhi samāgatam.»
30 Evam uktvā bahu|vidhaṃ tatas tau saṃnipetatuḥ
samare Vāli|Sugrīvau śāla|tāla|śil"|āyudhau.
Ubhau jaghnatur anyonyam ubhau bhūmau nipetatuḥ
ubhau vavalgatuś citraṃ muṣṭibhiś ca nijaghnatuḥ.
Ubhau rudhira|saṃsiktau nakha|danta|parikṣatau
śuśubhāte tadā vīrau puṣpitāv iva kiṃśukau.
Na viśeṣas tayor yuddhe tadā kaś cana dṛśyate.
Sugrīvasya tadā mālāṃ Hanūmān kaṇṭha āsajat.
Sa mālayā tadā vīraḥ śuśubhe kaṇṭha|saktayā
śrīmān iva mahā|śailo Malayo megha|mālayā.
35 Kṛta|cihnaṃ tu Sugrīvaṃ Rāmo dṛṣṭvā mahā|dhanuḥ
vicakarṣa dhanuḥ śreṣṭhaṃ Vālim uddiśya lakṣyavat.
Visphāras tasya dhanuṣo yantrasy' êva tadā babhau,
vitatrāsa tadā Vālī śareṇ' âbhihat' ôrasi.
Sa bhinna|hṛdayo Vālī vaktrāc choṇitam udvaman
dadarś' âvasthitaṃ Rāmam tataḥ Saumitriṇā saha.
Garhayitvā sa Kākutsthaṃ papāta bhuvi mūrchitaḥ.
Tārā dadarśa taṃ bhūmau tārā|patim iva cyutam.*
Hate Vālini Sugrīvaḥ Kiṣkindhāṃ pratyapadyata
tāṃ ca tārā|pati|mukhīṃ Tārāṃ nipatit'|ēśvarām.
40 Rāmas tu caturo māsān pṛṣṭhe Mālyavataḥ śubhe
nivāsam akarod dhīmān Sugrīveṇ' âbhyupasthitaḥ.

ing you to be a relative. Who are you to hurry toward death again?"

Addressed in this way, Sugríva the enemy-killer spoke a tendentious speech to his brother, as though alerting Rama that the time had come: "King, I have had my kingdom usurped and my wife abducted by you. What is the meaning of my life? Know that this is what I've come to."

After uttering many things of this kind, Valin and Su- 30
gríva fell on each other in battle, using *shala* and palm trees, and stones as weapons. They struck one another, fell on the ground together, executed extraordinary leaps and pummelled each other with their fists. Sprayed with blood, wounded by claws and teeth, the heroes then shone like *kímshuka* blossoms: there was no visible difference between them in battle.

Then Hanúmat placed a garland on Sugríva's neck. And the hero with the garland around his neck shone like the
radiant great Mount Málaya, garlanded with clouds. And 35
when Rama saw that Sugríva had been marked out, the great bowman drew his best bow, making Valin his target. The bow vibrated like an engine. Then Valin shook, struck in the chest by the arrow. Valin, hit in the heart, vomiting blood from his mouth, saw Rama standing there with Sumítra's son. Reviling Kakútstha, he fell on the ground, unconscious. Tará saw him lying on the earth like a fallen moon.

With Valin slain, Sugríva returned to Kishkíndha and
to moon-faced Tará, whose lord had fallen. But wise Rama 40
made his dwelling on the shining peak of Mount Mályavata for four months, attended on by Sugríva.

Rāvaṇo 'pi purīṃ gatvā Laṅkāṃ kāma|balāt kṛtaḥ
Sītāṃ niveśayām āsa bhavane Nandan'|ôpame
Aśoka|vanik"|âbhyāśe tāpas'|āśrama|saṃnibhe.
bhartṛ|smaraṇa|tanv|aṅgī tāpasī|veṣa|dhāriṇī
Upavāsa|tapaḥ|śīlā tatr'|āsā pṛthul'|ēkṣaṇā,
uvāsa duḥkha|vasatīṃ phala|mūla|kṛt'|âśanā.
Dideśa rākṣasīs tatra rakṣaṇe rākṣas'|âdhipaḥ
prās'|âsi|śūla|paraśu|mudgar'|âlāta|dhāriṇīḥ
45 Dvy|akṣīṃ try|akṣīṃ lalāṭ'|âkṣīṃ dīrgha|jihvām ajihvikām
tri|stanīm eka|pādāṃ ca tri|jaṭām eka|locanām.
Etāś c' ânyāś ca dīpt'|âkṣyaḥ karabh'|ôtkaṭa|mūrdha|jāḥ
parivāry' āsate Sītāṃ divā|rātram atandritāḥ.
Tās tu tām āyat'|âpāṅgīṃ piśācyo dāruṇa|svarāḥ
tarjayanti sadā raudrāḥ paruṣa|vyañjana|svarāḥ:
«Khādāma pāṭayām' âināṃ tilaśaḥ pravibhajya tām
y" êyaṃ bhartāram asmākam avamany' êha jīvati!»
Ity evaṃ paribhartsantīs trāsyamānā punaḥ punaḥ
bhartṛ|śoka|samāviṣṭā niḥśvasy' êdam uvāca tāḥ:
50 «Āryāḥ khādata māṃ śīghraṃ! na me lobho 'sti jīvite
vinā taṃ puṇḍarīk'|âkṣaṃ nīla|kuñcita|mūrdhajam.
Apy ev' âhaṃ nirāhārā jīvita|priya|varjitā
śoṣayiṣyāmi gātrāṇi vyālī tāla|gatā yathā.
Na tv anyam abhigaccheyaṃ pumāṃsaṃ Rāghavād ṛte
iti jānīta satyaṃ me kriyatāṃ yad anantaram!»
Tasyās tad vacanaṃ śrutvā rākṣasyas tāḥ khara|svanāḥ
ākhyātuṃ rākṣas'|êndrāya jagmus tat sarvam āditaḥ.*

Now, under the sway of the force of his lust, Rávana had gone to his city Lanka. He installed Sita in his Nándana-like abode,* near an *ashóka** grove that looked like an ascetic's hermitage. Her limbs thin from remembering her husband, wearing the dress of an ascetic, the wide-eyed woman's practice was austerity and fasting. There she spent miserable nights on a diet of fruit and edible roots.

There too the demon-king assigned female demons to guard her, bearing spears, swords, spikes, axes and flaming brands. Some were two-eyed, some three-eyed; some had an eye in their forehead; some had long tongues, some were tongueless; some had three breasts, some a single foot; some had their hair in three braids above a solitary eye. These, and others, with blazing eyes and hair as thick as an elephant's trunk, sat around Sita day and night, without tiring. These horrible-sounding, terrible demonesses continuously threatened the long-eyed woman, rasping out their consonants: "Let's eat her! Let's tear her into seed-sized bits—this woman who lives here despising our lord!"

Terrified ever anew, sighing with grief for her husband, she said this to those threatening her so: "Noble ladies, eat me quickly! Without that lotus-eyed man with the dark curling hair, I have no wish to live. Indeed, without food, separated from him who is as dear as life to me, I shall dry out my limbs like a snake in a palm tree. Besides Rághava I would never go to any man. Know that this is the truth—you can do what you like to me!" When they had heard her speech, those harsh-voiced demonesses went to report it all from the beginning to the demon-lord.

Gatāsu tāsu sarvāsu Trijaṭā nāma rākṣasī
sāntvayām āsa Vaidehīṃ dharma|jñā priya|vādinī.
55 «Sīte vakṣyāmi te kiṃ cid, viśvāsaṃ kuru me sakhi.
bhayaṃ taṃ tyaja vām'|ōru śṛṇu c' êdaṃ vaco mama.
Avindhyo nāma medhāvī vṛddho rākṣasa|puṃgavaḥ
sa Rāmasya hit'|ânveṣī tvad|arthe hi sa m" âvadat:
‹Sītā mad|vacanād vācyā samāśvāsya prasādya ca:
«bhartā te kuśalī Rāmo Lakṣmaṇ' ânugato balī
Sakhyaṃ vānara|rājena śakra|pratima|tejasā
kṛtavān Rāghavaḥ śrīmāṃs tvad|arthe ca samudyataḥ.
Mā ca te 'stu bhayaṃ bhīru Rāvaṇāl loka|garhitāt
Nalakūbara|śāpena rakṣitā hy asy nandini.
60 Śapto hy eṣa purā pāpo vadhūṃ Rambhāṃ parāmṛśan
na śaknoty avaśāṃ nārīm upaitum ajit'|êndriyaḥ.
Kṣipram eṣyati te bhartā Sugrīveṇ' âbhirakṣitaḥ
Saumitri|sahito dhīmāṃs tvāṃ c' êto mokṣayiṣyati.
Svapnā hi sumahā|ghorā dṛṣṭā me 'niṣṭa|darśanāḥ
vināśāy' âsya durbuddheḥ Paulastya|kula|ghātinaḥ.
Dāruṇo hy eṣa duṣṭ'|ātmā kṣudra|karmā niśā|caraḥ
sva|bhāvāc chīla|doṣeṇa sarveṣāṃ bhaya|vardhanaḥ.
Spardhate sarva|devair yaḥ kāl'|ôpahata|cetanaḥ
mayā vināśa|liṅgāni svapne dṛṣṭāni tasya vai.
65 Tail'|âbhiṣikto vikaco majjan paṅke daś'|ānanaḥ
asakṛt khara|yukte tu rathe nṛtyann iva sthitaḥ.

While they were all gone, a demoness called Tri·jata,
who knew the Law and spoke sweetly, consoled the Vi-
déha princess:

"Sita, let me tell you something—have confidence in me, 55
my friend. Drop your fear, woman of the lovely thighs, and
hear this, my speech. There is an old, wise bull of a demon,
called Avíndhya. He desires Rama's welfare, and, for your
sake, he said to me:

'Calm and console her, then give Sita my message: "Your
mighty husband—and Lákshmana too—is well. The radi-
ant Rághava has contracted a friendship with the monkey-
king, whose luster is like Shakra's, and he is striving for
your sake. Timid woman, don't be afraid of Rávana, who is
denounced by the world, since you, my daughter, are pro-
tected by Nala·kúbara's curse. For in the past, this evildoer 60
was cursed when he assaulted his nephew's wife, Rambha:
incapable of controlling his senses, he is unable to approach
a woman against her will. Protected by Sugríva, your hus-
band will soon arrive, along with the canny son of Sumítra,
and he will liberate you from here. For I have seen the
most terrible unwanted sights in dreams, presaging the de-
struction of this most evil-minded destroyer of Pulástya's
son's family. This bad-souled, mean creature, who ranges
the night, spreads fear to all, through his own essential be-
ing and his flawed character.

In a dream I have seen signs of his destruction—he whose
consciousness has been damaged by Death, who challenges
all the gods: ten-headed, bald, smeared with sesame oil, 65
frequently standing on a donkey cart, seeming to dance
while sinking in the mud. Here Kumbha·karna and others

Kumbhakarṇ'|ādayaś c' ême nagnāḥ patita|mūrdha|jāḥ
gacchanti dakṣiṇām āśāṃ rakta|māly'|ânulepanāḥ.
Śvet'|ātapatraḥ s'|ôṣṇīṣaḥ śukla|māly'|ânulepanāḥ
śveta|parvatam ārūḍha eka eva Vibhīṣaṇaḥ
Sacivāś c' âsya catvāraḥ śukla|māly'|ânulepanāḥ
śveta|parvatam ārūḍhā mokṣyante 'smān mahā|bhayāt.
Rāmasy' âstreṇa pṛthivī parikṣiptā sa|sāgarā;
yaśasā pṛthivīṃ kṛtsnāṃ pūrayiṣyati te patiḥ.
70 Asthi|saṃcayam ārūḍho bhuñjāno madhu|pāyasam
Lakṣmaṇaś ca mayā dṛṣṭo didhakṣuḥ sarvato diśam.
Rudatī rudhir'|ārdr'|âṅgī vyāghreṇa parirakṣitā
asakṛt tvaṃ mayā dṛṣṭā gacchantī diśam uttarām.
Harṣam eṣyasi Vaidehi kṣipraṃ bhartrā samanvitā
Rāghaveṇa saha bhrātrā Sīte tvam acirād iva.»›
Ity etan mṛga|śāv'|âkṣī tac chrutvā Trijaṭā|vacaḥ
babhūv' āśāvatī bālā punar bhartṛ|samāgame.
Yāvad abhyāgatā raudrāḥ piśācyas tāḥ sudāruṇāḥ
dadṛśus tāṃ Trijaṭayā sah' āsīnāṃ yathā purā.

Mārkaṇḍeya uvāca:

281.1 Tatas tāṃ bhartṛ|śok'|ārtāṃ dīnāṃ malina|vāsasam
maṇi|śeṣ'|âbhyalaṃkārāṃ rudatīṃ ca pati|vratām
Rākṣasībhir upāsyantīṃ samāsīnāṃ śilā|tale
Rāvaṇaḥ kāma|bāṇ'|ārto dadarś' ôpasasarpa ca.
Deva|dānava|gandharva|yakṣa|kiṃpuruṣair yudhi
ajito 'śoka|vanikāṃ yayau kandarpa|pīḍitaḥ.
Divyā'|âmbara|dharaḥ śrīmān su|mṛṣṭa|maṇi|kuṇḍalaḥ
vicitra|mālya|mukuṭo vasanta iva mūrtimān.

too are going, to the southern region, naked, their hair fallen out, garlanded and anointed in red.

Only Vibhíshana, under a white umbrella, wearing a turban, garlanded and anointed in white, who has ascended White Mountain, and his four counsellors, garlanded and anointed in white, who have also climbed White Mountain, shall escape this great terror. The earth and its oceans are surrounded by Rama's missile; your husband shall fill the
whole earth with glory. And I saw Lákshmana, who had 70
mounted a pile of bones, eating honeyed rice, desperate to scorch in all directions. Many times I saw you going in the northern direction, weeping, your limbs drenched in blood, protected by a tiger. Princess of Vidéha, Sita, soon you shall be joyful, soon you shall be reunited with Rághava your husband, together with his brother.'"

Hearing this speech of Tri·jata, the doe-eyed woman became hopeful that she would be reunited with her husband. When those cruel and dreadful demonesses came back, they saw her, as before, sitting with Tri·jata.

MARKANDÉYA said:

Then Rávana, pierced by the god of love's arrows, saw 281.1
her served by the demonesses, sitting on a flat stone, depressed with grief for her husband, distressed, wearing soiled clothes, left with just a remnant of her bridal jewels, weeping, a devoted wife. And he approached her.

Undefeated in battle by gods, *dánava*s, *gandhárva*s, *yaksha*s, and *kim·púrushas*, he entered the *ashóka** grove, distressed by love. Dressed in divine robes, lustrous, his earrings made of polished gems, crowned with colored garlands, he

5 Sa* kalpa|vṛkṣa|sadṛśo yatnād api vibhūṣitaḥ
śmaśāna|caitya|drumavad bhūṣito 'pi bhayaṃ|karaḥ.
Sa tasyās tanu|madhyāyāḥ samīpe rajanī|caraḥ
dadṛśe Rohiṇīm etya śanaiś|cara iva grahaḥ.
Sa tām āmantrya su|śroṇīṃ puṣpa|ketu|śar'|āhataḥ
idam ity abravīd vākyaṃ trastāṃ rauhīm iv' âbalām:
«Sīte paryāptam etāvat, kṛto bhartur anugrahaḥ.
prasādaṃ kuru tanv|aṅgi kriyatāṃ parikarma te.
Bhajasva māṃ var'|ārohe mah"|ârh'|ābharaṇ'|âmbarā
bhava me sarva|nārīṇām uttamā vara|varṇinī.
10 Santi me deva|kanyāś ca gandharvāṇāṃ ca yoṣitaḥ
santi dānava|kanyāś ca daityānāṃ c' âpi yoṣitaḥ.
Caturdaśa piśācānāṃ koṭyo me vacane sthitāḥ
dvis tāvat puruṣā'|âdānāṃ rakṣasāṃ bhīma|karmaṇām.
Tato me tri|guṇā yakṣā ye mad|vacana|kāriṇaḥ,
ke cid eva dhan'|âdhyakṣaṃ bhrātaraṃ me samāśritāḥ.
gandharv'|âpsaraso bhadre mām āpāna|gataṃ sadā
upatiṣṭhanti vām'|ôru yath" âiva bhrātaraṃ mama.
Putro 'ham api vipra'|rṣeḥ sākṣād Viśravaso muneḥ,
pañcamo loka|pālānām iti me prathitaṃ yaśaḥ.
15 Divyāni bhakṣya|bhojyāni pānāni vividhāni ca
yath" âiva tridaś'|ēśasya tath" âiva mama bhāvini.
Kṣīyatāṃ duṣkṛtaṃ karma vana|vāsa|kṛtaṃ tava.
bhāryā me bhava su|śroṇi yathā Mandodarī tathā.»

was like the embodiment of spring. Even though he had made the effort to dress himself like the wish-giving tree, even though he had adorned himself, he was terrifying, like a tree on a funeral mound in a cemetery. Next to that slim-waisted woman, the night-walker looked like the planet Saturn approaching Róhini. Greeting that fair-hipped woman, and pierced by the arrow of love, he made this speech to her, powerless like a frightened doe:

"Sita, enough of this! You have favored your husband—it's finished! Be gracious to me, slender woman. Let your body be prepared. Love me, fair-hipped woman! Be supreme among my wives—with the best complexion, with the most precious clothes and ornaments. I have god-maidens and *gandhárva* girls, *dánava* maidens and *daitya* girls. One hundred and forty million *pisháchas* wait at my command, twice as many man-eating demons, who do terrible things. I have three times as many *yaksha*s to do my command; just a few have gone to my brother the lord of wealth. *Gandhárva*s and *ápsarases* always attend on me in my drinking hall, beautiful-thighed lady, just as they do on my brother. I am actually the son of the brahmin sage and seer Víshravas. My fame extends to being called the fifth guardian of the world-regions. Beautiful woman, I have all kinds of divine foodstuffs and drink, just like the lord of the gods. Fair-hipped lady, let the ill effects of your stay in the forest be destroyed. Like Mandódari, become my wife."

Ity uktā tena Vaidehī parivṛtya śubh'|ānanā
tṛṇam antarataḥ kṛtvā tam uvāca niśā|caram.
A|śiven' âtivām'|ōrūr ajasraṃ netra|vāriṇā
stanāv a|patitau bālā sahitāv abhivarṣatī.
Uvāca vākyaṃ taṃ kṣudraṃ Vaidehī pati|devatā:
«asakṛd vadato vākyam īdṛśaṃ rākṣas'|ēśvara.
20 Viṣāda|yuktam etat te mayā śrutam a|bhāgyayā.
tad bhadra|sukha bhadraṃ te! mānasaṃ vinivartyatām.
Para|dār" âsmy alabhyā ca satataṃ ca pati|vratā
na c' âiv' āupayikī* bhāryā mānuṣī kṛpaṇā tava.
Vivaśāṃ dharṣayitvā ca kāṃ tvaṃ prītim avāpsyasi?
Prajāpati|samo vipro Brahma|yoniḥ pitā tava:
Na ca pālayase dharmaṃ loka|pāla|samaḥ katham?
bhrātaraṃ rāja|rājānaṃ mah"|ēśvara|sakhaṃ prabhum
Dhan'|ēśvaraṃ vyapadiśan kathaṃ tv iha na lajjase?»
ity uktvā prārudat Sītā kampayantī payo|dharau
25 Śiro|dharāṃ ca tanv|aṅgī mukhaṃ pracchādya vāsasā.
tasyā rudatyā bhāvinyā dīrghā veṇī susaṃyatā
Dadṛśe svasitā snigdhā kālī vyālīva mūrdhani.
śrutvā tad Rāvaṇo vākyaṃ Sītay" ôktaṃ su|niṣṭhuram
Pratyākhyāto 'pi dur|medhāḥ punar ev' âbravīd vacaḥ:
«kāmam aṅgāni me Sīte dunotu Makara|dhvajaḥ.
Na tvām akāmāṃ suśroṇīṃ sameṣye cāru|hāsinīm.
kiṃ nu śakyaṃ mayā kartuṃ yat tvam ady' âpi mānuṣam
Āhāra|bhūtam asmākaṃ Rāmam ev' ânurudhyase?»
30 Ity uktvā tām anindy'|âṅgīṃ sa rākṣasa|mah"|ēśvaraḥ

Addressed by him in this way, the fair-faced Vidéha princess turned away; considering him in her heart worthless as chaff, she spoke to the creature of the night—with inauspicious tears incessantly drenching her close, firm breasts, the young woman with such beautiful thighs, the Vidéha princess, so devoted to her husband, said to that cruel one: "Demon-lord, you have often given this speech before, full of despair, and I, unfortunately, have had to listen to it. Hail to you, blessed and happy one! Restrain your thoughts. I am another's wife, unobtainable, and forever devoted to my husband. Besides, a miserable human wife is unsuitable for you. And what pleasure will you obtain in assaulting an unwilling woman? Your father is a brahmin, equal to Praja·pati, born of Brahma. How is it that one who is the equal of a world guardian doesn't protect the Law? Your lordly brother, the king of kings, a friend of the great lord, the lord of wealth—how is it you are not ashamed to represent him?" Saying this, Sita began to weep, her breasts trembling—the slender-limbed woman—covering her throat and face with her scarf. The long tight braid of that weeping lady looked like a dark black snake, hugging her head.

Having heard such harsh words, uttered by Sita, Rávana, although rejected, kept on talking, the fool: "Sita, let the Mákara-bannered* god burn my limbs at will. I will not unite with you if you are unwilling, fair-hipped, sweet-smiling woman. What can I do, if even now you stick to the human, to our food, to Rama?" Saying this to the woman of flawless limbs, the great demon-lord vanished on the spot and went in his chosen direction. So, surrounded by

tatr' âiv' ântarhito bhūtvā jagām' âbhimatāṃ diśam.
Rākṣasībhiḥ parivṛtā Vaidehī śoka|karśitā
sevyamānā Trijaṭayā tatr' âiva nyavasat tadā.

MĀRKAṆḌEYA uvāca:

282.1 Rāghavaḥ saha Saumitriḥ Sugrīveṇ' âbhipālitaḥ
vasan Mālyavataḥ pṛṣṭhe dadarśe vimalaṃ nabhaḥ.
Sa dṛṣṭvā vimale vyomni nirmalaṃ śaśa|lakṣaṇam
graha|nakṣatra|tārābhir anuyātam amitra|hā
Kumud'|ôtpala|padmānāṃ gandham ādāya vāyunā
mahīdhara|sthaḥ śītena sahasā pratibodhitaḥ.
Prabhāte Lakṣmaṇaṃ vīram abhyabhāṣata dur|manāḥ
Sītāṃ saṃsmṛtya dharm'|ātmā ruddhāṃ rākṣasa|veśmani.
5 «Gaccha Lakṣmaṇa jānīhi Kiṣkindhāyāṃ kap'|īśvaram
pramattaṃ grāmya|dharmeṣu kṛtaghnaṃ sv'|ârtha|paṇḍitam,
Yo 'sau kul'|âdhamo mūḍho mayā rājye 'bhiṣecitaḥ
sarva|vānara|go|pucchā yam ṛkṣāś ca bhajanti vai.
Yad|arthaṃ nihato Vālī mayā Raghu|kul'|ôdvaha
tvayā saha mahā|bāho Kiṣkindh"|ôpavane tadā.
Kṛtaghnaṃ tam ahaṃ manye vānar'|âpasadaṃ bhuvi
yo māṃ evaṃgato mūḍho na jānīte 'dya Lakṣmaṇa.
Asau manye na jānīte samaya|pratipālanam
kṛt'|ôpakāraṃ māṃ nūnam avamany' âlpayā dhiyā.
10 Yadi tāvad anudyuktaḥ śete kāma|sukh'|ātmakaḥ
netavyo Vāli|mārgeṇa sarva|bhūta|gatiṃ tvayā.
Ath' âpi ghaṭate 'smākam arthe vānara|puṃgavaḥ
tam ādāy' âihi Kākutstha tvarāvān bhava mā ciram!»

demonesses, the Vidéha princess, thin with sorrow, attended by Tri·jata, went on living there.

Markandéya said:

Rághava, protected by Sugríva, and residing, along with 282.1
Sumítra's son, on the top of Mount Mályavat, looked at the clear sky. The enemy-killer, seeing the unblemished moon, followed by the planets, constellations and stars in the cloudless sky, was suddenly roused, as he stood on the mountain, by a cool breeze wafting the fragrance of blue and white lotuses and water lilies. Remembering that Sita was a captive in the house of a demon, the dispirited soul of the Law spoke at dawn to the hero Lákshmana:

"Go, Lákshmana! Find out about Kishkíndha, the lord of 5
monkeys, who is distracted by vulgar matters, ungrateful, obsessed with his own advantage —that lowborn fool who was consecrated ruler by me, and who is loved by all the cow-tailed monkeys and the bears. For his sake, great-armed support of the family of Raghu, I, with you at my side, killed Valin in the Kishkíndha forest. I consider him ungrateful, an outcast of monkeys on earth; in this deluded state, he no longer knows me, Lákshmana. I don't think he knows how to observe an agreement; with his small brain, he surely despises me, for assisting him. If he is lying so dormant, so 10
lust- and pleasure-obsessed, you must lead him down Valin's path to the goal that awaits all beings. If, on the other hand, the bullish monkey is intent on our purpose, Kakútstha, bring him here. Be quick! No delay!"

Ity ukto Lakṣmaṇo bhrātrā guru|vākya|hite rataḥ
pratasthe ruciraṃ gṛhya sa|mārgaṇa|guṇaṃ dhanuḥ.
Kiṣkindhā|dvāram āsādya praviveś' ânivāritaḥ.
sakrodha iti taṃ matvā rājā pratyudyayau hariḥ.
Taṃ sa|dāro vinīt'|ātmā Sugrīvaḥ plavag'|âdhipaḥ
pūjayā pratijagrāha prīyamāṇas tad|arhayā.
15 Tam abravīd Rāma|vacaḥ Saumitrir akuto|bhayaḥ.
sa tat sarvam aśeṣeṇa śrutvā prahvaḥ kṛtāñjaliḥ
Sa|bhṛtya|dāro rāj'|êndra Sugrīvo vānar'|âdhipaḥ
idam āha vacaḥ prīto Lakṣmaṇaṃ nara|kuñjaram:
«N' âsmi Lakṣmaṇa dur|medhā n' âkṛta|jño na nirghṛṇaḥ.
śrūyatāṃ yaḥ prayatno me Sītā|paryeṣaṇe kṛtaḥ.
Diśaḥ prasthāpitāḥ sarve vinītā harayo mayā
sarveṣāṃ ca kṛtaḥ kālo māsen' âgamanaṃ punaḥ.
Yair iyaṃ sa|vanā s'|âdriḥ sa|purā sāgar'|âmbarā
vicetavyā mahī vīra sa|grāma|nagar'|ākarā.
20 Sa māsaḥ pañca|rātreṇa pūrṇo bhavitum arhati.
tataḥ śroṣyasi Rāmeṇa sahitaḥ sumahat priyam.»
Ity ukto Lakṣmaṇas tena vānar'|êndreṇa dhīmatā
tyaktvā roṣam adīn'|ātmā Sugrīvaṃ pratyapūjayat.
Sa Rāmaṃ saha|Sugrīvo Mālyavat|pṛṣṭham āsthitam
abhigamy' ôdayaṃ tasya kāryasya pratyavedayat.
Ity evaṃ vānar'|êndrās te samājagmuḥ sahasraśaḥ
diśas tisro vicity' âtha na tu ye dakṣiṇāṃ gatāḥ.
Ācakhyus tatra Rāmāya mahīṃ sāgara|mekhalām
vicitāṃ na tu Vaidehyā darśanaṃ Rāvaṇasya vā.

Thus addressed by his brother, devoted to following the of his elder, Lákshmana took his bright bow, his bowstring and arrows, and set out. Reaching the gateway to Kishkíndha, he entered unobstructed. The monkey-king, thinking he was angry, went out to meet him. The well-bred monkey-lord, Sugríva, along with his wife, went up to him and received him with appropriate honor.

Fearing nothing, Sumítra's son relayed Rama's speech. Having heard it all without exception, bowing, with the palms of his hands joined, the monkey-lord, Sugríva, with his wife and servants, was pleased, king of kings; he uttered this speech to Lákshmana, an elephant of a man:

"Lákshmana, I am not stupid, ungrateful or cold. Hear about the effort I have made searching for Sita. I have dispatched all well-trained monkeys in all directions and a time limit of one month has been set for all to return. Hero, they are to search this earth, bounded by the oceans—its forests, mountains and cities, its villages, towns and mines. In five nights that month will be up. Then you and Rama shall hear something most precious."

Thus addressed by the wise monkey-lord, Lákshmana stopped being angry, and, in high spirits, honored Sugríva in return. With Sugríva, he went to Rama, waiting on the top of Mount Mályavat, and reported the outcome of his endeavors. And so the monkey-lords, having scoured the three directions, came together in their thousands—but not those who had gone south. There, they told Rama they had searched the earth, bounded by the ocean, but without a glimpse of the Vidéha princess or of Rávana. Yet afflicted Kakútstha kept himself alive, hopeful

25 Gatās tu dakṣiṇām āśāṃ ye vai vānara|puṃgavāḥ
āśāvāṃs teṣu Kākutsthaḥ prāṇān ārto 'bhyadhārayat.
Dvi|mās'|oparame kāle vyatīte plava|gās tataḥ
Sugrīvam abhigamy' êdaṃ tvaritā vākyam abruvan:
«Rakṣitaṃ Vālinā yat tat sphītaṃ Madhuvanaṃ mahat
tvayā ca plava|ga|śreṣṭha tad bhuṅkte pavan'|ātma|jaḥ.
Vāli|putro 'ṅgadaś c' âiva ye c' ânye plava|ga'|rṣabhāḥ
vicetuṃ dakṣiṇām āśāṃ rājan prasthāpitās tvayā.»
Teṣāṃ apanayaṃ śrutvā mene sa kṛta|kṛtyatām
kṛt'|ârthānāṃ hi bhṛtyānām etad bhavati ceṣṭitam.
30 Sa tad Rāmāya medhāvī śaśaṃsa plava|ga'|rṣabhaḥ
Rāmaś c' âpy anumānena mene dṛṣṭāṃ tu maithilīm.
Hanūmat|pramukhāś c' âpi viśrāntās te plavaṃ|gamāḥ
abhijagmur har'|îndraṃ taṃ Rāma|Lakṣmaṇa|saṃnidhau.
Gatiṃ ca mukha|varṇaṃ ca dṛṣṭvā Rāmo Hanūmataḥ
agamat pratyayaṃ bhūyo «dṛṣṭā Sīt" êti» Bhārata.
Hanūmat|pramukhās te tu vānarāḥ pūrṇa|mānasāḥ
praṇemur vidhivad Rāmaṃ Sugrīvaṃ Lakṣmaṇaṃ tathā.
Tān uvāc' ānatān Rāmaḥ pragṛhya sa|śaraṃ dhanuḥ:
«api māṃ jīvayiṣyadhvam? api vaḥ kṛta|kṛtyatā?
35 Api rājyam Ayodhyāyāṃ kārayiṣyāmy ahaṃ punaḥ
nihatya samare śatrūn āhṛtya Janak'|ātma|jām?
Amokṣayitvā Vaidehīm ahatvā ca raṇe ripūn
hṛta|dāro 'vadhūtaś ca n' âhaṃ jīvitum utsahe.»
Ity ukta|vacanaṃ Rāmaṃ pratyuvāc' ânil'|ātma|jaḥ:
«priyam ākhyāmi te Rāma dṛṣṭā sā Jānakī mayā.
Vicitya dakṣiṇām āśāṃ sa|parvata|van'|ākarām
śrāntāḥ kāle vyatīte sma dṛṣṭavanto mahā|guhām.

about the bullish monkeys that had gone to the southern quarter. Then, when two months had passed, the monkeys approached Sugríva in haste, and said this:

"The great thriving wood, Madhu·vana, which was protected by Valin, and by you, best of monkeys, is being consumed by the son of the Wind,* and by Valin's son Ángada, and other bullish monkeys sent out by you, king, to scour the southern direction." Hearing about their bad behavior, he supposed they must have achieved their object, for this was the conduct of servants who had done their job.

That intelligent bullish monkey told this to Rama, and 30
Rama too inferred that the princess of Míthila* had been
seen. With Hanúmat at their head, the rested monkeys
approached the monkey-lord in Rama's and Lákshmana's
presence. And, seeing Hanúmat's walk and complexion, Rama
was even more certain that Sita had been seen, Bhárata.
Then those contented monkeys, led by Hanúmat, bowed
properly to Rama, Sugríva and Lákshmana. Rama took his
bow and arrows and said to those bowing creatures:

"Will you bring me back to life? Have you done what you
set out to do? Shall I, having killed my enemies in battle, and 35
recovered Jánaka's daughter, rule in Ayódhya again? Unless
I can liberate the Vidéha princess and kill my enemies in
battle, I cannot bear to live, a slighted man whose wife has
been abducted."

To Rama, who had spoken in this way, the son of the Wind replied: "I shall tell you something precious, Rama. I have seen Jánaka's daughter. After searching through the southern region, with its mountains, forests and mines, time

Praviśāmo vayaṃ tāṃ tu bahu|yojanam āyatām
andha|kārāṃ suvipināṃ gahanāṃ kīṭa|sevitām.
40 Gatvā sumahad|adhvānam ādityasya prabhāṃ tataḥ
dṛṣṭavantaḥ sma, tatr' âiva bhavanaṃ divyam antarā.
Mayasya kila daityasya tad āsīd veśma Rāghava.
tatra Prabhāvatī nāma tapo 'tapyata tāpasī.
Tayā dattāni bhojyāni pānāni vividhāni ca.
bhuktvā labdha|balāḥ santas tay" ôktena pathā tataḥ
Niryāya tasmād uddeśāt paśyāmo lavaṇ'|âmbhasaḥ
samīpe Salya|malayau Darduraṃ ca mahā|girim.
Tato Malayam āruhya paśyanto Varuṇ'|ālayam
viṣaṇṇā vyathitāḥ khinnā nirāśā jīvite bhṛśam
45 Aneka|śata|vistīrṇaṃ yojanānāṃ mah"|ôdadhim
timi|nakra|jhaṣ'|āvāsaṃ cintayantaḥ suduḥkhitāḥ.
Tatr' ânaśana|saṃkalpaṃ kṛtv" āsīnā vayaṃ tadā
tataḥ kath"|ânte gṛdhrasya Jaṭāyor abhavat kathā.
Tataḥ parvata|śṛṅg'|ābhaṃ ghora|rūpaṃ bhay'|āvaham
pakṣiṇaṃ dṛṣṭavantaḥ sma vainateyam iv' âparam.
So 'smān atarkayad bhoktum ath' âbhyetya vaco 'bravīt:
‹bhoḥ ka eṣa mama bhrātur Jaṭāyoḥ kurute kathām.
Saṃpātir nāma tasy' âhaṃ jyeṣṭho bhrātā khag'|âdhipaḥ
anyonya|spardhay" ārūḍhāv āvām āditya|satpadam.
50 Tato dagdhāv imau pakṣau na dagdhau tu Jaṭāyuṣaḥ
tadā me cira|dṛṣṭaḥ sa bhrātā gṛdhra|patiḥ priyaḥ.
Nirdagdha|pakṣaḥ patito hy aham asmin mahā|girau.›

had passed and we were tired. Seeing a great cave, we entered it. Extending for many *yójanas*,* it was pitch black, very tangled, deep and infested with insects. After going a very long way, we saw sunlight; and there, inside, was a heavenly palace. Rághava, it was the home of the *daitya*, Maya, himself. There a female ascetic called Prabhávati was practicing austerities. She gave us all kinds of food and drink. Having consumed it, our strength returned, and then we took the path she described. Issuing from that place, according to the directions, we saw, close by the saltwater sea, Mount Salya, Mount Málaya and great Mount Dárdura.

Then, having climbed Málaya, looking at Váruna's realm, we became depressed, agitated, crushed, quite hopeless about life; thinking about the great ocean, stretching out for many hundreds of *yójanas*, the realm of whales, crocodiles and fish. We were utterly miserable. We were sitting there, determined to starve ourselves, when, at the end of a conversation, the story of the vulture Jatáyu came up. Then we saw a horrible, terrifying bird, big as a mountain peak, like another son of Vínata.*

He had decided to eat us; but then, coming closer, said: 'Ho! Who is this, telling the tale of my brother Jatáyu? I am his eldest brother, called Sampáti, lord of the birds. Vying with each other, we climbed toward the sun. Both my wings were burnt then, but not Jatáyu's. It's a long time since I've seen my brother, the vulture lord, for with my wings burnt up, I fell on this high mountain.'

tasy' âivaṃ vadato 'smābhir hato bhrātā niveditaḥ
Vyasanaṃ bhavataś c' êdaṃ saṃkṣepād vai niveditam.
sa Saṃpātis tadā rājañ śrutvā sumahad apriyam
Viṣaṇṇa|cetāḥ papraccha punar asmān ariṃ|dama:
‹kaḥ sa Rāmaḥ? kathaṃ Sītā? Jaṭāyuś ca kathaṃ hataḥ?
Icchāmi sarvam ev' âitac chrotuṃ plava|ga|sattamāḥ.›
tasy' âhaṃ sarvam ev' âitad bhavato vyasan'|āgamam
55 Prāy'|opaveśane c' âiva hetuṃ vistaraśo 'bruvam.
so 'smān utthāpayām āsa vākyen' ânena pakṣi|rāṭ.
‹Rāvaṇo vidito mahyaṃ Laṅkā c' âsya mahā|purī
dṛṣṭā pāre samudrasya Trikūṭa|giri|kandare.
Bhavitrī tatra Vaidehī—na me 'sty atra vicāraṇā.›
iti tasya vacaḥ śrutvā vayam utthāya sat|varāḥ
Sāgara|kramaṇe mantraṃ mantrayāmaḥ paraṃ|tapa.
n' âdhyavasyad yadā kaś cit sāgarasya vilaṅghanam.
Tataḥ pitaram āviśya pupluve 'haṃ mah"|ârṇavam
śata|yojana|vistīrṇaṃ nihatya jala|rākṣasīm.
60 Tatra Sītā mayā dṛṣṭā Rāvaṇ'|ântaḥpure satī
upavāsa|tapaḥ|śīlā bhartṛ|darśana|lālasā.
Jaṭilā mala|digdh'|âṅgī kṛśā dīnā tapasvinī.
nimittais tām ahaṃ Sītām upalabhya pṛthag|vidhaiḥ
Upasṛty' âbruvaṃ c' āryām abhigamya raho|gatām:
‹Sīte Rāmasya dūto 'haṃ vānaro mārut'|ātma|jaḥ.
Tvad|darśanam abhiprepsur iha prāpto vihāyasā.
rāja|putrau kuśalinau bhrātarau Rāma|Lakṣmaṇau.
Sarva|śākhā|mṛg'|êndreṇa Sugrīveṇ' âbhipālitau.

We made it known to him, who had been addressing us,
that his brother had been killed, and also briefly told him
about your lordship's misfortune. Then, king, on hearing
such extremely bad news, Sampáti, low in spirits, ques-
tioned us again, enemy-tamer: 'Who is this Rama? How is
Sita? And how was Jatáyu killed? I want to hear all this,
best of monkeys.' I told him all this—how your lordship
encountered misfortune, and the reason for our sitting in a 55
death fast, in detail. With this speech the bird-king caused
us to rise:

'Rávana is known to me, and his great city, Lanka, has
been spied by me on the far shore of the ocean, in a valley
on Mount Tri·kuta. The Vidéha princess will be there—I
have no doubt of it.'

Having heard his speech, we rose up quickly, and took
counsel together about a way to cross the ocean, incinerator
of the foe. When no one resolved to leap over the ocean,
I entered my father* and, having killed a water demoness,
flew across the great sea, extending for hundreds of *yójanas*.
There, I saw Sita in Rávana's women's quarters, practicing 60
austerities and fasting, pining to see her husband.

Her hair was matted, her limbs caked with dirt, wretched,
and afflicted. Establishing by various signs that she was Sita,
I approached, and spoke to the noble lady, going up to her
when she was by herself:

'Sita, I am Rama's messenger, the monkey son of the
Wind. Wanting to catch sight of you, I came here through
the air. The princely brothers, Rama and Lákshmana, are
well, protected by Sugríva, the lord of all the monkeys. Sita,
Rama, together with Sumítra's son, sends greeting, and, out 65

kuśalaṃ tv" âbravīd Rāmaḥ Sīte Saumitriṇā saha
65 Sakhi|bhāvāc ca Sugrīvaḥ kuśalaṃ tv" ânupṛcchati.
kṣipram eṣyati te bhartā sarva|śākhā|mṛgaiḥ saha.
Pratyayaṃ kuru me devi vānaro 'smi na rākṣasaḥ.›
muhūrtam iva ca dhyātvā Sītā māṃ pratyuvāca ha:
‹Avaimi tvāṃ Hanūmantam Avindhya|vacanād aham.
Avindhyo hi mahā|bāho rākṣaso vṛddha|saṃmataḥ.
Kathitas tena Sugrīvas tvad|vidhaiḥ sacivair vṛtaḥ.›
‹gamyatām› iti c' ôktvā māṃ Sītā prādād imaṃ maṇim.
Dhāritā yena Vaidehī kālam etam aninditā.
pratyay'|ârthaṃ kathāṃ c' êmāṃ kathayām āsa Jānakī
70 Kṣiptām iṣīkāṃ kākāya Citrakūṭe mahā|girau
bhavatā puruṣa|vyāghra pratyabhijñāna|kāraṇāt.
Grāhayitvā 'ham ātmānaṃ tato dagdhvā ca tāṃ purīm
saṃprāpta iti». taṃ Rāmaḥ priya|vādinam arcayat.

MĀRKAṆḌEYA uvāca:

283.1 Tatas tatr' âiva Rāmasya samāsīnasya taiḥ saha
samājagmuḥ kapi|śreṣṭhāḥ Sugrīva|vacanāt tadā.
Vṛtaḥ koṭi|sahasreṇa vānarāṇāṃ tarasvinām
śvaśuro Vālinaḥ śrīmān Suṣeṇo Rāmam abhyayāt.
Koṭī|śata|vṛtau v" âpi Gajo Gavaya eva ca
vānar'|êndrau mahā|vīryau pṛthak pṛthag adṛśyatām.
ṣaṣṭi|koṭi|sahasrāṇi prakarṣan pratyadṛśyata
go|lāṅgūlo mahā|rāja Gavākṣo bhīma|darśanaḥ.
5 Gandhamādana|vāsī tu prathito Gandhamādanaḥ
koṭī|śata|sahasrāṇi* harīṇāṃ samakarṣata.

of friendship, Sugríva asks about your health. Your husband will come swiftly, together with all the monkeys. Believe me, queen, I am a monkey not a demon.'

Seeming to ponder for a moment, Sita then answered me: 'From Avíndhya's speech, I know that you are Hanúmat, for Avíndhya, Great Arm, is a demon respected by the elders. He told me about Sugríva, surrounded by counsellors such as you.'

Then, telling me to go, Sita gave me this jewel, which
has sustained the blameless Vidéha princess throughout this
time. And as a means of proof, Jánaka's daughter told this
story—of the arrow thrown at the crow on Chitra·kuta 70
peak*—so that you would recognize it, tigerish man. Al-
lowing myself to be seized, I set fire to that city, and then I
came back." Rama honored him for speaking good news.

Markandéya said:

Then, while Rama was sitting there with them, the best 283.1
of monkeys gathered together at Sugríva's command.

Valin's esteemed father-in-law, Sushéna, surrounded by ten billion swift monkeys, came to Rama. The powerful monkey-lords Gaja and Gávaya appeared separately, each surrounded by a billion.

Cow-tailed Gaváksha, terrible to behold, great king, was
seen bringing six hundred billion. But famous Gandha·má- 5
dana, who lived on Mount Gandha·mádana, led a thousand
billion monkeys.

Panaso nāma medhāvī vānaraḥ sumahā|balaḥ
koṭīr daśa dvādaśa ca triṃśatpañca prakarṣati.
Śrīmān Dadhimukho nāma hari|vṛddho 'tivīryavān
pracakarṣa mahā|sainyaṃ harīṇāṃ bhīma|tejasām.
Kṛṣṇānāṃ mukha|puṇḍrāṇām ṛkṣāṇāṃ bhīma|karmaṇām
koṭī|śata|sahasreṇa Jāmbavān pratyadṛśyata.
Ete c' ânye ca bahavo hari|yūtha|pa|yūtha|pāḥ
asaṃkhyeyā mahā|rāja samīyū Rāma|kāraṇāt.
10 Giri|kūṭa|nibh"|âṅgānāṃ siṃhānām iva garjatām
śrūyate tumulaḥ śabdas tatra tatra pradhāvatām.
Giri|kūṭa|nibhāḥ ke cit ke cin mahiṣa|saṃnibhāḥ
śarad|abhra|pratīkāśāḥ kecidd hiṅgulak'|ānanāḥ.
Utpatantaḥ patantaś ca plavamānāś ca vānarāḥ
uddhunvanto 'pare reṇūn samājagmuḥ samantataḥ.
Sa vānara|mahā|sainyaḥ pūrṇa|sāgara|saṃnibhaḥ
niveśam akarot tatra Sugrīv'|ânumate tadā.
Tatas teṣu har'|îndreṣu samāvṛtteṣu sarvaśaḥ
tithau praśaste nakṣatre muhūrte c' âbhipūjite
15 Tena vyūḍhena sainyena lokān udvartayann iva
prayayau Rāghavaḥ śrīmān Sugrīva|sahitas tadā.
Mukham āsīt tu sainyasya Hanūmān mārut'|ātma|jaḥ
jaghanaṃ pālayām āsa Saumitrir akuto|bhayaḥ.
Baddha|godh"|âṅguli|trāṇau Rāghavau tatra jagmatuḥ
vṛtau hari|mahā|mātraiś candra|sūryau grahair iva.
Prababhau hari|sainyaṃ tat śāla|tāla|śil"|āyudham
sumahac chāli|bhavanaṃ yathā sūry'|ôdayaṃ prati.
Nala|Nīl'|Aṅgada|Krātha|Mainda|Dvivida|pālitā
yayau sumahatī senā Rāghavasy' ârtha|siddhaye.

The intelligent, exceptionally strong monkey, called Pánasa, led five hundred and seventy million. The esteemed, exceptionally heroic monkey elder, called Dadhi·mukha, led a great army of brilliantly terrible monkeys.

Jámbavat appeared with a thousand billion black, streak-faced bears, terrible in action.

These, and innumerable other marshals of monkey generals, united, great king, in Rama's cause.

The tumultous sound was heard of them running hither and thither, roaring like lions, their bodies like mountain peaks—some like mountain peaks, some like buffalo, some looked like autumn clouds, their faces vermilion. Monkeys were leaping up, flying, falling, others raising the dust, as they gathered from all directions.

Then that great monkey-army, like a brimming ocean, set up camp there with Sugríva's approval. Once those monkey-lords had collected from all directions, at a recommended hour, on a date under an auspicious star, illustrious Rághava set out, accompanied by Sugríva, as though overwhelming the worlds with that marshalled army. The vanguard was Hanúmat, son of the Wind; protecting the rear was Sumítra's son, who feared nothing. Raghu's two descendants advanced there, their wrist- and finger-guards strapped on, surrounded by those monkey ministers, like the sun and the moon surrounded by planets. That monkey-army, armed with *shala* trees, palm trees and stones, shone like the great sweep of a paddy field at sunrise. The huge army, protected by Nala, Nila, Ángada, Kratha, Mainda and Dvi·vida, went to accomplish Rághava's purpose.

20 Vividheṣu praśasteṣu bahu|mūla|phaleṣu ca
prabhūta|madhu|māṃseṣu vārimatsu śiveṣu ca
Nivasantī nirābādhā tath" âiva giri|sānuṣu
upāyādd hari|senā sā kṣār'|ôdam atha sāgaram.
Dvitīya|sāgara|nibhaṃ tad balaṃ bahula|dhvajam
velā|vanaṃ samāsādya nivāsam akarot tadā.
Tato Dāśarathiḥ śrīmān Sugrīvaṃ pratyabhāṣata
madhye vānara|mukhyānāṃ prāpta|kālam idaṃ vacaḥ:
«Upāyaḥ ko nu bhavatāṃ mataḥ sāgara|laṅghane?
iyaṃ ca mahatī senā sāgaraś c' âtidustaraḥ.»
25 Tatr' ânye vyāharanti sma vānarā bahu|māninaḥ:
«samarthā laṅghane sindhor na tu tat|kṛtsna|kārakam»
Ke cin naubhir vyavasyanti kecic ca vividhaiḥ plavaiḥ»
«n' êti» Rāmas tu tān sarvān sāntvayan pratyabhāṣata:
«Śata|yojana|vistāraṃ na śaktāḥ sarva|vānarāḥ
krāntuṃ toya|nidhiṃ vīrā n' âiṣā vo naiṣṭhikī matiḥ.
Nāvo na santi senāyā bahvyas tārayituṃ tathā
vaṇijām upaghātaṃ ca katham asmad|vidhaś caret?
Vistīrṇaṃ c' âiva naḥ sainyaṃ hanyāc chidreṇa vai paraḥ.
plav'|ôḍupa|pratāraś ca n' âiv' âtra mama rocate.
30 Ahaṃ tv imaṃ jala|nidhiṃ samārapsyāmy upāyataḥ.
pratiśeṣyāmy upavasan, darśayiṣyati māṃ tataḥ.
Na ced darśayitā mārgaṃ dhakṣyāmy enam ahaṃ tataḥ
mah"|âstrair apratihatair atyagni|pavan'|ôjjvalaiḥ.»
Ity uktvā saha|Saumitrir upaspṛśy' âtha Rāghavaḥ
pratiśiśye jala|nidhiṃ vidhivat kuśa|saṃstare.

Camping in various renowned, auspicious places, full 20
of roots and fruits, rich in meat, honey and water, free of
trouble—and similarly on mountain ridges—that monkey-
army approached the saltwater sea. Like a second ocean, that
force, with its many banners, reached the coastal forest and
set up camp.

Then, in the middle of the monkey leaders, Dasha·ratha's
eminent son uttered this timely speech to Sugríva: "What
means have you thought of to cross the ocean? This army
is large, and the ocean is very hard to span."

Some monkeys there thought themselves great, saying: 25
"We are capable of leaping the ocean, but not everyone can
do that." Some are planning to cross by boats, and some by
various rafts.

But Rama soothingly answered them all: "No—not all
the monkey heroes are able to cross an expanse of water
stretching for hundreds of *yójana*s. Your thought on this is
not conclusive. In the same way, the army doesn't have so
many ships to ferry it across, and how can the likes of us
wrong the merchants? Moreover, the enemy would strike at
a gap when our army is spread out. And crossing by boat
and raft doesn't appeal to me here. But I have a method for 30
tackling this expanse of water. Fasting, I shall importune
him, then he will show me. And if he doesn't show me a path,
I shall set him alight with mighty, unstoppable missiles,
greater than a fire stoked by the wind." So saying, Rághava,
together with Sumítra's son, touched water on a layer of *ku-
sha* grass,* according to ritual prescription, and importuned
the ocean.

Sāgaras tu tataḥ svapne darśayām āsa Rāghavam
devo nada|nadī|bhartā śrīmān yādo|gaṇair vṛtaḥ.
«Kausalyā|mātar ity» evam ābhāṣya madhuraṃ vacaḥ
idam ity āha ratnānām ākaraiḥ śataśo vṛtaḥ.
35 «Brūhi kiṃ te karomy atra sāhāyyaṃ puruṣa'|rṣabha?»
«aikṣvāko hy asmi te jñātir» iti. Rāmas tam abravīt:
«Mārgam icchāmi sainyasya dattaṃ nada|nadī|pate
yena gatvā daśa|grīvaṃ hanyāṃ Paulastya|pāṃsanam.
Yady evaṃ yācato mārgaṃ na pradāsyati me bhavān
śarais tvāṃ śoṣayiṣyāmi divy'|âstra|pratimantritaiḥ.»

Ity evaṃ bruvataḥ śrutvā Rāmasya Varuṇ'|ālayaḥ
uvāca vyathito vākyam iti baddh'|âñjaliḥ sthitaḥ:
«N' êcchāmi pratighātaṃ te n' âsmi vighna|karas tava.
śṛṇu c' êdaṃ vaco Rāma, śrutvā kartavyam ācara.
40 Yadi dāsyāmi te mārgaṃ sainyasya vrajato "|jñayā
anye 'py ājñāpayiṣyanti mām evaṃ dhanuṣo balāt.
Asti tv atra Nalo nāma vānaraḥ śilpi|saṃmataḥ
tvaṣṭur devasya tanayo balavān Viśvakarmaṇaḥ.
Sa yat kāṣṭhaṃ tṛṇaṃ v" âpi śilāṃ vā kṣepsyate mayi
sarvaṃ tad dhārayiṣyāmi, sa te setur bhaviṣyati.»

Ity uktv" ântarhite tasmin Rāmo Nalam uvāca ha:
«kuru setuṃ samudre tvaṃ śakto hy asi mato mama.»
Ten' ôpāyena Kākutsthaḥ setu|bandham akārayat
daśa|yojana|vistāram āyataṃ śata|yojanam
45 Nala|setur iti khyāto yo 'dy' âpi prathito bhuvi
Rāmasy' ājñāṃ puras|kṛtya niryāto giri|saṃnibhaḥ.

But then the sea god, the illustrious lord of rivers and
streams, surrounded by troops of sea monsters, showed him-
self to Rághava in a dream. He addressed him as "Son of
Kausálya," and, covered with piles of gems in their hun-
dreds, spoke this sweet speech: "Tell me, bullish man, since 35
I am descended from your relative, Ikshváku, what can I do
to help you here?" "Lord of rivers and streams, I want to be
given a path for the army, going by which I may kill the dis-
grace of the Páulastyas, the ten-necked Rávana. If, despite
my asking in this way, you don't give me a path, I shall dry
you up, lord, with arrows that have been empowered with
divine missiles."

Hearing Rama talking in this way, Váruna's resort,* stand-
ing with folded hands, said in agitation: "I do not wish to
obstruct you. I am not one to put obstacles in your way.
Listen to something, Rama. Once you have heard it, do
what you have to. If, at your command, I give you a path 40
for your marching army, others too will command me in
the same way, by force of bow. But there is a powerful mon-
key here called Nala; respected by artisans, he is the son
of the builder god, Vishva·karman. What he throws into
me—wood, grass, or stone—all that I shall support. That
will be your causeway."

Saying this, he disappeared. Rama said to Nala: "Build
a bridge over the sea, for I believe you can do it." By this
means Kakútstha had a causeway built, ten *yójanas* wide,
a hundred *yójanas* long, which, even today, is known as 45
Nala's causeway, famed on earth, looking like a mountain,
and procured at Rama's command.

Tatra|stham sa tu dharm'|ātmā samāgacchad Vibhīṣaṇaḥ
bhrātā vai rākṣas'|êndrasya caturbhiḥ sacivaiḥ saha.
Pratijagrāha Rāmas taṃ svāgatena mahā|manāḥ
Sugrīvasya tu śaṅk" âbhūt praṇidhiḥ syād iti sma ha.
Rāghavaḥ satya|ceṣṭābhiḥ samyak ca carit'|êṅgitaiḥ
yadā tattvena tuṣṭo 'bhūt tata enam apūjayat.
Sarva|rākṣasa|rājye c' âpy abhyaṣiñcad Vibhīṣaṇam
cakre ca mantra|sacivaṃ suhṛdaṃ Lakṣmaṇasya ca.
50 Vibhīṣaṇa|mate c' âiva so 'tyakrāman mah"|ârṇavam
sasainyaḥ setunā tena māsen' âiva nar'|âdhipa.
Tato gatvā samāsādya Laṅk"|ôdyānāny anekaśaḥ
bhedayām āsa kapibhir mahānti ca bahūni ca.
Tatas tau Rāvaṇ'|âmātyau mantriṇau Śuka|Sāraṇau
cārau vānara|rūpeṇa tau jagrāha Vibhīṣaṇaḥ.
Pratipannau yadā rūpaṃ rākṣasaṃ tau niśā|carau
darśayitvā tataḥ sainyaṃ Rāmaḥ paścād avāsṛjat.
Niveśy' ôpavane sainyaṃ tat puraḥ prājña|vānaram
preṣayām āsa dautyena Rāvaṇasya tato 'ṅgadam.

MĀRKAṆḌEYA uvāca:

284.1 Prabhūt'|ânn'|ôdake tasmin bahu|mūla|phale vane
senāṃ niveśya Kākutstho vidhivat paryarakṣata.
Rāvaṇaḥ saṃvidhiṃ cakre Laṅkāyāṃ śāstra|nirmitam,
prakṛty" âiva durādharṣā dṛḍha|prākāra|toraṇā.
Agādha|toyāḥ parikhā mīna|nakra|samākulāḥ
babhūvuḥ sapta durdharṣāḥ khādiraiḥ śaṅkubhiś citāḥ.
Kapāṭa|yantra|durdharṣā babhūvuḥ sa|huḍ'|ôpalāḥ

The Law-spirited Vibhíshana, brother of the demon-king, came with four of his counsellors to where he was standing. The great-minded Rama received him with a welcome, but Sugríva feared that he might be spying. When, from his truthful behavior and his proper movements and actions, Rághava was satisfied as to his true nature, he honored him. And he also consecrated Vibhíshana king of all the demons, and made him the counsellor and friend of
Lákshmana. And on Vibhíshana's advice, by means of that 50
causeway he crossed the great sea with the army in just a month, lord of men.

Having arrived there, he reached the plentiful and numerous great gardens of Lanka, and had them devastated by the monkeys. Then those two counsellors, Shuka and Sárana, ministers of Rávana, were spies in the likeness of monkeys. Vibhíshana captured them. Once those creatures of the night had resumed their demonic form, Rama showed them to the army, and afterward released them. After encamping the army in a small forest, that leader sent out the bright monkey, Ángada, as an envoy to Rávana.

MARKANDÉYA said:

With the army camped in that forest full of food and 284.1
water, roots and fruit, Kakútstha guarded it properly. Rávana made preparation in Lanka, as laid down in the manuals. It was naturally difficult to attack, its gateways and ramparts were strong. There were seven bottomless moats, crowded with fish and crocodiles, built with piles of *khádira* wood,* hard to assault. Because of gates and catapults they

s'|āśīviṣa|ghaṭ'|āyodhāḥ sa|sarja|rasa|pāṃsavaḥ
5 Musal'|âlāta|nārāca|tomar'|âsi|paraśvadhaiḥ
anvitāś ca śata|ghnībhiḥ sa|madh'|ûcchiṣṭa|mudgarāḥ
Pura|dvāreṣu sarveṣu gulmāḥ sthāvara|jaṅgamāḥ
babhūvuḥ patti|bahulāḥ prabhūta|gaja|vājinaḥ.
Aṅgadas tv atha Laṅkāyā dvāra|deśam upāgataḥ
vidito rākṣas'|êndrasya praviveśa gata|vyathaḥ.
Madhye rākṣasa|koṭīnāṃ bahvīnāṃ sumahā|balaḥ
śuśubhe megha|mālābhir āditya iva saṃvṛtaḥ.
Sa samāsādya Paulastyam amātyair abhisaṃvṛtam
Rāma|saṃdeśam āmantrya vāgmī vaktuṃ pracakrame:
10 «Āha tvāṃ Rāghavo rājan Kosal'|êndro mahā|yaśāḥ
prāpta|kālam idaṃ vākyaṃ tad ādatsva kuruṣva ca.
Akṛt'|ātmānam āsādya rājānam anaye ratam
vinaśyanty anay'|āviṣṭā deśāś ca nagarāṇi ca.
Tvay" âiken' âparāddhaṃ me Sītām āharatā balāt
vadhāy' ânaparāddhānām anyeṣāṃ tad bhaviṣyati.
Ye tvayā bala|darpābhyām āviṣṭena vane|carāḥ
ṛṣayo hiṃsitāḥ pūrvaṃ devāś c' âpy avamānitāḥ.
Rāja'|rṣayaś ca nihatā rudantyaś ca hatāḥ striyaḥ
tad idaṃ samanuprāptaṃ phalaṃ tasy' ânayasya te.
15 Hantāsmi tvāṃ sah' âmātyair. yudhyasva, puruṣo bhava!
paśya me dhanuṣo vīryaṃ mānuṣasya niśā|cara.
Mucyatāṃ Jānakī Sītā! na me mokṣyasi karhi cit!
arākṣasam imaṃ lokaṃ kartāsmi niśitaiḥ śaraiḥ.»

were difficult to storm; there were iron bars and rocks, soldiers with jars of venomous snakes and resinous powders,
supported with clubs, coals, iron arrows, spears, swords and 5
axes, hundred-killers and hammers coated in beeswax. At all the city gates there were stationary and mobile forts, full of infantry, elephants and horses.

But then Ángada, coming to the entrance to Lanka, was announced to the demon-lord, and entered, untouched by fear. In the midst of demons in their tens of millions, that exceptionally strong one shone like the sun surrounded by garlands of clouds. He approached Pulástya's son surrounded by his ministers, saluted him, and began, eloquently, to speak Rama's message:

"King, the most glorious Rághava, lord of Kósala, sends 10
you this timely word. Accept it and act on it! Countries and cities securing a king who is spiritually imperfect, and devoted to bad conduct, are filled with misfortune, and destroyed. You alone have transgressed against me by taking Sita by force. But that will mean the death of others who have not transgressed. Full of strength and insolence, you have already injured forest-wandering seers, and even insulted the gods. You have killed royal sages and stricken weeping women; now the fruit of your bad conduct has
ripened: I shall kill you with your ministers. Fight! Be a 15
man! Behold, creature of the night, the power of my bow—of a human being! Free Sita, Jánaka's daughter! You will never be free of me! With my sharp arrows I shall rid this world of demons."

Iti tasya bruvāṇasya dūtasya paruṣaṃ vacaḥ
śrutvā na mamṛṣe rājā Rāvaṇaḥ krodha|mūrchitaḥ.
Iṅgita|jñās tato bhartuś catvāro rajanī|carāḥ
caturṣv aṅgeṣu jagṛhuḥ śārdūlam iva pakṣiṇaḥ.
Tāṃs tath" âṅgeṣu saṃsaktān Aṅgado rajanī|carān
ādāy' âiva kham utpatya prāsāda|talam āviśat.
20 Vegen' ôtpatatas tasya petus te rajanī|carāḥ
bhuvi saṃbhinna|hṛdayāḥ prahāra|vara|pīḍitāḥ.
Saṃsakto harmya|śikharāt tasmāt punar avāpatat
laṅghayitvā purīṃ Laṅkāṃ sva|balasya samīpataḥ.
Kosal'|êndram ath' āgamya sarvam āvedya vānaraḥ
viśaśrāma sa tejasvī Rāghaveṇ' âbhinanditaḥ.
Tataḥ sarv'|âbhisāreṇa harīṇāṃ vāta|raṃhasām
bhedayām āsa Laṅkāyāḥ prākāraṃ Raghu|nandanaḥ.
Vibhīṣaṇa'|rkṣ'|âdhipatī puras|kṛty' âtha Lakṣmaṇaḥ
dakṣiṇaṃ nagara|dvāram avāmṛdnād durāsadam.
25 Karabh'|âruṇa|pāṇḍūṇāṃ harīṇāṃ yuddha|śālinām
koṭī|śata|sahasreṇa Laṅkām abhyapatat tadā.
Pralamba|bāh'|ūru|kara|jaṅgh"|ântara|vilambinām
ṛkṣāṇāṃ dhūmra|varṇānāṃ tisraḥ koṭyo vyavasthitāḥ.
Utpatadbhiḥ patadbhiś ca nipatadbhiś ca vānaraiḥ
n' âdṛśyata tadā sūryo rajasā nāśita|prabhaḥ.
Śāli|prasūna|sadṛśaiḥ śirīṣa|kusuma|prabhaiḥ
taruṇ'|āditya|sadṛśaiḥ śaṇa|gauraiś ca vānaraiḥ
Prākāraṃ dadṛśus te tu samantāt kapilī|kṛtam
rākṣasā vismitā rājan sa|strī|vṛddhāḥ samantataḥ.
30 Bibhidus te maṇi|stambhān karṇ'|âṭṭa|śikharāṇi ca
bhagn'|ônmathita|śṛṅgāṇi yantrāṇi ca vicikṣipuḥ.

Hearing this harsh speech uttered by the messenger, King Rávana, stunned with rage, could not tolerate it. So, understanding their lord's gestures, four creatures of darkness fastened onto his four limbs, like birds on a tiger. Then, taking the creatures of darkness attached to his limbs, Ángada leaped through the air onto the roof of the palace. With the speed at which he rose, those night prowlers fell to the ground, heartbroken, painfully bruised by the blow. He jumped down again from the palace roof on which he had perched, and leaped over the city of Lanka to the outskirts of his own army. So coming to the lord of Kósala and informing him of everything, the lustrous monkey rested, applauded by Rághava.

Then the joy of Raghu* had Lanka's wall breached by the total attack of the monkeys, fast as the wind. After which Lákshmana placed Vibhíshana and the bear king in the front, and smashed down the near impregnable southern gate of the city. Then he fell upon Lanka with a billion battle-hardened monkeys, white and tan like elephant trunks. Thirty million gray bears were drawn up in battle, supported on long arms and thighs and pendulous paws. Then the sun disappeared, its light blocked by the dust, as monkeys jumped up, flew about and fell down.

But the demons, with their women and elders, watched astonished, my king, as their rampart was turned entirely and completely brown by hemp-white monkeys, the color of the young sun, like rice blossoms, like *shirísha* flowers.* They shattered the bejewelled pillars and catapult towers, and scattered the machines, whose turrets were broken and plucked down. And grasping the hundred-killers, with their

Parigṛhya śata|ghnīś ca sa|cakrāḥ sa|huḍ'|ôpalāḥ
cikṣipur bhuja|vegena Laṅkā|madhye mahā|svanāḥ.
Prākāra|sthāś ca ye ke cin niśā|cara|gaṇās tathā
pradudruvus te śataśaḥ kapibhiḥ samabhidrutāḥ.

Tatas tu rāja|vacanād rākṣasāḥ kāma|rūpiṇaḥ
niryayur vikṛt'|ākārāḥ sahasra|śata|saṃghaśaḥ.
Śastra|varṣāṇi varṣanto drāvayitvā van'|âukasaḥ
prākāraṃ śobhayantas te paraṃ vikramam āsthitāḥ.
35 Sa māṣa|rāśi|sadṛśair babhūva kṣaṇadā|caraiḥ
kṛto nirvānaro bhūyaḥ prākāro bhīma|darśanaiḥ.
Petuḥ śūla|vibhinn'|âṅgā bahavo vānara'|rṣabhāḥ
stambha|toraṇa|bhagnāś ca petus tatra niśā|carāḥ.
Keśā|keśy abhavad yuddhaṃ rakṣasāṃ vānaraiḥ saha
nakhair dantaiś ca vīrāṇāṃ khādatāṃ vai paras|param.
Niṣṭananto hy ubhayatas tatra vānara|rākṣasāḥ
hatā nipatitā bhūmau na muñcanti paras|param.
Rāmas tu śara|jālāni vavarṣa jalado yathā,
tāni Laṅkāṃ samāsādya jaghnus tān rajanī|carān.
40 Saumitrir api nārācair dṛḍha|dhanvā jita|klamaḥ
ādiśy' âdiśya durga|sthān pātayām āsa rākṣasān.
Tataḥ pratyavahāro 'bhūt sainyānāṃ Rāghav'|ājñayā
kṛte vimarde Laṅkāyāṃ labdha|lakṣo jay'|ôttaraḥ.

MĀRKAṆḌEYA uvāca:

285.1 Tato niviśamānāṃs tān sainikān Rāvaṇā'|ânugāḥ
abhijagmur gaṇ'|âneke piśāca|kṣudra|rakṣasām
Parvaṇaḥ Patano Jambhaḥ Kharaḥ Krodhavaśo Hariḥ
Prarujaś c' Arujaś c' âiva Praghasaś c' âivam ādayaḥ.

wheels, iron bars and rocks, through the speed of their arms the great roarers threw them to the middle of Lanka. Attacked by the monkeys, those troops of night-prowlers stationed on the ramparts fled in their hundreds.

But then, on their king's order, the demons who can change shape at will came out in groups of hundreds and thousands with their appearances transformed. Raining showers of weapons, they drove off the forest-dwellers; glow-
ing on the ramparts, they displayed supreme bravery. The 35
rampart was again made free of monkeys by the terrible-looking creatures of the night, resembling great heaps of beans. Many bullish monkeys fell, their bodies skewered by spears, and creatures of darkness too fell there, crushed by pillars and crossbeams. Head to head was the battle of monkeys and demons, nail and tooth, heroes eating one another. Monkeys and demons roared there alike, and, never letting one another go, fell dead on the ground. But Rama, like a cloud, rained sheets of arrows. Assailing Lanka, they killed
those creatures of the night. Sumítra's son* as well, over- 40
coming fatigue, aimed a stream of arrows with his steady bow at the demons standing on the citadel, and felled them. Then, by Rághava's command, the armies withdrew, their goal attained—they had the upper hand in the destruction of Lanka.

MARKANDÉYA said:

Then some troops of *pisháchas* and low demons, follow- 285.1
ers of Rávana—Párvana, Pátana, Jambha, Khara, Krodha·vasha, Hari, Práruja, Áruja, Prághasa and company—fell on those soldiers while they were resting but, as those evil-

Tato 'bhipatatāṃ teṣām adṛśyānāṃ durātmanām
antardhāna|vadhaṃ taj|jñaś cakāra sa Vibhīṣaṇaḥ.
Te dṛśyamānā haribhir balibhir dūra|pātibhiḥ
nihatāḥ sarvaśo rājan mahīṃ jagmur gat'|âsavaḥ.

5 Amṛṣyamāṇaḥ sa|balo Rāvaṇo niryayāv atha
rākṣasāṇāṃ balair ghoraiḥ piśācāṇāṃ ca saṃvṛtaḥ.
Yuddha|śāstra|vidhāna|jña Uśanā iva c' âparaḥ
vyūhya c' āuśanasaṃ vyūhaṃ harīn abhyavahārayat.
Rāghavas tv viniryāntaṃ vyūḍh'|ânīkaṃ daś'|ānanam
bārhaspatyaṃ vidhiṃ kṛtvā pratyavyūhan niśā|caram.
Sametya yuyudhe tatra tato Rāmeṇa Rāvaṇaḥ
yuyudhe Lakṣmaṇaś c' âpi tath" âiv' Êndrajitā saha,
Virūpākṣeṇa Sugrīvas Tāreṇa ca Nikharvaṭaḥ
Tuṇḍena ca Nalas tatra Paṭuśaḥ Panasena ca.
10 Viṣahyaṃ yaṃ hi yo mene sa sa tena sameyivān
yuyudhe yuddha|velāyāṃ sva|bāhu|balam āśritaḥ.

Sa saṃprahāro vavṛdhe bhīrūṇāṃ bhaya|vardhanaḥ
loma|saṃharṣaṇo ghoraḥ purā dev'|âsure yathā.

Rāvaṇo Rāmam ānarchac chakti|śūl'|âsi|vṛṣṭibhiḥ
niśitair āyasais tīkṣṇai Rāvaṇaṃ c' âpi Rāghavaḥ.
Tath" âiv' Êndrajitaṃ yattaṃ Lakṣmaṇo marma|bhedibhiḥ
Indrajic c' âpi Saumitriṃ bibheda bahubhiḥ śaraiḥ.
Vibhīṣaṇaḥ Prahastaṃ ca Prahastaś ca Vibhīṣaṇam
khaga|patraiḥ śarais tīkṣṇair abhyavarṣad gata|vyathaḥ.
15 Teṣāṃ balavatām āsīn mah"|âstrāṇāṃ samāgamaḥ
vivyathuḥ sakalā yena trayo lokāś car'|âcarāḥ.

natured invisible creatures attacked, Vibhíshana destroyed their invisibility and identified them. Seen by the powerful, far-leaping monkeys, they were slain on all sides, my king, and fell lifeless on the earth.

Unable to take this, Rávana marched out with his army, surrounded by a terrible force of demons and *pisháchas.* Knowing the rules and dispositions of warfare, like another Úshanas,* he drew them up in the Úshanas formation, and attacked the monkeys. But Rághava, making the Brihas·pati* formation, opposed the ten-necked night-prowler, who was advancing with his armed formation. Then, coming up on him there, Rávana fought with Rama, and, in the same way, Lákshmana fought with Indra·jit, Sugríva with Virupáksha, Nikhárvata with Tara, Nala with Tunda, and Pátusha with Pánasa. Each came together with whomsoever he considered his match, and fought with him in the hour of battle, relying on the strength of his own arms.

The battle swelled, dilating the fear of the fearful; it was as hair-raising and terrible as that in the past between gods and anti-gods.

Rávana went at Rama with showers of spears, spikes and swords, and Rághava at Rávana with filed iron arrows. In the same way Lákshmana pierced the stretched Indra·jit, cutting his vitals, and Indra·jit split Sumítra's son with multiple arrows. Impervious to fear, Vibhíshana showered Prahásta, and Prahásta, Vibhíshana, with sharp, bird-feathered shafts. There was a clash of those strong, great weapons, and, as a result, the three worlds in their entirety, whether static or moving, were shaken.

MĀRKAṆḌEYA uvāca:

286.1 Tataḥ Prahastaḥ sahasā samabhyetya Vibhīṣaṇam
gadayā tāḍayām āsa vinadya raṇa|karkaśaḥ.
Sa tay" âbhihato dhīmān gadayā bhīma|vegayā
n' âkampata mahā|bāhur himavān iva susthiraḥ.
Tataḥ pragṛhya vipulāṃ śata|ghaṇṭāṃ Vibhīṣaṇaḥ
abhimantrya mahā|śaktiṃ cikṣep' âsya śiraḥ prati.
Patantyā sa tayā vegād rākṣaso 'śani|vegayā
hṛt'|ôttam'|âṅgo dadṛśe vāta|rugna iva drumaḥ.
5 Taṃ dṛṣṭvā nihataṃ saṃkhye Prahastaṃ kṣaṇa|dā|caram
abhidudrāva Dhūmrākṣo vegena mahatā kapīn.
Tasya megh'|ôpamaṃ sainyam āpatad bhīma|darśanam,
dṛṣṭv" âiva sahasā dīrṇā raṇe vānara|puṃgavāḥ.
Tatas tān sahasā dīrṇān dṛṣṭvā vānara|puṃgavān
niryāyau kapi|śārdūlo Hanūmān mārut'|ātma|jaḥ.
Taṃ dṛṣṭv" âvasthitaṃ saṃkhye harayaḥ pavan'|ātma|jam
mahatyā tvarayā rājan saṃnyavartanta sarvaśaḥ.
Tataḥ śabdo mahān āsīt tumulo loma|harṣaṇaḥ
Rāma|Rāvaṇa|sainyānām anyonyam abhidhāvatām.
10 Tasmin pravṛtte saṃgrāme ghore rudhira|kardame
Dhūmrākṣaḥ kapi|sainyaṃ tad drāvayām āsa patribhiḥ.
Taṃ rakṣo|mahā|mātram āpatantaṃ sapatna|jit
pratijagrāha Hanūmāṃs tarasā pavan'|ātma|jaḥ.
Tayor yuddham abhūd ghoraṃ hari|rākṣasa|vīrayoḥ
jigīṣator yudhā 'nyonyam Indra|Prahlādayor iva.
Gadābhiḥ parighaiś c' âiva rākṣaso jaghnivān kapim
kapiś ca jaghnivān rakṣaḥ sa|skandha|viṭapair drumaiḥ.

MARKANDÉYA said:

Then Prahásta, who was a savage fighter, suddenly came 286.1
roaring at Vibhíshana and struck him with a mace. Wise,
and strong-armed, thumped by the terrifying velocity of
the club, he was rooted like the Himálaya, and did not
waver. Then, lifting up a huge hundred-bell spear, Vibhí-
shana armed the great missile with a spell, and threw it
toward his head. Like a tree snapped by the wind, the demon
was summarily decapitated by that flying missile, swift as
a thunderbolt.

Seeing the night-prowler Prahásta felled in battle, Dhu- 5
mráksha bore down on the monkeys with great speed. Like
a cloud, his terrifying army attacked. Seeing it, the bullish
monkeys suddenly scattered on the battlefield. Witnessing
those bullish monkeys suddenly dispersed, the son of the
Wind, the tigerish monkey, Hanúmat, advanced. At the
sight of the Wind's son standing solidly in battle, the mon-
keys came together again, my king, with great speed from
all sides. Then there was the great, tumultuous, hair-raising
noise of Rama's and Rávana's armies attacking each other.

As that frightful, bloody, muddy battle proceeded, Dhu- 10
mráksha put that monkey-army to flight with his arrows.
Hanúmat, the Wind's rival-defeating son, quickly confron-
ted that extraordinary attacking demon. It turned into a
frightful fight between those two, the monkey and demon
heroes, striving to overcome each other in battle, like Indra
and Prahláda. The demon struck the monkey with clubs
and maces, and the monkey struck the demon with trees,
complete with trunks and branches. Provoked, the Wind's
son, Hanúmat, in extreme wrath killed Dhumráksha, along

Tatas tam atikopena s'|âśvaṃ sa|ratha|sārathim
Dhūmrākṣam avadhīd kruddho Hanūmān mārut'|ātma|jaḥ.
15 Tatas taṃ nihataṃ dṛṣṭvā Dhūmrākṣaṃ rākṣas'|ottamam
harayo jāta|visrambhā jaghnur anye ca sainikān.
Te vadhyamānā haribhir balibhir jita|kāśibhiḥ
rākṣasā bhagna|saṃkalpā Laṅkām abhyapatan bhayāt.
Te 'bhipatya puraṃ bhagnā hata|śeṣā niśā|carāḥ
sarvaṃ rājñe yathā vṛttaṃ Rāvaṇāya nyavedayan.
Śrutvā tu Rāvaṇas tebhyaḥ Prahastaṃ nihataṃ yudhi
Dhūmrākṣaṃ ca mah"|êṣvāsaṃ sa|sainyaṃ vānara'|rṣabhaiḥ
Sudīrgham iva niḥśvasya samutpatya var'|āsanāt
uvāca: «Kumbhakarṇasya karma|kālo 'yam āgataḥ!»
20 Ity evam uktvā vividhair vāditraiḥ su|mahā|svanaiḥ
śayānam atinidrāluṃ Kumbhakarṇam abodhayat.
Prabodhya mahatā c' âinaṃ yatnen' āgata|sādhvasaḥ
svastham āsīnam avyagraṃ vinidraṃ rākṣas'|âdhipaḥ
Tato 'bravīd daśa|grīvaḥ Kumbhakarṇaṃ mahā|balam:
«Dhanyo 'si yasya te nidrā Kumbhakarṇ' êyam īdṛśī, ya
imaṃ dāruṇ'|ākāraṃ na jānīṣe mahā|bhayam.
eṣa tīrtv" ârṇavaṃ Rāmaḥ setunā haribhiḥ saha
Avamany' êha naḥ sarvān karoti kadanaṃ mahat.
mayā tv apahṛtā bhāryā Sītā nām' âsya Jānakī.
25 Tāṃ netuṃ sa ih' āyāto baddhvā setuṃ mah" ârṇave.
tena c' âiva Prahast'|ādir mahān naḥ sva|jano hataḥ.
Tasya n' ânyo nihant" âsti tvāṃ ṛte śatru|karśana,
sudaṃśito 'bhiniryāya tvam adya balināṃ vara

with his horses, chariot, and charioteer. Once they saw that that supreme demon Dhumráksha had been slain, the other monkeys' confidence returned, and they slaughtered his soldiers. Stricken by the powerful monkeys, who were radiant with victory, the demons' resolve was broken; they fled in fear to Lanka.

Those creatures of the night who had survived the slaughter fled, broken, to the city, and informed King Rávana of everything that had happened. But on hearing from them that Prahásta and the great bowman Dhumráksha, along with his army, had been destroyed in battle by the bullish monkeys, Rávana exhaled violently, leaped up from his throne, and cried: "It's arrived—the time for Kumbha·karna to act!"

This pledged, he awoke the lethargic, sleeping Kumbha·karna with a selection of exceptionally loud musical instruments. Having, with a great effort, roused him, so that he was sitting at ease, undisturbed and alert, the ten-necked demon-lord, full of anxiety, said to the mighty Kumbha·karna:

"You are fortunate,Kumbha·karna, to be able to sleep in this way. You're ignorant of this terrifying disaster. This Rama has crossed the sea by a causeway, together with the monkeys; despising all of us here, he is wreaking great havoc. Because I abducted Sita, the daughter of Jánaka, his wife, he has built a causeway over the ocean and come here to take her home. He has killed our great kinsman, Prahásta, and others. None other than you can kill him, thinner of enemies. Go out, well-armored to meet him today, best of the strong. Kill Rama and all the rest in battle, enemy-tamer, and Dúshana's younger brothers, Vajra·vega and Pramáthin,

Rām'|ādīn samare sarvāñ jahi śatrūn ariṃ|dama,
Dūṣaṇ'|âvarajau c' âiva Vajravega|Pramāthinau
Tau tvāṃ balena mahatā sahitāv anuyāsyataḥ.»
ity uktvā rākṣasa|patiḥ Kumbhakarṇaṃ tarasvinam
saṃdideś' êti|kartavye Vajravega|Pramāthinau.
«Tath" êty» uktvā tu tau vīrau Rāvaṇaṃ Dūṣaṇ'|ânujau
Kumbhakarṇaṃ puras|kṛtya tūrṇaṃ niryayatuḥ purāt.

MĀRKAṆḌEYA uvāca:

287.1 Tato niryāya svapurāt Kumbhakarṇaḥ sah'|ânugaḥ
apaśyat kapi|sainyaṃ taj jita|kāśy agrataḥ sthitam.
Sa vīkṣamāṇas tat sainyaṃ Rāma|darśana|kāṅkṣayā
apaśyac c' âpi saumitraṃ dhanuṣ|pāṇiṃ vyavasthitam.
Tam abhyety' āśu harayaḥ parivavruḥ samantataḥ
abhyaghnaṃś ca mahā|kāyair bahubhir jagatī|ruhaiḥ.
Kara|jair atudaṃś c' ânye vihāya bhayam uttamam
bahudhā yudhyamānās te yuddha|mārgaiḥ plavaṃ|gamāḥ
5 Nānā|praharaṇair bhīmai rākṣas'|êndram atāḍayan.
sa tāḍyamānaḥ prahasan bhakṣayām āsa vānarān
Balaṃ Caṇḍabal'|ākhyaṃ ca Vajrabāhuṃ ca vānaram.
tad dṛṣṭvā vyathanaṃ karma Kumbhakarṇasya rakṣasaḥ
Udakrośan paritrastās Tāra|prabhṛtayas tadā.
tān uccaiḥ krośataḥ sainyān śrutvā sa hari|yūtha|pān,
Abhidudrāva Sugrīvaḥ Kumbhakarṇam apeta|bhīḥ.
tato nipatya vegena Kumbhakarṇaṃ mahā|manāḥ.
Śālena jaghnivān mūrdhni balena kapi|kuñjaraḥ
sa mah"|ātmā mahā|vegaḥ Kumbhakarṇasya mūrdhani.
10 Bibheda śālaṃ Sugrīvo na c' âiv' âvyathayat kapiḥ
tato vinadya sahasā śāla|sparśa|vibodhitaḥ
Dorbhyām ādāya Sugrīvaṃ Kumbhakarṇo 'harad balāt.

shall follow you with a great force!" Once he had said this to the powerful Kumbha·karna, the demon-lord assigned Vajra·vega and Pramáthin to the task in hand.

With a "So be it!" to Rávana, those two heroes, Dúshana's younger brothers, placed Kumbha·karna at the front and set out quickly from the city.

MARKANDÉYA said:

Once he was outside his own city with his followers, 287.1
Kumbha·karna saw the monkey-army in front of him, glowing with victory. Scrutinizing that army in the hope of catching sight of Rama, he saw Sumítra's son, standing bow in hand. The monkeys quickly came up, surrounded him on all sides and hit him with many thick-trunked trees.

Others, ignoring the great danger, struck him with their 4–5
claws. Attacking with many different martial strategies, the 5
monkeys beat the demon-lord with a variety of terrible weapons. Laughing while being beaten, he devoured the monkeys, known as Bala and Chanda·bala, and the ape Vajra·bahu. Witnessing the demon Kumbha·karna's dismaying act, Tara and the others cried out in fear. Hearing the monkey-led forces crying aloud, Sugríva rushed fearlessly toward Kumbha·karna.

The great-minded elephant of a monkey descended at speed on Kumbha·karna and struck him on the head forcefully with a *shala* tree. The great-spirited, super-swift mon- 10
key, Sugríva, broke the *shala* on Kumbha·karna's head, and failed even to shake him. Then, immediately aroused by the contact of the *shala*, Kumbha·karna grasped Sugríva with his arms and took hold of him by force. But the heroic

hriyamāṇaṃ tu Sugrīvaṃ Kumbhakarṇena rakṣasā
Avekṣy' âbhyadravad vīraḥ Saumitrir mitra|nandanaḥ
so 'bhipatya mahā|vegaṃ rukma|puṅkhaṃ mahā|śaram
Prāhiṇot Kumbhakarṇāya Lakṣmaṇaḥ para|vīra|hā.
sa tasya dehā|varaṇaṃ bhittvā dehaṃ ca sāyakaḥ
Jagāma dārayan bhūmiṃ rudhireṇa samukṣitaḥ.
tathā sa bhinna|hṛdayaḥ samutsṛjya kap'|īśvaram
Kumbhakarṇo mah"|êṣv|āsaḥ pragṛhīta|śil"|āyudhaḥ
abhidudrāva Saumitrim udyamya mahatīṃ śilām.
Tasy' âbhipatatas tūrṇaṃ kṣurābhyām ucchritau karau
ciccheda niśit'|âgrābhyāṃ. sa babhūva catur|bhujaḥ.
Tān apy asya bhujān sarvān pragṛhīta|śil"|āyudhān
kṣuraiś ciccheda laghv astraṃ Saumitriḥ pratidarśayan.
Sa babhūv' âtikāyaś ca bahu|pāda|śiro|bhujaḥ
taṃ Brahm'|âstreṇa Saumitrir dadāh' âdri|cay'|ôpamam.
Sa papāta mahā|vīryo divy'|âstr'|âbhihato raṇe
mah"|âśani|vinirdagdhaḥ pādapo 'ṅkuravān iva.
Taṃ dṛṣṭvā Vṛtra|saṃkāśaṃ Kumbhakarṇaṃ tarasvinam
gat'|âsuṃ patitaṃ bhūmau rākṣasāḥ prādravan bhayāt.
Tathā tān dravato yodhān dṛṣṭvā tau Dūṣaṇ'|ânujau
avasthāpy' âtha Saumitriṃ saṃkruddhāv abhyadhāvatām.
Tāv ādravantau saṃkruddhau Vajravega|Pramāthinau
abhijagrāha Saumitrir vinady' ôbhau patatribhiḥ.
Tataḥ su|tumulaṃ yuddham abhaval loma|harṣaṇam
Dūṣaṇ'|ânujayoḥ Pārtha Lakṣmaṇasya ca dhīmataḥ.
Mahatā śara|varṣeṇa rākṣasau so 'bhyavarṣata
tau c' âpi vīrau saṃkruddhāv ubhau tau samavarṣatām.
Muhūrtam evam abhavad Vajravega|Pramāthinoḥ

son of Sumítra, the joy of his friends, saw Sugríva being taken away by the demon Kumbha·karna, and ran forward. Arriving, Lákshmana, killer of enemy heroes, shot an extra-swift, gold-shafted arrow at Kumbha·karna. The arrow cut through his armor and body, and plowed up the ground, smeared in blood. Pierced through the heart, Kumbha·karna, the great archer, released the monkey-lord, acquired a boulder as a weapon, and ran at Sumítra's son, holding the mighty stone aloft.

With two sharpened razors, the latter cut off the upraised arms of the creature as it rushed swiftly toward him. He became four-armed. Even those, his mutiple arms armed with boulders, were cut off with razors by Sumítra's son, wielding a nimble weapon. He outgrew his body with many feet, heads and arms. Looking like a cairn of stones, he was burned by Sumítra's son with the Brahma weapon. Stricken by the divine weapon, he fell, hugely potent, in battle, like a branching tree incinerated by a great bolt of lightning. Seeing that the strong Kumbha·karna, who looked like Vritra, had fallen lifeless to the ground, the demons fled in terror.

Seeing those fleeing warriors, Dúshana's younger brothers stopped them and fell furiously upon Sumítra's son. Sumítra's son roared, and greeted Vajra·vega and Pramáthin, who were rushing frenziedly toward him, with arrows.

Then, Partha, there was a tumultuous and hair-raising battle between Dúshana's younger brothers and the wise Lákshmana. He showered those two demons with a huge shower of arrows, and those two furious heroes both showered him. And in this way the dreadful battle of Vajra·vega and Pramáthin with Sumítra's strong-armed son lasted for

Saumitreś ca mahā|bāhoḥ saṃprahāraḥ su|dāruṇaḥ.
Ath' âdri|śṛṅgam ādāya Hanūmān mārut'|ātma|jaḥ
abhidruty' ādade prāṇān Vajravegasya rakṣasaḥ.
Nīlaś ca mahatā grāvṇā Dūṣaṇ'|âvara|jaṃ hariḥ
Pramāthinam abhidrutya pramamātha mahā|balaḥ.
Tataḥ prāvartata punaḥ saṃgrāmaḥ kaṭuk'|ôdayaḥ
Rāma|rāvaṇa|sainyānām anyonyam abhidhāvatām.
Śataśo Nairṛtān vanyā jaghnur vanyāṃś ca Nairṛtāḥ
Nairṛtās tatra vadhyante prāyeṇa na tu vānarāḥ.

MĀRKAṆḌEYA uvāca:

288.1 Tataḥ śrutvā hataṃ saṃkhye Kumbhakarṇaṃ sah'|ânugam
Prahastaṃ ca mah"|êṣv|āsaṃ Dhūmrākṣaṃ c' âtitejasam
Putram Indrajitaṃ vīraṃ Rāvaṇaḥ pratyabhāṣata:
«jahi Rāmam amitra|ghna Sugrīvaṃ ca sa|Lakṣmaṇam.
Tvayā hi mama sat|putra yaśo dīptam upārjitam
jitvā vajra|dharaṃ saṃkhye sahasr'|âkṣaṃ Śacī|patim.
Antarhitaḥ prakāśo vā divyair datta|varaiḥ śaraiḥ
jahi śatrūn amitra|ghna mama śastra|bhṛtāṃ vara.
5 Rāma|Lakṣmaṇa|Sugrīvāḥ śara|sparśaṃ na te 'nagha
samarthāḥ pratisoḍhuṃ ca kutas tadanuyāyinaḥ?
Agatā yā Prahastena Kumbhakarṇena c' ânagha
Kharasy' âpacitiḥ saṃkhye tāṃ gaccha tvaṃ mahā|bhuja.
Tvam adya niśitair bāṇair hatvā śatrūn sa|sainikān
pratinandaya māṃ putra purā jitv" êva Vāsavam.»

some time. Then the Wind's son, Hanúmat, seizing a mountain peak, rushed up and took the life of the demon Vajra·vega. And the mighty monkey Nila rushed up and crushed Dúshana's younger brother, Pramáthin, with a huge rock. Then, attacking each other, a fierce battle between Rama's and Rávana's armies erupted again. The forest creatures slew Nírriti's sons, and Nírriti's sons the forest creatures in their hundreds; but it was mostly Nírriti's sons who were killed there, not the monkeys.

MARKANDÉYA said:

Then, hearing that Kumbha·karna had, with his follow- 288.1
ers, been killed in battle, along with Prahásta, the great archer, and the fierce Dhumráksha, Rávana said to his son, the heroic Indra·jit:

"Enemy-killer, kill Rama and Sugríva, and Lákshmana too! For you, my good son, have acquired glowing fame, you have conquered the thunderbolt-wielder, the thousand-eyed husband of Shachi,* in battle. Now, enemy-killer, visible or invisible, kill my enemies with divine, gift-given
arrows, best of my men bearing arms. Rama, Lákshmana 5
and Sugríva are unable to stand the touch of your arrows, sinless being—so how can their followers? Sinless being, what neither Prahásta nor Kumbha·karna could manage in battle—the revenge for Khara—you take it, Great Arm! Delight me, son, by killing our enemies and their soldiers with your whetted arrows today, just as you did before in conquering Vásava."

Ity uktaḥ sa «tath" êty» uktvā ratham āsthāya daṃśitaḥ
prayayāv Indrajid rājaṃs tūrṇam āyodhanaṃ prati.
Tato viśrāvya vispaṣṭaṃ nāma rākṣasa|puṃgavaḥ
āhvayām āsa samare Lakṣmaṇaṃ śubha|lakṣaṇam.
10 Taṃ Lakṣmaṇo 'py abhyadhāvat pragṛhya sa|śaraṃ dhanuḥ
trāsayaṃs tala|ghoṣeṇa siṃhaḥ kṣudra|mṛgān yathā.
Tayoḥ samabhavad yuddhaṃ su|mahaj jaya|gṛddhinoḥ
divy'|âstra|viduṣos tīvram anyonya|spardhinos tadā.
Rāvaṇis tu yadā n' âivaṃ viśeṣayati sāyakaiḥ
tato gurutaraṃ yatnam ātiṣṭhad balināṃ varaḥ.
Tata enaṃ mahā|vegair ardayām āsa tomaraiḥ,
tān āgatān sa ciccheda Saumitrir niśitaiḥ śaraiḥ,
Te nikṛttāḥ śarais tīkṣṇair nyapatan dharaṇī|tale.
tam Aṅgado Vāli|sutaḥ śrīmān udyamya pādapam
15 Abhidrutya mahā|vegas tāḍayām āsa mūrdhani.
tasy' Êndrajid asaṃbhrāntaḥ prāsen' ôrasi vīryavān
Prahartum aicchat, taṃ c' âsya prāsaṃ ciccheda Lakṣmaṇaḥ.
tam abhyāśa|gataṃ vīram Aṅgadaṃ Rāvaṇ'|ātma|jaḥ
Gaday" âtāḍayat savye pārśve* vānara|puṃgavam.
tam acintya prahāraṃ sa balavān Vālinaḥ sutaḥ
Sasarj' Êndrajitaḥ krodhāc chāla|skandham tath" Aṅgadaḥ
so 'ṅgadena ruṣ" ôtsṛṣṭo vadhāy' Êndrajitas taruḥ
Jaghān' Êndrajitaḥ Pārtha rathaṃ s'|âśvaṃ sa|sārathim.
tato hat'|âśvāt praskandya rathāt sa hata|sārathiḥ
20 Tatr' âiv' ântardadhe rājan māyayā Rāvaṇ'|ātma|jaḥ.

Thus addressed, Indra·jit replied: “So be it!,” mounted
his chariot in armor, my king, and went forward quickly
to battle. Then, boldly announcing his name, the bullish
demon challenged Lákshmana, marked by good fortune, to
a fight. Lákshmana too grabbed his bow and arrows, and ran 10
toward him, spreading terror with a slapping sound, like a
lion petrifying tiny animals. Both gluttons for victory, both
au fait with divine weapons and in competition with each
other, there was a huge and intense battle between them.

But when he could not overcome him in this way with
his arrows, then Rávana’s son, the greatest of the strong,
made the weightiest of efforts: he bombarded him with
very swift javelins. As they arrived, Sumítra’s son split them
with whetted arrows. Mown down with sharp arrows, they
fell flat on the earth. Ángada, Valin’s glorious son, lifted
up a tree, rushed toward him at high speed and struck 15
him on the head. Unruffled, the potent Indra·jit wanted
to strike him on his chest with a spear, but Lákshmana cleft
his spear. When that bullish, heroic monkey Ángada ap-
proached, Rávana’s son struck him on the left side with a
club. Thinking nothing of that blow, the strong son of Va-
lin, Ángada, thereupon angrily hurled the trunk of a *shala*
tree at Indra·jit. That tree, released by Ángada in a rage
to kill Indra·jit, destroyed Indra·jit’s chariot, Partha, along
with his horses and his charioteer. Then, his charioteer slain,
having leaped from the chariot with its slaughtered horses,
Rávana’s son disappeared on the spot, my king, through his 20
magical power.

antarhitaṃ viditvā taṃ bahu|māyaṃ ca rākṣasam
Rāmas taṃ deśam āgamya tat sainyaṃ paryarakṣata.
sa Rāmam uddiśya śarais tato datta|varais tadā
Vivyādha sarva|gātreṣu Lakṣmaṇaṃ ca mahā|balam.
tam adṛśyaṃ śaraiḥ śūrau māyay" ântarhitaṃ tadā
Yodhayām āsatur ubhau Rāvaṇiṃ Rāma|Lakṣmaṇau.
sa ruṣā sarva|gātreṣu tayoḥ puruṣa|siṃhayoḥ
Vyasṛjat sāyakān bhūyaḥ śataśo 'tha sahasraśaḥ.
tam adṛśyaṃ vicinvantaḥ sṛjantam aniśaṃ śarān
25 Harayo viviśur vyoma pragṛhya mahatīḥ śilāḥ.
tāṃś ca tau c' âpy adṛśyaḥ sa śarair vivyādha rākṣasaḥ.
Tān bhṛśaṃ tāḍayām āsa Rāvaṇir māyayā vṛtaḥ.
tau śarair ācitau vīrau bhrātarau Rāma|Lakṣmaṇau
petatur gaganād bhūmiṃ sūryā|candramasāv iva.

MĀRKAṆḌEYA uvāca:

289.1 Tāv ubhau patitau dṛṣṭvā bhrātarāv Rāma|Lakṣmaṇau
babandha Rāvaṇir bhūyaḥ śarair datta|varais tadā.
Tau vīrau śara|bandhena baddhāv Indrajitā raṇe
rejatuḥ puruṣa|vyāghrau śakuntāv iva pañjare.
Tau dṛṣṭvā patitau bhūmau śataśaḥ sāyakaiś citau
Sugrīvaḥ kapibhiḥ sārdhaṃ parivārya tataḥ sthitaḥ
Suṣeṇa|Mainda|Dvividaiḥ Kumuden' Aṅgadena ca
Hanūman|Nīla|Tāraiś ca Nalena ca kap'|īśvaraḥ.

Realizing that the demon, who had many powers, had disappeared, Rama came to that place and protected the army. Then he aimed at Rama with gift-given arrows, and pierced him and the hugely strong Lákshmana in all their limbs. Then the heroes, Rama and Lákshmana, both fought with arrows against Rávana's invisible son, who had disappeared through his magical power. In a rage, he once more discharged arrows in their hundreds and thousands into all the limbs of those leonine men. Searching for the invisible creature that was continuously shooting arrows, the monkeys armed themselves with great stones and took to the sky. And as well as those two, the invisible demon pierced them with arrows too. Concealed by his magical power, Rávana's son beat them severely. Covered in arrows, those heroic brothers, Rama and Lákshmana, fell like the sun and the moon from the sky to the earth.

MARKANDÉYA said:

Seeing that both those brothers, Rama and Lákshmana, had fallen, Rávana's son then bound them further with gift-given arrows. The two heroes, tigerish men trapped by Indra·jit with a row of arrows, looked like a couple of caged birds. Seeing those two fallen on the ground, covered with hundreds of arrows, Sugríva, together with the monkeys, stood around them—the monkey-king together with Sushéna, Mainda, Dvi·vida, Kúmuda, Ángada, Hanúmat, Nila, Tara and Nala. 289.1

5 Tatas taṃ deśam āgamya kṛta|karmā Vibhīṣaṇaḥ
bodhayām āsa tau vīrau prajñ"|âstreṇa prabodhitau.
Viśalyau c' âpi Sugrīvaḥ kṣaṇen' âitau cakāra ha
viśalyayā mah"|âuṣadhyā divya|mantra|prayuktayā.
Tau labdha|saṃjñau nṛ|varau viśalyāv udatiṣṭhatām
gata|tandrī|klamau c' âpi kṣaṇen' âitau mahā|rathau.

Tato Vibhīṣaṇaḥ Pārtha Rāmam Ikṣvāku|nandanam
uvāca vijvaraṃ dṛṣṭvā kṛt'|âñjalir idaṃ vacaḥ:
«Idam ambho gṛhītvā tu rāja|rājasya śāsanāt
Guhyako 'bhyāgataḥ śvetāt tvat|sakāśam ariṃ|dama.
10 Idam ambhaḥ Kuberas te mahā|rājaḥ prayacchati
antarhitānāṃ bhūtānāṃ darśan'|ârthaṃ paraṃ|tapa.
Anena spṛṣṭa|nayano bhūtāny antarhitāny uta
bhavān drakṣyati yasmai ca pradāsyati naraḥ sa tu.»

«Tath" êti» Rāmas tad vāri pratigṛhy' âbhisaṃskṛtam
cakāra netrayoḥ śaucaṃ Lakṣmaṇaś ca mahā|manāḥ.
Sugrīva|Jāmbavantau ca Hanūmān Aṅgadas tathā
Mainda|Dvivida|Nīlāś ca prāyaḥ plava|ga|sattamāḥ.
Tathā samabhavac c' âpi yad uvāca Vibhīṣaṇaḥ,
kṣaṇen' âtīndriyāṇy eṣāṃ cakṣūṃṣy āsan Yudhiṣṭhira.
15 Indrajit kṛta|karmā ca pitre karma tad ātmanaḥ
nivedya punar āgacchat tvaray" āji|śiraḥ prati.

Tam āpatantaṃ saṃkruddhaṃ punar eva yuyutsayā
abhidudrāva Saumitrir Vibhīṣaṇa|mate sthitaḥ.
Akṛt'|āhnikam ev' âinaṃ jighāṃsur jita|kāśinam
śarair jaghāna saṃkruddhaḥ kṛta|saṃjño 'tha Lakṣmaṇaḥ.

Arriving at that place, Vibhíshana, who knew what he was doing, woke those two heroes, bringing them back to consciousness with the consciousness weapon. Then Sugríva freed them of arrows in an instant with the great herb *vishálya*, prepared with a divine spell. Freed from arrows, their consciousness restored, those paragons of men stood up, and in an instant the weariness and fatigue of such great warriors had gone.

Then, Partha, when Vibhíshana had seen Rama, the delight of Ikshváku, free from affliction, he greeted him with joined hands and made this speech: "Enemy-subduer, instructed by the king of kings, a Gúhyaka took this water and came to you from the White Mountain. Great King Kubéra offers you this water, incinerator of the foe, so that you can see invisible beings. Your eyes touched with this, you shall see even invisible creatures, as will anyone you give it to."

Saying "So be it!," Rama accepted that purified water and washed his eyes, as did great-minded Lákshmana, Sugríva and Jámbavat, Hanúmat, Ángada, Mainda, Dvi·vida and Nila, and most of the eminent monkeys. Then what Vibhíshana had described happened: in an instant, Yudhi·shthira, their eyes became clairvoyant. And Indra·jit, his work done, letting his father know of his action, came again at speed to the front line of battle.

On Vibhíshana's advice, Sumítra's son bore down on him, attacking furiously, full of the desire to fight again. So the furious Lákshmana, who had been tipped off in this way, struck him with arrows, wanting to kill that one who had the look of victory about him before he had performed

Tayoḥ samabhavad yuddhaṃ tad" ânyonyaṃ jigīṣatoḥ
atīva citram āścaryaṃ Śakra|Prahlādayor iva.
Avidhyad Indrajit tīkṣṇaiḥ Saumitriṃ marma|bhedibhiḥ
Saumitriś c' ânala|sparśair avidhyad Rāvaṇiṃ śaraiḥ.
20 Saumitri|śara|saṃsparśād Rāvaṇiḥ krodha|mūrchitaḥ
asṛjal Lakṣmaṇāy' âṣṭau śarān āśī|viṣ'|ôpamān.
Tasy' âsūn pāvaka|sparśaiḥ Saumitriḥ patribhis tribhiḥ
yathā niraharad vīras tan me nigadataḥ śṛṇu.
Eken' âsya dhanuṣmantaṃ bāhuṃ dehād apātayat
dvitīyena sa|nārācaṃ bhujaṃ bhūmau nyapātayat.
Tṛtīyena tu bāṇena pṛthu|dhāreṇa bhāsvatā
jahāra su|nasaṃ c' âpi śiro bhrājiṣṇu|kuṇḍalam.
Vinikṛtta|bhuja|skandhaṃ kabandhaṃ bhīma|darśanam
taṃ hatvā sūtam apy astrair jaghāna balināṃ varaḥ.
25 Laṅkāṃ praveśayām āsus taṃ rathaṃ vājinas tadā
dadarśa Rāvaṇas taṃ ca rathaṃ putra|vinākṛtam.
Sa putraṃ nihataṃ dṛṣṭvā trāsāt saṃbhrānta|mānasaḥ
Rāvaṇaḥ śoka|moh'|ārto Vaidehīṃ hantum udyataḥ.
Aśoka|vanikā|sthāṃ tāṃ Rāma|darśana|lālasām
khaḍgam ādāya duṣṭ'|ātmā javen' âbhipapāta ha.

Taṃ dṛṣṭvā tasya durbuddher Avindhyaḥ pāpa|niścayam
śamayām āsa saṃkruddhaṃ śrūyatāṃ yena hetunā.
«Mahā|rājye sthito dīpte na striyaṃ hantum arhasi
hat" âiv' âiṣā yadā strī ca bandhana|sthā ca te vaśe.
30 Na c' âiṣā deha|bhedena hatā syād iti me matiḥ.

his daily rites.* So a very striking and rare battle ensued
between the two of them, like that between Shakra and Pra-
hláda, each desiring to overcome the other. Indra·jit pierced
Sumítra's son with sharp arrows, splitting his vital organs,
and Sumítra's son pierced Rávana's son with arrows whose
touch was like fire.

Senseless with anger at the touch of Sumítra's son's arrows, 20
Rávana's son released eight venomous, snake-like shafts at
Lákshmana. Listen, as I tell how the hero, Sumítra's son,
took his life with three arrows whose touch was like fire:
with one, he shot his bow-bearing arm from his body; with
the second he brought his arrow-bearing arm to the ground;
but with the third, broad, shining shaft, he took off his head
with its fine nose and sparkling earrings. Once he had slain
that headless trunk—a terrible sight with its arms lopped
from its shoulders—the strongest of the strong killed the
charioteer too with arrows.

Then the horses brought the chariot back to Lanka, and 25
Rávana saw that chariot minus his son. Seeing his son slain,
his mind reeling with fear, afflicted by grief and confusion,
Rávana prepared to kill the Vidéha princess. Grabbing his
sword, the evil-natured creature rushed quickly toward her
as she waited in the *ashóka** grove, ardently hoping for a
glimpse of Rama.

Listen to the reasoning with which Avíndhya, seeing the
evil intention of that bad-minded one, calmed the angry
creature: "Stationed in a glorious great kingdom, you must
not kill a woman—a woman who has been killed already,
captive in your power. In my opinion she won't be killed by 30
the destruction of her body. But kill her husband—killing

jahi bhartāram ev' âsyā. hate tasmin hatā bhavet.
Na hi te vikrame tulyaḥ sākṣād api śata|kratuḥ
asakṛdd hi tvayā s'|Êndrās trāsitās tridaśā yudhi.»
Evaṃ bahu|vidhair vākyair Avindhyo Rāvaṇaṃ tadā
kruddhaṃ saṃśamayām āsa, jagṛhe ca sa tad vacaḥ.
Niryāṇe sa matiṃ kṛtvā nidhāy' âsiṃ kṣapā|caraḥ
ājñāpayām āsa tadā «ratho me kalpyatām» iti.

MĀRKAṆḌEYA uvāca:

290.1 Tataḥ kruddho daśa|grīvaḥ priye putre nipātite
niryayau ratham āsthāya hema|ratna|vibhūṣitam.
Sa vṛto rākṣasair ghorair vividh'|āyudha|pāṇibhiḥ
abhidudrāva Rāmaṃ sa yodhayan hari|yūthapān.
Tam ādravantaṃ saṃkruddhaṃ Mainda|Nīla|Nal'|Aṅgadāḥ
Hanūmāñ Jāmbavāṃś c' âiva sa|sainyāḥ paryavārayan.
Te daśa|grīva|sainyaṃ tad ṛkṣa|vānara|puṅgavāḥ
drumair vidhvaṃsayāṃ cakrur daśa|grīvasya paśyataḥ.
5 Tataḥ sva|sainyam ālokya vadhyamānam arātibhiḥ
māyāvī c' âsṛjan māyāṃ Rāvaṇo rākṣas'|âdhipaḥ.
Tasya deha|viniṣkrāntāḥ śataśo 'tha sahasraśaḥ
rākṣasāḥ pratyadṛśyanta śara|śakty|ṛṣṭi|pāṇayaḥ.
Tān Rāmo jaghnivān sarvān divyen' âstreṇa rākṣasān.
atha bhūyo 'pi māyāṃ sa vyadadhād rākṣas'|âdhipaḥ.
Kṛtvā Rāmasya rūpāṇi Lakṣmaṇasya ca Bhārata
abhidudrāva Rāmaṃ ca Lakṣmaṇaṃ ca daś'|ānanaḥ.
Tatas te Rāmam arcchanto Lakṣmaṇaṃ ca kṣapā|carāḥ
abhipetus tadā Rāmaṃ pragṛhīta|śar'|āsanāḥ.

him would be killing her. For clearly not even the god of a hundred sacrifices himself is equal to your prowess, since it's not just the once that you've upset Indra and the gods in battle." Thus Avíndhya calmed the furious Rávana with all kinds of arguments, and he took his advice. Deciding to march out, the creature of darkness sheathed his sword, then gave the order for his chariot to be made ready.

MARKANDÉYA said:

Then the furious ten-necked one, whose dear son had 290.1
been slain, mounted his gold and jewel-encrusted chariot, and rode out. Surrounded by terrible demons, his hands full of all kinds of weapons, fighting the monkey generals, he bore down on Rama.

As he rushed at them furiously, Mainda, Nila, Nala and Ángada, Hanúmat and Jámbavat surrounded him with their armies. Before the eyes of the ten-necked one, those heroic bears and monkeys scattered the ten-necked one's army with trees.

Then, seeing his own army being killed by his enemies, 5
Rávana, lord of demons, the possessor of magical power, discharged his magic. Demons in their hundreds and thousands, brandishing arrows, spears and swords, were seen to issue from his body. Rama killed all those demons with a divine weapon. So again the demon-lord resorted to magic. Producing materializations of Rama and Lákshmana, Bhárata, the ten-headed one bore down on Rama and Lákshmana. So those night-prowlers rushed at Rama and Lákshmana, and then fell upon Rama, their bows at the ready.

10 Tāṃ dṛṣṭvā rākṣas'|êndrasya māyām Ikṣvāku|nandanaḥ
uvāca Rāmaṃ Saumitrir asaṃbhrānto bṛhad vacaḥ:
«Jah' îmān rākṣasān pāpān ātmanaḥ pratirūpakān!»
jaghāna Rāmas tāṃś c' ânyān ātmanaḥ pratirūpakān.
Tato hary|aśva|yuktena rathen' āditya|varcasā
upatasthe raṇe Rāmaṃ Mātaliḥ Śakra|sārathiḥ.

MĀTALIR uvāca:

«Ayaṃ hary|aśva|yug jaitro maghonaḥ syandan'|ôttamaḥ
anena Śakraḥ Kākutstha samare daitya|dānavān
Śataśaḥ puruṣa|vyāghra rath'|ôdāreṇa jaghnivān.
tad anena nara|vyāghra may" āyattena saṃyuge
15 Syandanena jahi kṣipraṃ Rāvaṇaṃ. mā ciraṃ kṛthāḥ!»
ity ukto Rāghavas tathyaṃ vaco 'śaṅkata Mātaleḥ:
«Māy" âiṣā rākṣasasy' êti». tam uvāca Vibhīṣaṇaḥ:
«n' êyaṃ māyā nara|vyāghra Rāvaṇasya dur|ātmanaḥ.
Tad ātiṣṭha rathaṃ śīghram imam Aindraṃ mahā|dyute.»
tataḥ prahṛṣṭaḥ Kākutsthas «tath" êty» uktvā Vibhīṣaṇam
Rathen' âbhipapāt' âtha daśa|grīvaṃ ruṣ" ânvitaḥ.
hāhā|kṛtāni bhūtāni Rāvaṇe samabhidrute
Siṃha|nādāḥ sa|paṭahā divi divyāś tath" ânadan.
daśa|kandhara|rāja|sūnvos tathā yuddham abhūn mahat.
20 Alabdh' ôpamam anyatra tayor eva tath" âbhavat.
sa Rāmāya mahā|ghoraṃ visasarja niśā|caraḥ
Śūlam Indr'|âśani|prakhyaṃ Brahma|daṇḍam iv' ôdyatam.
tac chūlam satvaraṃ Rāmaś ciccheda niśitaiḥ śaraiḥ.

Witnessing that magical power of the demon-lord, Ikshváku's delight, Sumítra's son made this great, unruffled speech to Rama: "Kill those evil demons which look like you!" And Rama killed those which looked like him.

Then, on a chariot brilliant as the sun, yoked with bay horses, Mátali, Shakra's charioteer, approached Rama in the battle.

MÁTALI said:

"This victory chariot, drawn by bay horses, is the bountiful one's best chariot. Kakútstha, tigerish man, with this noble chariot Shakra killed *daitya*s and *dánava*s in their hundreds in battle. So with this chariot driven by me, tigerish man, quickly kill Rávana in the battle. Don't delay!" Addressed in this way, Rághava was suspicious of Mátali's true speech:

"This is some magic of the demon!" But Vibhíshana told him: "This is not the evil-natured Rávana's magic, tigerish man! So, splendid being, swiftly mount this chariot of Indra." Then Kakútstha was delighted.

Saying "So be it!" to Vibhíshana, full of rage, he then drove at the ten-necked one with the chariot. When Rávana was attacked, beings screamed "Haha!"; then divine lion roars thundered in the sky with kettledrums. And the fight between the ten-necked one and the prince was great—nothing to exceed it had happened anywhere else. The night-prowler hurled at Rama a most terrible spear, like Indra's thunderbolt, like Brahma's staff held aloft. Rama split that spear quickly with his sharp arrows.

Tad dṛṣṭvā duṣkaraṃ karma Rāvaṇaṃ bhayam āviśat.
tataḥ kruddhaḥ sasarj' āśu daśa|grīvaḥ śitāṃś charān
Sahasr'|âyutaśo Rāme śastrāṇi vividhāni ca
tato bhuśuṇḍīḥ śūlāni ca musalāni paraśvadhān
Śaktīś ca vividh'|ākārāḥ śata|ghnīś ca śitān kṣurān.
tāṃ māyāṃ vikṛtāṃ dṛṣṭvā daśa|grīvasya rakṣasaḥ
25 Bhayāt pradudruvuḥ sarve vānarāḥ sarvato diśam.
tataḥ su|patraṃ su|mukhaṃ hema|puṅkhaṃ śar'|ôttamam
Tūṇād ādāya Kākutstho brahm'|âstreṇa yuyoja ha.
taṃ bāṇa|varyaṃ Rāmeṇa brahm'|âstreṇ' ânumantritam
Jahṛṣur deva|gandharvā dṛṣṭvā Śakra|purogamāḥ
alp'|âvaśeṣam āyuś ca tato 'manyanta rakṣasaḥ
Brahm'|âstr'|ôdīraṇāc chatror deva|dānava|kiṃnarāḥ.
tataḥ sasarja taṃ Rāmaḥ śaram apratim'|âujasam
Rāvaṇ'|ântakaraṃ ghoraṃ Brahma|daṇḍam iv' ôdyatam.
mukta|mātreṇa Rāmeṇa dūr'|ākṛṣṭena Bhārata
30 Sa tena rākṣasa|śreṣṭhaḥ sa|rathaḥ s'|âśva|sārathiḥ
prajajvāla mahā|jvālen' âgnin" âbhipariplutaḥ.
Tataḥ prahṛṣṭās tridaśāḥ saha|gandharva|cāraṇāḥ
nihataṃ Rāvaṇaṃ dṛṣṭvā Rāmeṇ' âkliṣṭa|karmaṇā.
Tatyajus taṃ mahā|bhāgaṃ pañca bhūtāni Rāvaṇam
bhraṃśitaḥ sarva|lokeṣu sa hi brahm'|âstra|tejasā.
Śarīra|dhātavo hy asya māṃsaṃ rudhiram eva ca
neśur brahm'|âstra|nirdagdhā na ca bhasm' âpy adṛśyata.

Seeing that almost impossible feat, Rávana was filled with fear. Then, angered, the ten-necked one quickly fired off sharp arrows and various weapons at Rama in their tens of millions—such as bhushúndis, spears, clubs, axes, lances of various kinds, hundred-killers and sharpened blades. Seeing
the ten-necked demon's unnatural power, all the monkeys 25
scattered, out of fear, in every direction. Then Kakútstha, taking a well-feathered, fine-headed, gold-shafted superarrow from his quiver, joined it to Brahma's weapon. Rama charged this supreme arrow with the Brahma weapon.

Seeing this, the gods and *gandhárva*s, led by Shakra, rejoiced. And they thought the enemy demon's life almost over—the gods, *dánavas*, *kim·naras*—because of the charging of Brahma's weapon. Then Rama released that terrible arrow—its energy immeasurable, like Brahma's staff held aloft—and finished off Rávana. For as soon, Bhárata, as it was released by Rama, drawing his bowstring from far
above him into a circle, it ignited the best of demons, with 30
his chariot, horses and charioteer; he was engulfed by a great blazing fire.

Then the gods rejoiced, together with the *gandhárva*s and *chárana*s, on seeing Rávana killed by Rama, the unimpeachable actor. The five elements abandoned the most fortunate Rávana, for he was ousted in all the worlds by the brilliance of Brahma's weapon. His bodily elements, even his flesh and blood, perished, burned up by Brahma's weapon, and not even his ashes were seen.

MĀRKAṆḌEYA uvāca:

291.1 Sa hatvā Rāvaṇaṃ kṣudraṃ rākṣas'|êndraṃ sura|dviṣam
babhūva hṛṣṭaḥ sa|suhṛd Rāmaḥ Saumitriṇā saha.
Tato hate daśa|grīve devāḥ sa|ṛṣi|purogamāḥ
āśīrbhir jaya|yuktābhir ānarcus taṃ mahā|bhujam.
Rāmaṃ kamala|patr'|âkṣaṃ tuṣṭuvuḥ sarva|devatāḥ
Gandharvāḥ puṣpa|varṣaiś ca vāgbhiś ca tridaś'|ālayāḥ.
Pūjayitvā tathā Rāmaṃ pratijagmur yath"|āgatam.
tan mah"|ôtsava|saṃkāśam āsīd ākāśam acyuta.
5 Tato hatvā daśa|grīvaṃ Laṅkāṃ Rāmo mahā|yaśāḥ
Vibhīṣaṇāya pradadau prabhuḥ para|puraṃ|jayaḥ.
Tataḥ Sītāṃ puras|kṛtya Vibhīṣaṇa|puras|kṛtām
Avindhyo nāma su|prajño vṛddh'|âmātyo viniryayau.
Uvāca ca mah"|ātmānaṃ Kākutsthaṃ dainyam āsthitaḥ:
«pratīccha devā sad|vṛttāṃ mah"|ātmañ Jānakīm iti.»
Etac chrutvā vacas tasmād avatīrya rath'|ôttamāt
bāṣpeṇ' âpihitāṃ Sītāṃ dadarś' Êkṣvāku|nandanaḥ.
Tāṃ dṛṣṭvā cāru|sarv'|âṅgīṃ yāna|sthāṃ śoka|karśitām
mal'|ôpacita|sarv'|âṅgīṃ jaṭilāṃ kṛṣṇa|vāsasam
10 Uvāca Rāmo Vaidehīṃ parāmarśa|viśaṅkitaḥ:
«gaccha Vaidehi muktā tvaṃ. yat kāryaṃ tan mayā kṛtam
Mām āsādya patiṃ bhadre na tvaṃ rākṣasa|veśmani
jarāṃ vrajethā iti me nihato 'sau niśā|caraḥ.
Kathaṃ hy asmad|vidho jātu jānan dharma|viniścayam
para|hasta|gatāṃ nārīṃ muhūrtam api dhārayet?
Su|vṛttām a|su|vṛttāṃ v" âpy ahaṃ tvām adya maithili

MARKANDÉYA said:

Having killed the low, god-hating demon-lord, Rávana, 291.1
Rama was delighted, as was Sumítra's son, and their friends.
Once the ten-necked one had been killed, then the gods, led
by the seers, honored that great-armed one with blessings
for his victory.

All the gods, *gandhárvas*, and those living in heaven,
praised Rama of the lotus-petal eyes with downpours of
flowers and words. After honoring Rama in this way, they
returned as they had come. The sky looked like one great
festival, imperishable one.* So, having killed the ten-necked 5
one, the most glorious Rama, conqueror of the enemy city,
gave Lanka to Vibhíshana. Then, preceded by Sita and Vi-
bhíshana, the most wise and ancient minister, Avíndhya,
issued out. And he said to the great-souled Kakútstha, sunk
in depression: "Great soul, receive back your virtuous queen,
Jánaka's daughter."

Having listened to this speech, the delight of Ikshváku
stepped down from that supreme chariot and looked at Sita,
veiled in tears. Seeing her, all her limbs beautiful, standing
on a vehicle, thin from grief, her body caked with dirt, her
hair matted, wearing a black robe, Rama, suspicious that 10
she had been violated, said to the Vidéha princess:

"Go, princess of Vidéha! You have been freed. I have done
what I had to. Good lady, since I was your husband I could
not let you wander into old age in a demon's house, so I
killed that creature of the night. For how could someone
like me, who knows what the Law decrees, tolerate his wife's
being in another man's power even for a hour? Whether you

n' ôtsahe paribhogāya śv'|âvalīḍhaṃ havir yathā.»
Tataḥ sā sahasā bālā tac chrutvā dāruṇaṃ vacaḥ
papāta devī vyathitā nikṛttā kadalī yathā.
15 Yo 'pi asyā harṣa|saṃbhūto mukha|rāgas tad" âbhavat
kṣaṇena sa punar bhraṣṭo niḥśvāsa iva darpaṇe.
Tatas te harayaḥ sarve tac chrutvā Rāma|bhāṣitam
gat'|âsu|kalpā niśceṣṭā babhūvuḥ saha|Lakṣmaṇāḥ.
Tato devo viśuddh'|ātmā vimānena catur|mukhaḥ
padma|yonir jagat|sraṣṭā darśayām āsa Rāghavam,
Śakraś c' âgniś ca Vāyuś ca Yamo Varuṇa eva ca
Yakṣ'|âdhipaś ca bhagavāṃs tathā sapta'|rṣayo 'malāḥ
Rājā Daśarathaś c' âiva divya|bhāsvara|mūrtimān
vimānena mah"|ârheṇa haṃsa|yuktena bhāsvatā.
20 Tato 'ntarikṣaṃ tat sarvaṃ deva|gandharva|saṃkulam
śuśubhe tārakā|citraṃ śarad' îva nabhas|talam.
Tata utthāya Vaidehī teṣāṃ madhye yaśasvinī
uvāca vākyaṃ kalyāṇī Rāmaṃ pṛthula|vakṣasam.
«Rāja|putra na te doṣaṃ karomi viditā hi te
gatiḥ strīṇāṃ narāṇāṃ ca. śṛṇu c' êdaṃ vaco mama.
Antaś carati bhūtānāṃ mātariśvā sadā|gatiḥ
sa me vimuñcatu prāṇān yadi pāpaṃ carāmy aham.
Agnir āpas tath" ākāśaṃ pṛthivī vāyur eva ca
vimuñcantu mama prāṇān yadi pāpaṃ carāmy aham.
25 Yath" âhaṃ tvad|ṛte vīra n' ânyaṃ svapne 'py acintayam
tathā me deva|nirdiṣṭas tvam eva hi patir bhava.»
Tato 'ntarikṣe vāg āsīt su|bhagā loka|sākṣiṇī
puṇyā saṃharṣaṇī teṣāṃ vānarāṇāṃ mahātmanām.

have behaved well or not, princess of Míthila, you are like an oblation licked by a dog—I cannot enjoy you now."

When the young queen heard this dreadful speech, she fell juddering down, like a cut banana tree. Then the color that had risen in her face from joy disappeared again in a moment, like breath from a mirror. And all the monkeys, and Lákshmana too, hearing what Rama had said, became motionless, as if dead.

Then the four-faced, pure-spirited god,* born from a lotus, creator of the universe, showed himself with his vehicle to Rághava, as did Shakra, Agni, Vayu, Yama, Váruna, the lordly king of the *yakshas*, and the stainless seven seers, and King Dasha·ratha, shining and divine in form, with his greatly worthy, glorious vehicle, yoked with geese. The entirety of space was filled with gods and *gandhárvas*; it shone like the surface of the sky bright with autumnal stars. Then the glorious and beautiful princess of Vidéha stood up in their midst and made a speech to broad-chested Rama:

"Prince, I find no fault with you, for you are familiar with the way of men and women. Listen to what I have to say. The ever-moving wind that moves in beings—let him liberate my life breaths if I have done wrong! Let fire, water, space, earth and wind liberate my life breaths if I have done wrong! As even in my dreams, hero, I have never thought of anyone but you, so you should be my husband, as was determined by the gods."

Then there was a beautiful, auspicious voice in the sky, a universal witness, gladdening those great-spirited monkeys.

VĀYUR uvāca:

«Bho bho Rāghava satyaṃ vai vāyur asmi sad|āgatiḥ.
apāpā maithilī rājan. saṃgaccha saha bhāryayā.»

AGNIR uvāca:

«Aham antaḥ|śarīra|stho bhūtānāṃ Raghu|nandana.
su|sūkṣmam api Kākutstha maithilī n' âparādhyati.»

VARUṆA uvāca:

«Rasā vai mat|prasūtā hi bhūta|deheṣu Rāghava.
ahaṃ vai tvāṃ prabravīmi maithilī pratigṛhyatām.»

BRAHM"ôvāca

30 «Putra n' âitad ih' āścaryaṃ tvayi rāja'|rṣi|dharmiṇi.
sādho sadvṛtta Kākutstha śṛṇu c' êdaṃ vaco mama.
Śatrur eṣa tvayā vīra deva|gandharva|bhoginām
Yakṣāṇāṃ dānavānāṃ ca maha"|rṣīṇāṃ ca pātitaḥ.
Avadhyaḥ sarva|bhūtānāṃ mat|prasādāt pur" âbhavat.
kasmāc cit kāraṇāt pāpaḥ kaṃ cit kālam upekṣitaḥ.
Vadh'|ârtham ātmanas tena hṛtā Sītā dur|ātmanā
Nalakūbara|śāpena rakṣā c' âsyāḥ kṛtā mayā.
Yadi hy akāmām āsevet striyam anyām api dhruvam
śatadh" âsya phalen mūrdhā ity uktaḥ so 'bhavat purā.
35 N' âtra śaṅkā tvayā kāryā. pratīcch' êmāṃ mahā|dyute.
kṛtaṃ tvayā mahat kāryaṃ devānām amara|prabha.»

VAYU said:

"Oh, Oh, Rághava! It's true—I am the ever-moving Wind —the princess of Míthila is without sin, king. Be reunited with your wife!"

AGNI said:

"I am in the body of beings, Raghu's delight. The princess of Míthila has not, even in the slightest, strayed, Kakútstha."

VÁRUNA said:

"The juices in creatures' bodies are produced by me, Rághava. Truly, I tell you, take the princess of Míthila back!"

BRAHMA said:

"Good son, virtuous Kakútstha, for you, who have the 30
law of the royal seers, there is nothing extraordinary about
this. Listen to my words. You have felled this enemy of the
gods, *gandhárva*s, snakes, *yaksha*s, *dánava*s and great seers.
Hitherto, by my grace, no beings could kill him. For some
reason the evil one was overlooked for some time. Sita was
abducted by the evil-natured one in order to bring about his
own death, and I protected her by means of Nala·kúbara's
curse. For he had been told in the past that, if he were to
approach any unwilling woman, it would certainly result
in his head splitting into a hundred pieces. You should 35
be in no doubt about this. Take her back, glorious man.
You have done a great deed for the gods, you who are like
an immortal!"

DAŚARATHA uvāca:

«Prīto 'smi vatsa bhadraṃ te pitā Daśaratho 'smi te
anujānāmi rājyaṃ ca praśādhi puruṣ'|ôttama!»

RĀMA uvāca:

«Abhivādaye tvāṃ rāj'|êndra. yadi tvaṃ janako mama
gamiṣyāmi purīṃ ramyām Ayodhyāṃ śāsanāt tava.»

MĀRKAṆḌEYA uvāca:

Tam uvāca pitā bhūyaḥ prahṛṣṭo Bharata'|rṣabha
«gacch' âyodhyāṃ praśādh' îti» Rāmaṃ rakt'|ânta|locanam
«Sampūrṇān' îha varṣāṇi caturdaśa mahā|dyute.»
tato devān namaskṛtya suhṛdbhir abhinanditaḥ
40 Mah"|êndra iva Paulomyā bhāryayā sa sameyivān.
tato varaṃ dadau tasmai Avindhyāya paraṃ|tapaḥ
Trijaṭāṃ c' ârtha|mānābhyāṃ yojayām āsa rākṣasīm.
tam uvāca tato Brahmā devaiḥ śakra|purogamaiḥ:
«Kausalyā|mātar iṣṭāṃs te varān adya dadāni kān?»
vavre Rāmaḥ sthitiṃ dharme śatrubhiś c' âparājayam
Rākṣasair nihatānāṃ ca vānarāṇāṃ samudbhavam.
tatas te Brahmaṇā prokte «tath" êti» vacane tadā
Samuttasthur mahā|rāja vānarā labdha|cetasaḥ
Sītā c' âpi mahā|bhāgā varaṃ Hanumate dadau:
45 «Rāma|kīrtyā samaṃ putra jīvitaṃ te bhaviṣyati,
divyās tvām upabhogāś ca mat|prasāda|kṛtāḥ sadā
Upasthāsyanti Hanumann iti sma hari|locana.»

DASHA·RATHA said:

"I am pleased, son. A blessing on you! I am your father, Dasha·ratha. I give permission. And govern the kingdom, outstanding man!"

RAMA said:

"I salute you, Indra of a king. If you are my father, I will go to the beautiful city of Ayódhya at your command."

MARKANDÉYA said:

Delighted, his father, bull of the Bharatas, again told him, Rama of the red-tipped eyes: "Go to Ayódhya and govern! Your fourteen years here have been completed, man of great glory."

Then having bowed to the gods, and greeted by his
friends, he was reunited with his wife, like great Indra with 40
Paulómi. Then the incinerator of the foe gave a gift to that Avíndhya, and provided the demoness Tri·jata with wealth and honor. Then Brahma, among the gods with Indra at their head, said to him:

"Kausálya's son, what gifts do you desire that I shall give you today?" Rama chose firmness in the Law, invincibility in the face of his enemies and the resurrection of the monkeys killed by the demons. And when Brahma had spoken the words "So be it!" the monkeys stood up, their consciousness restored, great king.

Then the most fortunate Sita gave a gift to Hanúmat:
"Your life, son, shall last as long as Rama's fame, and, fash- 45
ioned by my grace, divine refreshments shall ever wait on you, brown-eyed Hanúmat!" And while those whose actions were impeccable were looking on, all the gods, with Indra at

tatas te prekṣamāṇānāṃ teṣām akliṣṭa|karmaṇām
Antardhānaṃ yayur devāḥ sarve Śakra|purogamāḥ.
dṛṣṭvā Rāmaṃ tu jānakyā saṅgataṃ Śakra|sārathiḥ
Uvāca parama|prītaḥ suhṛn|madhya idaṃ vacaḥ:
«deva|gandharva|yakṣāṇāṃ mānuṣ'|âsura|bhoginām
Apanītaṃ tvayā duḥkham idaṃ satya|parākrama.
sa|dev'|âsura|gandharvā yakṣa|rākṣasa|pannagāḥ
50 Kathayiṣyanti lokās tvāṃ yāvad bhūmir dhariṣyati.»
ity evam uktv" ânujñāpya Rāmaṃ śastra|bhṛtāṃ varam
Saṃpūjy' âpākramat tena rathen' āditya|varcasā.
tataḥ Sītāṃ puras|kṛtya Rāmaḥ Saumitriṇā saha
Sugrīva|pramukhaiś c' âiva sahitaḥ sarva|vānaraiḥ
vidhāya rakṣāṃ Laṅkāyāṃ Vibhīṣaṇa|puras|kṛtaḥ
Saṃtatāra punas tena setunā makar'|ālayam
Puṣpakeṇa vimānena khecareṇa virājatā
Kāma|gena yathā mukhyair amātyaiḥ saṃvṛto vaśī.
tatas tīre samudrasya yatra śiśye sa pārthivaḥ
55 Tatr' âiv' ôvāsa dharm'|ātmā sahitaḥ sarva|vānaraiḥ.
ath' âinān Rāghavaḥ kāle samānīy' âbhipūjya ca
Visarjayām āsa tadā ratnaiḥ saṃtoṣya sarvaśaḥ.
gateṣu vānar'|êndreṣu gopuccha'|rkṣeṣu teṣu ca
Sugrīva|sahito Rāmaḥ Kiṣkindhāṃ punar āgamat.
Vibhīṣaṇen' ânugataḥ Sugrīva|sahitas tadā
Puṣpakeṇa vimānena Vaidehyā darśayan vanam
Kiṣkindhāṃ tu samāsādya Rāmaḥ praharatāṃ varaḥ
Aṅgadaṃ kṛta|karmāṇaṃ yauva|rājye 'bhyaṣecayat.

their head, disappeared. But seeing Rama reunited with Jánaka's daughter, Shakra's charioteer, extremely pleased, said this, in the midst of friends:

"You, whose strength is truth, have dispersed this sorrow of gods, *gandhárva*s, *yaksha*s, men, anti-gods and snakes. *Yaksha*s, demons, serpents, along with gods, anti-gods and *gandhárvas*, and the worlds will tell of you as long as the earth remains." Having said this, he asked for leave to depart, honored the best of weapon-bearers, Rama, and left with his chariot brilliant as the sun. Then, placing Sita before him, together with Sumítra's son, along with all the monkeys, with Sugríva at their head, and attended by Vibhíshana, Rama arranged for Lanka's protection.

And then he again crossed the sea monster's realm by that causeway, on the beautiful sky-going chariot, Púshpaka, which goes as he wills, a ruler surrounded by his chief ministers. Then, on the seashore where he, the king, had slept, the Law-spirited man stayed with all the monkeys. In time Rághava called them together and honored them, and, having completely satisfied them with jewels, dismissed them. And when the monkey-lords and the monkeys and bears had gone, Rama went back to Kishkíndha with Sugríva.

Followed by Vibhíshana, and accompanied by Sugríva, he showed the Vidéha princess the forest from the Púshpaka vehicle. After he had reached Kishkíndha, Rama, the greatest of warriors, had Ángada, who had done his duty, consecrated as crown prince.

tatas tair eva sahito Rāmaḥ Saumitriṇā saha
60 Yath"|āgatena mārgeṇa prayayau sva|puraṃ prati.
Ayodhyāṃ sa samāsādya purīṃ rāṣṭra|patis tataḥ
Bharatāya Hanūmantaṃ dūtaṃ prāsthāpayat tadā.
lakṣayitv" êṅgitaṃ sarvaṃ priyaṃ tasmai nivedya ca
Vāyu|putre punaḥ prāpte Nandigrāmam upāgamat.
sa tatra mala|digdh'|âṅgaṃ Bharataṃ cīra|vāsasam
Agrataḥ pāduke kṛtvā dadarś' āsīnam āsane.
saṅgato Bharaten' âtha Śatrughnena ca vīryavān
Rāghavaḥ saha|Saumitrir mumude Bharata'|rṣabha.
tato Bharata|Śatrughnau sametau guruṇā tadā
65 Vaidehyā darśanen' ôbhau praharṣaṃ samavāpatuḥ.
tasmai tad Bharato rājyam āgatāy' âtisatkṛtam
nyāsaṃ niryātayām āsa yuktaḥ paramayā mudā.

Tatas te Vaiṣṇave śūraṃ nakṣatre 'bhimate 'hani
Vasiṣṭho Vāmadevaś ca sahitāv abhyaṣiñcatām.
So 'bhiṣiktaḥ kapi|śreṣṭhaṃ Sugrīvaṃ sa|suhṛj|janam
Vibhīṣaṇaṃ ca Paulastyam anvajānād gṛhān prati.
Abhyarcya vividhai bhogaiḥ prīti|yuktau mudā yutau
samādhāy' êti|kartavyaṃ duḥkhena visasarja ha.
Puṣpakaṃ ca vimānaṃ tat pūjayitvā sa Rāghavaḥ
prādād Vaiśravaṇāy' âiva prītyā sa Raghu|nandanaḥ.
70 Tato deva'|rṣi|sahitaḥ saritaṃ Gomatīm anu
daś' âśva|medhān ājahre jārūthyān sa nirargalān.

Then, together with them, Rama, along with Sumítra's son, went toward his own city by the way he had come. On reaching Ayódhya city, the lord of the realm sent Hanúmat as a messenger to Bharata. Noting every gesture, the Wind's son told him the good news, and he returned again* to Nandi·grama. There he saw Bharata, wearing a bark tunic, his limbs smeared with dirt, sitting on a seat, with Rama's sandals in front of him. Then heroic Rághava, along with Sumítra's son, rejoiced on being reunited with Bharata and Shatru·ghna, O Bharata bull; and Bharata and Shatru·ghna, reunited with their elder, both became joyful on seeing the Vidéha princess. Filled with an overwhelming joy, Bharata restored his honored trust, the kingdom, to the one who had come back.

Then, on an auspicious day under the Váishnava constellation, Vasíshtha and Vama·deva together consecrated the hero. Consecrated, he gave the best of monkeys, Sugríva, and Vibhíshana, Pulástya's son, together with the friendly people, leave to go home. Having, with various luxuries, honored the two of them, who were pleased and filled with joy, he accepted his duty and sorrowfully let them go. Rághava, the delighter of Raghu, honored the Púshpaka vehicle and gave it with pleasure to Vaishrávana. Then, accompanied by the gods and the seers, without obstruction he offered ten horse sacrifices with donations of meat next to the Go·mati river.

MĀRKAṆḌEYA uvāca:

292.1 Evam etan mahā|bāho Rāmeṇ' âmita|tejasā
prāptaṃ vyasanam atyugraṃ vanavāsa|kṛtaṃ purā.
Mā śucaḥ puruṣa|vyāghra! kṣatriyo 'si paraṃ|tapa.
bāhu|vīry'|āśrite mārge vartase dīpta|nirṇaye.
Na hi te vṛjinaṃ kiṃ cid vartate param'|âṇv|api.
asmin mārge niṣīdeyuḥ s' Êndrā api sur'|âsurāḥ.
Saṃhatya nihato Vṛtro Marudbhir vajra|pāṇinā
Namuciś c' âiva durdharṣo Dīrghajihvā ca rākṣasī.
5 Sahāyavati sarv'|ârthāḥ saṃtiṣṭhant' îha sarvaśaḥ.
kiṃ nu tasy' âjitaṃ saṃkhye yasya bhrātā Dhanaṃjayaḥ
Ayaṃ ca balināṃ śreṣṭho Bhīmo bhīma|parākramaḥ
yuvānau ca mah"|êṣv|āsau vīrau mādravatī|sutau?
Ebhiḥ sahāyaiḥ kasmāt tvaṃ viṣīdasi paraṃ|tapa
ya ime vajriṇaḥ senāṃ jayeyuḥ saMarud|gaṇām?
Tvam apy ebhir mah"|êṣv|āsaiḥ sahāyair deva|rūpibhiḥ
vijeṣyasi raṇe sarvān amitrān Bharata'|rṣabha.
Itaś ca tvam imāṃ paśya Saindhavena dur|ātmanā
balinā vīrya|mattena hṛtām ebhir mah"|ātmabhiḥ
10 Ānītāṃ Draupadīṃ Kṛṣṇāṃ kṛtvā karma suduṣkaram
Jayadrathaṃ ca rājānaṃ vijitaṃ vaśam āgatam.
Asahāyena Rāmeṇa Vaidehī punar āhṛtā
hatvā saṃkhye daśa|grīvaṃ rākṣasaṃ bhīma|vikramam
Yasya śākhā|mṛgā mitrāṇy ṛkṣāḥ kāla|mukhās tathā
jāty|antara|gatā rājann etad buddhy" ânucintaya.

MARKANDÉYA said:

Great-arm, in this way Rama, whose luster is immeasur- 292.1
able, underwent this very great hardship in the past as a
result of living in the forest.

Don't grieve, tigerish man! You are a warrior-prince, in-
cinerator of the foe! You are on the path founded on strength
of arms, and fiery resolve. You show no signs of even the
minutest vice. Demons and gods—even Indra—would de-
spair on this path. Joining with the Maruts, the thunderbolt-
wielder* killed Vritra, and the unassailable demoness, Dir-
gha·jihva. Throughout this world all aims are accomplished 5
by the one who has companions. What is not won in bat-
tle by the man who has Dhanam·jaya for a brother? And
this strongest of the strong, the frighteningly bold Bhima?
And the great bowmen, the youthful and heroic twin sons
of Madri? With these companions who could conquer the
army of the thunderbolt-wielder along with his troops of
Maruts, why do you despair, incinerator of the foe? You
too, with these great, god-like archers as companions, will
conquer all enemies in battle, Bharata bull.

See how these great-spirited ones, accomplishing a most difficult feat, rescued Krishná Dráupadi, who had been abducted by the strong, evil-souled Sáindhava, drunk with power; and King Jayad·ratha was conquered and brought under control. Without such companions, Rama recovered the Vidéha princess, having killed the terrifyingly strong ten-necked demon in battle. His friends were monkeys and black-faced bears —quite different kinds of creatures. Bear that in mind, my king. Therefore, best of Kurus, Bharata

Tasmāt sa tvaṃ Kuru|śreṣṭha mā śuco Bharata'|rṣabha!
tvad|vidhā hi mah"|ātmāno na śocanti paraṃ|tapa.

VAIŚAṂPĀYANA uvāca:

Evam āśvāsito rājā Mārkaṇḍeyena dhīmatā
tyaktvā duḥkham adīn'|ātmā punar apy enam abravīt.

bull, do not grieve! For great-spirited men like you do not grieve, incinerator of the foe.

VAISHAM·PÁYANA said:

Thus consoled by the wise Markandéya, the king relinquished his sorrow, and, undaunted in himself, addressed him again.

293–299
THE GLORIFICATION OF THE FAITHFUL WIFE

Yudhiṣṭhira uvāca:

293.1 N’ ātmānam anuśocāmi
n’ êmān bhrātṝn mahā|mune
haraṇaṃ c’ âpi rājyasya yath” êmāṃ Drupad’|ātmajām.
Dyūte durātmabhiḥ kliṣṭāḥ Kṛṣṇayā tāritā vayam
Jayadrathena ca punar vanāc c’ âpi hṛtā balāt.
Asti sīmantinī kā cid dṛṣṭa|pūrv” âpi vā śrutā
pativratā mahā|bhāgā yath” êyaṃ Drupad’|ātmajā?

Mārkaṇḍeya uvāca:

Śṛṇu rājan kula|strīṇāṃ mahā|bhāgyam Yudhiṣṭhira,
sarvam etad yathā prāptaṃ Sāvitryā rāja|kanyayā.
5 Āsīn Madreṣu dharm’|ātmā rājā parama|dharmikaḥ
Brahmaṇyaś ca mah”|ātmā ca satya|saṃdho jit’|êndriyaḥ
Yajvā dāna|patir dakṣaḥ paura|jānapada|priyaḥ
pārthivo ’śvapatir nāma sarva|bhūta|hite rataḥ.
Kṣamāvān an|apatyaś ca satya|vāg|vijit’|êndriyaḥ
atikrāntena vayasā saṃtāpam upajagmivān.
Apaty’|ôtpādan’|ârthaṃ ca tīvraṃ niyamam āsthitaḥ
kāle parimit’|āhāro brahmacārī jit’|êndriyaḥ.
Hutvā śata|sahasraṃ sa Sāvitryā rāja|sattama
ṣaṣṭhe ṣaṣṭhe tadā kāle babhūva mita|bhojanaḥ.
10 Etena niyamen’ āsīd varṣāṇy aṣṭādaś’ âiva tu
pūrṇe tv aṣṭādaśe varṣe Sāvitrī tuṣṭim abhyagāt.
Rūpiṇī tu tadā rājan darśayām āsa taṃ nṛpam
agnihotrāt samutthāya harṣeṇa mahat” ânvitā
uvāca c’ âinaṃ varadā vacanaṃ pārthivaṃ tadā:

YUDHI·SHTHIRA said:

I DON'T GRIEVE FOR MYSELF, nor for these brothers—no, 293.1
not even for the kingdom's theft, Great Sage—so much as I grieve for this daughter of Drúpada. At the dicing, when we were tormented by the wicked, it was Krishná* who saved us; and now she has been snatched once more and dragged from the forest by Jayad·ratha. Have you ever heard, or even caught sight of a woman—a wife—so pure, so devoted and virtuous as this, as Drúpada's daughter?

MARKANDÉYA said:

Listen, King Yudhi·shthira, to a story of the high purity of virtuous women—how all that follows was accomplished by a princess called Sávitri.

There was, among the Madras, a king, wonderfully 5
virtuous, the epitome of law, a friend to brahmins, a great spirit who kept his word and his self-control—a clever king called Ashva·pati, a sacrificer, a lord of liberality, dear to both town and country, dedicated to the welfare of all. He had self-control and spoke the truth; he was childless, and patient with it; but as he grew older his anguish increased. So to produce a child he undertook a hard penance: celibacy, part starvation, and control of the senses. With the Sávitri mantra,* Supreme Ruler, he offered a hundred thousand
oblations, and ate just a mouthful in any six hours. For 10
eighteen years he followed this vow, until, at the end of year eighteen, Sávitri* was satisfied. Then, my lord, rising from the flames of the Agni·hotra,* she, a wish-giving goddess filled with high joy, took on a body in front of that ruler, and said to the king:

Sāvitry uvāca:

12 «Brahmacaryeṇa śuddhena damena niyamena ca
sarv'|ātmanā ca bhaktyā ca tuṣṭ" âsmi tava pārthiva.
Varaṃ vṛṇīṣv' Âśvapate Madra|rāja yad īpsitam,
na pramādaś ca dharmeṣu kartavyas te kathaṃ cana.»

Aśvapatir uvāca:

«Apaty'|ârthaḥ* samārambhaḥ kṛto dharm'|ēpsayā mayā
putrā me bahavo devi bhaveyuḥ kula|bhāvanāḥ.
15 Tuṣṭ" âsi yadi me devi varam etaṃ vṛṇomy aham
santānaṃ paramo dharma ity āhur māṃ dvi|jātayaḥ.»

Sāvitry uvāca:

«Pūrvam eva mayā rājann abhiprāyam imaṃ tava
jñātvā putr'|ârtham ukto vai bhagavāṃs te pitā|mahaḥ.
Prasādāc c' âiva tasmāt te svayaṃbhu|vihitād bhuvi
kanyā tejasvinī saumya kṣipram eva bhaviṣyati.
Uttaraṃ ca na te kiṃ cid vyāhartavyaṃ kathaṃ cana,
pitā|maha|nisargeṇa tuṣṭā hy etad bravīmi te.»

Mārkaṇḍeya uvāca:

Sa «tath" êti» pratijñāya Sāvitryā vacanaṃ nṛpaḥ
prasādayām āsa punaḥ: «kṣipram etad bhaviṣyati?»
20 Antar|hitāyāṃ Sāvitryāṃ jagāma sva|puraṃ nṛpaḥ
sva|rājye c' âvasad vīraḥ prajā dharmeṇa pālayan.
Kasmiṃś cit tu gate kāle sa rājā niyata|vrataḥ
jyeṣṭhāyāṃ dharma|cāriṇyāṃ mahiṣyāṃ garbham ādadhe.
Rāja|putryās tu garbhaḥ sa Mānavyā Bharata'|rṣabha
vyavardhata tadā śukle tārā|patir iv' âmbare.
Prāpte kāle tu suṣuve kanyāṃ rājīva|locanām

SÁVITRI said:

"I am pleased, King, with your celibacy, your purity, your 12
self-control, your self-restraint and your complete and utter
devotion to me. So, Ashva·pati, king of the Madras, choose
a gift that you desire, but never grow careless with the law."

ASHVA·PATI said:

"I began this to engender a child, led by my yearning
for virtue. Goddess, for the sake of my family line, give me
plenty of sons! If you are pleased with me, Goddess, this is 15
the gift I ask for. The twice-born* have told me children are
the highest virtue."

SÁVITRI said:

"King, I already knew your intention, and I've spoken to the Grandsire* concerning your sons. And by that favor the Self-existent* bestowed on you on earth, good man, a lustrous girl shall be born to you soon. Don't reply! I am pleased, and I tell you this with the Grandsire's blessing."

MARKANDÉYA said:

The king consented to Sávitri's words: "So be it!" Then,
again he implored her: "Will this happen soon?" When Sá- 20
vitri vanished, the king returned to his city, where he lived
a hero in his own kingdom, his people protected by the
rule of Law. And after a while, that king, so strict to his
vow, gave rise to a child in the womb of his virtuous senior
queen. And then, Bharata bull, the embryo of that queen
of Manu's lineage waxed like the moon in a clear sky. And
when her time came, she gave birth to a lotus-eyed daughter,
and that greatest of kings performed her rites with joy. Then

kriyāś ca tasyā muditaś cakre sa nṛpa|sattamaḥ.
Sāvitryā prītayā dattā Sāvitryā hutayā hy api
Sāvitr" îty eva nām' âsyāś cakrur viprās tathā pitā.
25 Sā vigrahavat" îva Śrīr vyavardhata nṛp'|ātmajā
kālena c' âpi sā kanyā yauvana|sthā babhūva ha.
Tāṃ su|madhyāṃ pṛthu|śroṇiṃ pratimāṃ kāñcanīm iva
«prāpt" êyaṃ devakany" êti» dṛṣṭvā saṃmenire janāḥ.
Tāṃ tu padma|palāś'|âkṣīṃ jvalantīm iva tejasā
na kaś cid varayām āsa tejasā prativāritaḥ.
Ath' ôpoṣya śiraḥ snātā devatām abhigamya sā
hutv" âgniṃ vidhivad viprān vācayām āsa parvaṇi.
Tataḥ sumanasaḥ śeṣāḥ pratigṛhya mah"|ātmanaḥ
pituḥ samīpam agamad devī Śrīr iva rūpiṇī.
30 S" âbhivādya pituḥ pādau śeṣāḥ pūrvaṃ nivedya ca
kṛt'|âñjalir var'|ārohā nṛpateḥ pārśvam āsthitā.
Yauvana|sthāṃ tu tāṃ dṛṣṭvā svāṃ sutāṃ deva|rūpiṇīm
ayācyamānāṃ ca varair nṛ|patir duḥkhito 'bhavat.

RĀJ" ôvāca

«Putri pradāna|kālas te na ca kaś cid vṛṇoti mām.
svayam anviccha bhartāraṃ guṇaiḥ sadṛśam ātmanaḥ.
Prārthitaḥ puruṣo yaś ca sa nivedyas tvayā mama
vimṛśy' âhaṃ pradāsyāmi. varaya tvaṃ yath" ēpsitam.
Śrutaṃ hi dharma|śāstreṣu paṭhyamānaṃ dvi|jātibhiḥ
tathā tvam api kalyāṇi gadato me vacaḥ śṛṇu:
35 ‹A|pradātā pitā vācyo vācyaś c' ânupayan patiḥ
mṛte bhartari putraś ca vācyo mātur a|rakṣitā.›
Idaṃ me vacanaṃ śrutvā bhartur anveṣaṇe tvara.
devatānāṃ yathā vācyo na bhaveyaṃ tathā kuru.»

her father and the brahmins called her "Sávitri," since it was Sávitri, pleased with the Sávitri oblations, who gave her.

The princess grew up like the embodiment of Shri, and 25
in time that girl attained puberty. When people saw what seemed a golden image, with slender waist and rounded hips, they agreed, "A goddess has come among us!" Her eyes were like the lotus petal, as if blazing with energy, yet, inhibited by that luster, no man chose her. Then she fasted, bathed her head, and approaching the family god, made a proper offering into the fire and had brahmins recite on the day the moon changes. Then, taking up the remaining flowers, she went, like the goddess Shri incarnate, to her
great-souled father. Fair-hipped girl, she saluted her father's 30
feet, offered him the left-over flowers, then stood at the king's side with her hands joined. At the sight of his own adolescent daughter, beautiful as a goddess, yet unsought by suitors, the king was despondent.

The KING said:

"It is time, daughter, for me to give you in marriage, but no man chooses you. So seek out a husband yourself, whose qualities equal your own. Let me know which man you desire;I'll make inquiries, and give him to you. Make your own choice. Indeed, I have heard brahmins recite this from law books, so listen to me, lucky girl, as I repeat what
they say: "Blame a father whose daughter has not been given 35
away, a husband who does not consort with his wife, and a son who leaves his mother unprotected when her husband dies." Now you've heard my word, hurry to find a husband. Act so that the gods may not blame me!"

MĀRKAṆḌEYA uvāca:

Evam uktvā duhitaraṃ tathā vṛddhāṃś ca mantriṇaḥ
vyādideś' ânuyātraṃ ca «gamyatām» c' êty acodayat.
S" âbhivādya pituḥ pādau vrīḍit" êva tapasvinī
pitur vacanam ājñāya nirjagām' âvicāritam.
Sā haimaṃ ratham āsthāya sthaviraiḥ sacivair vṛtā
tapo|vanāni ramyāṇi rāja'|rṣīṇāṃ jagāma ha.
40 Mānyānāṃ tatra vṛddhānāṃ kṛtvā pād'|âbhivādanam
vanāni kramaśas tāta sarvāṇy ev' âbhyagacchata.
Evaṃ tīrtheṣu sarveṣu dhan'|ôtsargaṃ nṛp'|ātmajā
kurvatī dvija|mukhyānāṃ taṃ taṃ deśaṃ jagāma ha.

MĀRKAṆḌEYA uvāca:

294.1 Atha Madr'|âdhipo rājā Nāradena samāgataḥ
upaviṣṭaḥ sabhā|madhye kathā|yogena Bhārata.
Tato 'bhigamya tīrthāni sarvāṇy ev' āśramāṃs tathā
ājagāma pitur veśma Sāvitrī saha mantribhiḥ.
Nāradena sah' āsīnaṃ dṛṣṭvā sā pitaraṃ śubhā
ubhayor eva sirasā cakre pād'|âbhivādanam.

NĀRADA uvāca:

«Kva gat" âbhūt sut" êyaṃ te kutaś c' âiv' āgatā nṛpa?
kim|arthaṃ yuvatīṃ bhartre na c' âināṃ samprayacchasi?»

AŚVAPATIR uvāca:

5 «Kāryeṇa khalv anen' âiva preṣit" âdy' âiva c' āgatā.
etasyāḥ śṛṇu deva'|rṣe bhartāraṃ yo 'nayā vṛtaḥ.»

MARKANDÉYA said:

This said to his daughter, he appointed to her retinue experienced counsellors, and urged her to go. The ascetic girl, as if embarrassed, touched her father's feet and, understanding his words, set off without hesitation. Surrounded by ancient counsellors, she got into a golden chariot, and
went to the beautiful forest retreats of the royal seers. There, 40
my son, having saluted the feet of the venerable elders, she worked her way gradually around all the forests. Thus the princess went from place to place, making donations to the foremost twice-born at all the holy fords.

MARKANDÉYA said:

Then, Bhárata, when the king of the Madras was sitting 294.1
in the middle of his court, conversing with Nárada, Sávitri returned from all the holy fords and hermitages, and came with the counsellors to her father's house. Seeing her father seated with Nárada, the lovely girl saluted them both by lowering her head to their feet.

NÁRADA said:

"Where has this daughter of yours come from, and where has she been, my lord? She's a young girl—why don't you present her to a husband?"

ASHVA·PATI said:

"This was the very business on which she was sent out, 5
and has returned just now. Hear from her, heavenly sage, whom she has chosen as her husband."

Mārkaṇḍeya uvāca:

Sā «brūhi vistareṇ' êti» pitrā saṃcoditā śubhā
tad" âiva tasya vacanaṃ pratigṛhy' êdam abravīt:

Sāvitry uvāca:

«Āsīc Chālveṣu dharm'|ātmā kṣatriyaḥ pṛthivī|patiḥ
Dyumatsena iti khyātaḥ paścāc c' ândho babhūva ha.
Vinaṣṭa|cakṣuṣas tasya bāla|putrasya dhīmataḥ
sāmīpyena hṛtaṃ rājyaṃ chidre 'smin pūrva|vairiṇā.
Sa bāla|vatsayā sārdhaṃ bhāryayā prasthito vanam
mah"|āraṇyaṃ gataś c' âpi tapas tepe mahā|vrataḥ.
10 Tasya putraḥ pure jātaḥ saṃvṛddhaś ca tapo|vane
Satyavān anurūpo me bhart" êti manasā vṛtaḥ.»

Nārada uvāca:

«Aho bata! mahat pāpaṃ Sāvitryā nṛ|pate kṛtam
ajānantyā yad anayā guṇavān Satyavān vṛtaḥ.
Satyaṃ vadaty asya pitā satyaṃ mātā prabhāṣate
tato 'sya brāhmaṇāś cakrur nām' âitat Satyavān iti.
Bālasy' âśvāḥ priyāś c' âsya karoty aśvāṃś ca mṛn|mayān
citre 'pi vilikhaty aśvāṃś Citr'|âśva iti c' ôcyate.»

rāj" ôvāca

«Ap' îdānīṃ sa tejasvī buddhimān vā nṛp"|ātmajaḥ?
kṣamāvān api vā śūraḥ Satyavān pitṛ|vatsalaḥ?»

Nārada uvāca:

15 «Vivasvān iva tejasvī Bṛhaspati|samo matau
Mah"|Êndra iva vīraś ca vasudh" êva kṣam"|ânvitaḥ.»

MARKANDÉYA said:

Urged by her father to tell all in detail, the lovely girl noted his words, and then said this:

SÁVITRI said:

"There was among the Shalvas a warrior king, the soul of the Law, called Dyumat·sena; latterly he became blind. Preying on this weakness, a hostile neighbor seized the kingdom from the wise king, for his eyesight had gone and his son was still young. With his wife and her infant boy, he retired to the woods, and, once in the great forest, that man
of great vows chastened his flesh. It is Sátyavat, his son— 10
born in the city, raised in the ascetics' grove —I have chosen with my heart as the right husband for me."

NÁRADA said:

"Alas king! Sávitri has, in her ignorance, done a great wrong, in choosing the virtuous Sátyavat. His father speaks the truth, his mother speaks the truth; therefore brahmins gave him this name, "Sátyavat."* As a child he loved horses, and made horses of clay; he painted horses in pictures as well, and so he is called 'Chitráshva.'*"

The KING said:

"Does the prince now have luster and wisdom? Is Sátyavat patient and brave, and fond of his father?"

NÁRADA said:

"He is as lustrous as Vivásvat, as wise as Brihas·pati, as 15
heroic as great Indra, and as patient as Earth herself."

Aśvapatir uvāca:

«Api rāj'|ātmajo dātā brahmaṇyaś c' âpi Satyavān
rūpavān apy udāro v' âpy atha vā priya|darśanaḥ?»

Nārada uvāca:

«Sāṅkṛte Rantidevasya sva|śaktyā dānataḥ samaḥ,
brahmaṇyaḥ satya|vādī ca Śibir Auśīnaro yathā
Yayātir iva c' ôdāraḥ, somavat priya|darśanaḥ,
rūpeṇ' ânyatamo 'śvibhyāṃ Dyumatsena|suto balī.
Sa dāntaḥ sa mṛduḥ śūraḥ sa satyaḥ saṃyat'|êndriyaḥ
sa maitraḥ so 'nasūyaś ca sa hrīmān dyutimāṃś ca saḥ.
20 Nityaśaś c' ārjavaṃ tasmin sthitis tasy' âiva ca dhruvā
saṅkṣepatas tapo|vṛddhaiḥ śīla|vṛddhaiś ca kathyate.»

Aśvapatir uvāca:

«Guṇair upetaṃ sarvais taṃ bhagavan prabravīṣi me
doṣān apy asya me brūhi yadi sant' îha ke|cana.»

Nārada uvāca:

«Eka ev' âsya doṣo hi guṇān ākramya tiṣṭhati
sa ca doṣaḥ prayatnena na śakyam ativartitum.
Eko doṣo 'sti n' ânyo 'sya: so 'dya prabhṛti Satyavān
saṃvatsareṇa kṣīṇ'|āyur deha|nyāsaṃ kariṣyati.»

Rāj" ôvāca

«Ehi Sāvitri gacchasva anyaṃ varaya śobhane
tasya doṣo mahān eko guṇān ākramya ca sthitaḥ.
25 Yathā me bhagavān āha Nārado deva|satkṛtaḥ
saṃvatsareṇa so 'lp'|āyur deha|nyāsaṃ kariṣyati.»

Ashva·pati said:

"Is Prince Sátyavat a giver and devoted to religion? Is he handsome, upright and lovely to look at?"

Nárada said:

"According to his own ability, he is the equal of Ranti·deva Sánkriti in giving. He is devoted to religion and, like Shibi Aushínara, a speaker of the truth. As upright as Yayáti, as lovely to look at as the moon, as handsome as either of the Ashvins is the mighty son of Dyumat·sena. He is restrained, gentle, brave and truthful, he has his senses under control; he is friendly, he bears no grudges, he is
modest and dignified. In short, those who are old in virtue 20
and advanced in austerities describe him as ever constant and a home to integrity."

Ashva·pati said:

"You tell me, my lord, that he has all the good qualities, but speak to me of his faults too, if indeed he has any."

Nárada said:

"He has a single defectwhich outweighs his qualities; it is a defect that cannot be disposed of by effort. He has one defect and one alone: a year from today his span of life will be over and Sátyavat will lay down his body."

The King said:

"Come near, Sávitri. Beautiful girl, go and choose another. He has one great fault that outweighs his other qual-
ities. As Lord Nárada, who is honored by the gods has told 25
me—his life span is short: in a year's time he will lay down his body."

SĀVITRY uvāca:

«Sakṛd aṃśo nipatati sakṛt kanyā pradīyate
sakṛd āha: ‹dadān' îti› trīṇy etāni sakṛt sakṛt.
Dīrgh'|āyur atha v" âlp'|āyuḥ sa|guṇo nir|guṇo 'pi vā
sakṛd vṛto mayā bhartā na dvitīyaṃ vṛṇomy aham.
Manasā niścayaṃ kṛtvā tato vāc" âbhidhīyate
kriyate karmaṇā paścāt pramāṇaṃ me manas tataḥ.»

NĀRADA uvāca:

«Sthirā buddhir nara|śreṣṭha Sāvitryā duhitus tava.
n' âiṣā cālayituṃ śakyā dharmād asmāt kathaṃ cana.
30 N' ânyasmin puruṣe santi ye Satyavati vai guṇāḥ
pradānam eva tasmān me rocate duhitus tava.»

RĀJ" ôvāca

«Avicāryam etad uktaṃ hi tathyaṃ ca bhavatā vacaḥ.
kariṣyāmy etad evaṃ ca gurur hi bhagavān mama.»

NĀRADA uvāca:

«A|vighnam astu Sāvitryāḥ pradāne duhitus tava.
sādhayiṣyāmy ahaṃ tāvat sarveṣāṃ bhadram astu vaḥ!»

MĀRKAṆḌEYA uvāca:

Evam uktvā samutpatya Nāradas tridivaṃ gataḥ.
rāj" âpi duhituḥ sarvaṃ vaivāhikam akārayat.

Sávitri said:

"An inheritance falls to one just once; just once is a daughter given away; just once he says, "I give her away!"; each of these three just once. Long-lived or short-lived, with qualities, or even with none, I chose a husband just once; I shall not choose a second time. I have made my mind up; now I articulate it in speech; later I shall enact it; my authority for this is my mind."

Nárada said:

"Best of men, your daughter Sávitri's mind is made up. There is no way she can be made to choose anything other than this right and dutiful course. No other men have the 30
virtues that are Sátyavat's; therefore it seems to me right to give your daughter away."

The King said:

"The words spoken by your lordship are true, and require no deliberation. And so I shall do this, for you are my lord guru."

Nárada said:

"May the bestowal of your daughter Sávitri have no hindrance. I shall finish now. May you all be fortunate!"

Markandéya said:

On these words, Nárada rose up and flew to heaven. And the king had all preparations for his daughter's wedding put in train.

MĀRKAṆḌEYA uvāca:

295.1 Atha kanyā|pradāne sa tam ev' ârthaṃ vicintayan
samāninye ca tat sarvaṃ bhāṇḍaṃ vaivāhikaṃ nṛpaḥ.
Tato vṛddhān dvijān sarvān ṛtvijaḥ sa|purohitān
samāhūya dine puṇye prayayau saha kanyayā.
Medhy'|āraṇyaṃ sa gatvā ca Dyumatsen'|āśramaṃ nṛpaḥ
padbhyām eva dvijaiḥ sārdhaṃ rāja'|rṣiṃ tam upāgamat.
Tatr' âpaśyan mahā|bhāgaṃ śāla|vṛkṣam upāśritam
kauśyāṃ bṛsyāṃ samāsīnaṃ cakṣur|hīnaṃ nṛpaṃ tadā.
5 Sa rājā tasya rāja'|rṣeḥ kṛtvā pūjāṃ yath" ârhataḥ
vācā su|niyato bhūtvā cakār' ātma|nivedanam.
Tasy' ârghyam āsanaṃ c' âiva gāṃ c' āvedya sa dharma|vit
«kim āgamanam? ity» evaṃ rājā rājānam abravīt.
Tasya sarvam abhiprāyam itikartavyatāṃ ca tām
Satyavantaṃ samuddiśya sarvam eva nyavedayat.

AŚVAPATIR uvāca:

«Sāvitrī nāma rāja'|rṣe kany" êyaṃ mama śobhanā
tāṃ sva|dharmeṇa dharma|jña snuṣ"|ârthe tvaṃ gṛhāṇa me.»

DYUMATSENA uvāca:

«Cyutāḥ sma rājyād vana|vāsam āśritāś
carāma dharmaṃ niyatās tapasvinaḥ.
kathaṃ tv anarhā vana|vāsam āśrame
nivatsyate kleśam imaṃ sutā tava?»

MARKANDÉYA said:

So, wondering about the very purpose of giving away 295.1
his daughter, the king collected all those marriage vessels
together. Then, on an auspicious day, he assembled all the
brahmin elders, the sacrificial priests and chaplains, and set
out with his daughter. The king went to the sacred forest
and to Dyumat·sena's hermitage, where, together with the
brahmins, he approached that royal seer on foot.

There he saw the illustrious blind king, resting under
a *shala* tree, sitting on a cushion of *kusha** grass. Having 5
honored the royal seer, as was his due, King Ashva·pati
introduced himself in restrained speech. Knowing the Law,
the other king offered him a guest gift, a seat and a cow; then,
king to king, he asked, "What have you come for?" And he
told him everything—everything about the obligation and
his intention with regard to Sátyavat.

ASHVA·PATI said:

"Royal seer, this is my beautiful daughter; her name is Sávitri. You, who know the Law, take her from me as a daughter-in-law, in line with our inherent duty."

DYUMAT·SENA said:

"Expelled from our kingdom, we have taken up a
forest life.
We follow the Law as strict ascetics.
But how will your daughter, who does not
deserve it,
Withstand this hardship in a forest retreat?"

ASVAPATIR uvāca:

10 «Sukhaṃ ca duḥkhaṃ ca bhav'|âbhav'|ātmakaṃ
yadā vijānāti sut" âham eva ca
na mad|vidhe yujyati vākyam īdṛśaṃ
viniścayen'|âbhigato 'smi te nṛpa.
Āśāṃ n' ârhasi me hantuṃ sauhṛdāt praṇatasya ca
abhitaś c' āgataṃ premṇā pratyākhyātuṃ na m" ârhasi.
Anurūpo hi yuktaś ca tvaṃ mam' âhaṃ tav' âpi ca
snuṣāṃ pratīccha me kanyāṃ bhāryāṃ Satyavataḥ sutām.*»

DYUMATSENA uvāca:

«Pūrvam ev' âbhilaṣitaḥ saṃbandho me tvayā saha
bhraṣṭa|rājyas tv aham iti tata etad vicāritam.
Abhiprāyas tv ayaṃ yo me pūrvam ev' âbhikāṅkṣitaḥ
sa nirvartatu me 'dy' âiva kāṅkṣito hy asi me 'tithiḥ.»
15 Tataḥ sarvān samānāyya dvijān āśrama|vāsinaḥ
yathā|vidhi samudvāhaṃ kārayām āsatur nṛpau.
Dattvā so 'śvapatiḥ kanyāṃ yath"|ârhaṃ sa paricchadam
yayau svam eva bhavanaṃ yuktaḥ paramayā mudā.
Satyavān api tāṃ bhāryāṃ labdhvā sarva|gun'|ânvitām
mumude, sā ca taṃ labdhvā bhartāraṃ manas" ēpsitam.
Gate pitari sarvāṇi sannyasy' ābharaṇāni sā
jagṛhe valkalāny eva vastraṃ kāṣāyam eva ca.
Paricārair guṇaiś c' âiva praśrayeṇa damena ca
sarva|kāma|kriyābhiś ca sarveṣāṃ tuṣṭim āvahat
20 Śvaśrūṃ śarīra|satkāraiḥ sarvair ācchādanādibhiḥ
śvaśuraṃ deva|satkārair vācaḥ saṃyamanena ca.
Tath" âiva priya|vādena naipuṇena śamena ca

Ashva·pati said:

“Since my daughter knows—as well as I—
That happiness and misery come and go,
Such words do not apply to a man like me.
I have come to you decided, king.

Don’t kill my hope. I have bowed to you in friendship, and come to you in love. Do not deny me, for we match one another; accept my girl as your daughter-in-law and as Sátyavat’s wife.”

Dyumat·sena said:

“Long before this I wished for an alliance with you, but I lost my kingdom, and so I hesitated. So let this long-standing wish be granted me this very day, for you are my hoped-for guest.”

Then, assembling all the brahmins living in the hermitage, the two kings had the marriage performed as prescribed. And Ashva·pati, having given his daughter the dowry garments she merited, returned to his own palace in a spirit of great joy. Having gained such a wife, possessing all the qualities, Sátyavat, too, rejoiced, and so did she, having gained that husband her heart desired. Once her father had gone, she discarded all her ornaments and wore nothing but tree bark and an ochre robe.

She pleased them all with her services and her qualities, with her modesty and her self-control, with her attentiveness to the desires of all—caring for her mother-in-law’s body, for all her clothes, and everything else; honoring her father-in-law as though he were a god; controlling her

rahaś c' âiv' ôpacāreṇa bhartāraṃ paryatoṣayat.
Evaṃ tatr' āśrame teṣāṃ tadā nivasatāṃ satām
kālas tapasyatāṃ kaścid apākrāmata Bhārata.
Sāvitryās tu śayānāyās tiṣṭhantyāś ca* divā|niśam
Nāradena yad uktaṃ tad vākyaṃ manasi vartate.

MĀRKAṆḌEYA uvāca:

296.1 Tataḥ kāle bahu|tithe vyatikrānte kadā cana
prāptaḥ sa kālo martavyaṃ yatra Satyavatā nṛpa.
Gaṇayantyāś ca Sāvitryā divase divase gate
yad vākyaṃ Nāraden' ôktaṃ vartate hṛdi nityaśaḥ.
Caturthe 'hani martavyam iti saṃcintya bhāvinī
vrataṃ tri|rātram uddiśya diva|rātraṃ sthit" âbhavat.
Taṃ śrutvā niyamaṃ tasyā bhṛśaṃ duḥkh'|ânvito nṛpaḥ
utthāya vākyaṃ Sāvitrīm abravīt parisāntvayan:

DYUMATSENA uvāca:

5 «Atitīvro 'yam ārambhas tvay" ārabdho nṛp'|ātmaje
tisṛṇāṃ vasatīnāṃ hi sthānaṃ parama|duścaram.»

SĀVITRY uvāca:

«Na kāryas tāta saṃtāpaḥ. pārayiṣyāmy ahaṃ vratam.
vyavasāya|kṛtaṃ h' îdaṃ vyavasāyaś ca kāraṇam.»

DYUMATSENA uvāca:

«‹Vrataṃ bhindh' îti vaktuṃ tvāṃ
n' âsmi śaktaḥ katham cana.›
‹pārayasv' êti› vacanaṃ
yuktam asmad|vidho vadet.»

speech. Similarly she gratified her husband with her pleasing words, her skill, her calm, and with private acts of love. So, Bhárata,as they lived there, in the hermitage, as ascetic practitioners, some time went by. But for Sávitri, lying or standing, by day or by night, Nárada's speech churned in her mind.

MARKANDÉYA said:

When many days had passed, the time arrived for Sát- 296.1
yavat to die, my king. And every one of those days, as it passed, had been counted by Sávitri, Nárada's words ever in mind. When she knew he was to die four days hence, the beautiful woman stood night and day to fulfill a three-night vow. Hearing about her ascetic act, the king was very sad; arising, he spoke this soothing speech to Sávitri.

DYUMAT·SENA said:

"Princess, this exertion you've taken on is too severe: re- 5
maining stationary for three nights is exceptionally hard."

SÁVITRI said:

"You shouldn't worry, father: I shall bring the vow to its conclusion. This is done with perseverance, and perseverance is effective."

DYUMAT·SENA said:

"In no way can I tell you to break a vow. 'Complete it' is a fitting word for those like us."

Mārkaṇḍeya uvāca:

Evam uktvā Dyumatseno virarāma mahāmanāḥ
tiṣṭhantī c' âiva Sāvitrī kāṣṭha|bhūt" êva lakṣyate.
Śvo|bhūte bhartṛ|maraṇe Sāvitryā Bharata'|rṣabha
duḥkh'|ânvitāyās tiṣṭhantyāḥ sā rātrir vyatyavartata.
10 «Adya tad divasaṃ c' êti» hutvā dīptaṃ hut'|âśanam
yuga|mātr'|ôdite sūrye kṛtvā paurvāhṇikīḥ kriyāḥ.
Tataḥ sarvān dvijān vṛddhāñ śvaśrūṃ śvaśuram eva ca
abhivādy' ânupūrvyeṇa prāñjalir niyatā sthitā.
A|vaidhavy'|āśiṣas te tu Sāvitry|arthaṃ hitāḥ śubhāḥ
ūcus tapasvinaḥ sarve tapo|vanāni vāsinaḥ.
«Evam astv iti» Sāvitrī dhyāna|yoga|parāyaṇā
manasā tā giraḥ sarvāḥ pratyagṛhṇāt tapasvinām.
Taṃ kālaṃ taṃ muhūrtaṃ ca pratīkṣantī nṛp'|ātmajā
yath" ôktaṃ Nārada|vacaś cintayantī su|duḥkhitā.
15 Tatas tu śvaśrū|śvaśurāv ūcatus tāṃ nṛp'|ātmajām
ekāntam āsthitāṃ vākyaṃ prītyā Bharata|sattama:

Śvaśurāv ūcatuḥ

«Vrataṃ yath" ôpadiṣṭaṃ tu tathā tat pāritaṃ tvayā
āhāra|kālaḥ samprāptaḥ kriyatāṃ yad anantaram.»

Sāvitry uvāca:

«Astaṃ gate may" āditye bhoktavyaṃ kṛta|kāmayā,
eṣa me hṛdi saṃkalpaḥ samayaś ca kṛto mayā.»

MARKANDÉYA said:

So saying, the high-minded Dyumat·sena ceased, and Sávitri remained standing, looking like someone turned to wood. O Bharata bull, for Sávitri standing there, that night before her husband's death passed full of bitter sorrow. "Today is that day," she thought, offering an oblation in the fire, performing the morning ritual when the sun had risen a mere four hands. Then she bowed to all the brahmin elders, and to her mother-in-law and her father-in-law in due succession, and stood restrained with folded hands. And all the ascetics living in the forest retreat uttered auspicious blessings for Sávitri's sake, in the hope that she would never be a widow. "So be it!" said Sávitri to herself, sunk in yogic concentration, accepting all those words of the ascetics. Thinking on the words that Nárada had spoken, and anticipating that time and hour, the princess suffered deeply. Then, best of the Bharatas, her parents-in-law spoke loving words to that princess, as she stood apart.

The PARENTS-IN-LAW said:

"Do the next thing: now that the vow has been fulfilled by you as prescribed, it is time to eat."

SÁVITRI said:

"I shall take my food when the sun has set, and my wish has been fulfilled. This is my heart's resolve, and the covenant made by me."

Mārkaṇḍeya uvāca:

Evaṃ sambhāṣamāṇāyāḥ Sāvitryā bhojanaṃ prati
skandhe paraśum ādāya Satyavān prasthito vanam.
Sāvitrī tv āha bhartāraṃ «n' âikas tvaṃ gantum arhasi
saha tvay" āgamiṣyāmi na hi tvām hātum utsahe.»

Satyavān uvāca:

20 «Vanaṃ na gata|pūrvaṃ te, duḥkhaḥ pathāś ca bhāvini,
vrat'|ôpavāsa|kṣāmā ca kathaṃ padbhyāṃ gamiṣyasi?»

Sāvitry uvāca:

«Upavāsān na me glānir n' âsti c' âpi pariśramaḥ.
gamane ca kṛt'|ôtsāhāṃ pratiṣeddhuṃ na m" ârhasi.»

Satyavān uvāca:

«Yadi te gaman'|ôtsāhaḥ kariṣyāmi tava priyam
mama tv āmantraya gurūn na māṃ doṣaḥ spṛśed ayam.»

Mārkaṇḍeya uvāca:

S" âbhivādy' âbravīc chvaśrūṃ śvaśuraṃ ca mahā|vratā:
«ayaṃ gacchati me bhartā phal'|āhāro mahā|vanam.
Iccheyam abhyanujñātā āryayā śvaśureṇa ha
anena saha nirgantuṃ, na me 'dya virahaḥ kṣamaḥ.
25 Gurv|agnihotr'|ârtha|kṛte prasthitaś ca sutas tava
na nivāryo nivāryaḥ syād anyathā prasthito vanam.
Saṃvatsaraḥ kiṃ cid ūno na niṣkrānt" âham āśramāt.
vanaṃ kusumitaṃ draṣṭum paraṃ kautūhalaṃ hi me.»

MARKANDÉYA said:

While Sávitri was conversing concerning her meal, Sátyavat set out for the forest, an axe on his shoulder. But Sávitri said to her husband: "You shouldn't go alone. I'll come with you, for I cannot bear to lose you."

SÁTYAVAT said:

"You have never gone into the forest before, and the path 20
is difficult for you, noble lady. Plus, you've just endured a fasting vow —how will you go on foot?"

SÁVITRI said:

"I am not exhausted by the fast, nor do I feel fatigue. I have made up my mind to go—you should not prevent me!"

SÁTYAVAT said:

"Since you are determined to go, I shall do what pleases you. But take leave of my parents first, so I am touched by no blame."

MARKANDÉYA said:

Addressing them reverently, that woman, so strong in her vows, said to her parents-in-law: "This husband of mine is going to the great forest to gather fruit. I wish that the lady and my father-in-law would permit me to go with him, for
today I cannot bear to be separated. He might be stopped if 25
he had set out for some other reason, but since he has gone for the sake of his parents and the Agni·hotra, your son will not be dissuaded. For nearly a year I have not left the hermitage—I am most curious to see the flowering forest."

DYUMATSENA uvāca:

Yataḥ prabhṛti Sāvitrī pitrā dattā snuṣā mama
n' ânay" âbhyarthan'|âyuktam ukta|pūrvaṃ smarāmy aham.
Tad eṣā labhatāṃ kāmaṃ yath" âbhilaṣitaṃ vadhūḥ.
apramādaś ca kartavyaḥ putri Satyavataḥ pathi.

MĀRKAṆḌEYA uvāca:

Ubhābhyām abhyanujñātā sā jagāma yaśasvinī
saha bhartrā hasant" îva hṛdayena vidūyatā.
30 Sā vanāni vicitrāṇi ramaṇīyāni sarvaśaḥ
mayūra|gaṇa|juṣṭāni dadarśa vipul'|ēkṣaṇā.
«Nadīḥ puṇya|vahāś c' âiva puṣpitāṃś ca nag'|ôttamān»
Satyavān āha «paśy' êti» Sāvitrīṃ madhuraṃ vacaḥ.
Nirīkṣamāṇā bhartāraṃ sarv'|âvastham aninditā
mṛtam eva hi bhartāraṃ kāle muni|vaco 'smarat.
Anuvrajantī bhartāraṃ jagāma mṛdu|gāminī
dvidh" êva hṛdayaṃ kṛtvā taṃ ca kālam avekṣatī.

MĀRKAṆḌEYA uvāca:

297.1 Atha bhāryā|sahāyaḥ sa phalāny ādāya vīryavān
kaṭhinaṃ pūrayām āsa, tataḥ kāṣṭhāny apāṭayat.
Tasya pāṭayataḥ kāṣṭhaṃ svedo vai samajāyata
vyāyāmena ca ten' âsya jajñe śirasi vedanā.
So 'bhigamya priyāṃ bhāryām uvāca śrama|pīḍitaḥ:

SATYAVĀN uvāca:

«vyāyāmena mam'|ânena jātā śirasi vedanā,
Aṅgāni c' âiva Sāvitri hṛdayaṃ dūyat' îva ca
asvastham iva c' ātmānaṃ lakṣaye mita|bhāṣiṇi.
5 Śūlair iva śiro viddham idaṃ saṃlakṣayāmy aham,
tat svaptum icche kalyāṇi, na sthātuṃ śaktir asti me.»

Dyumat·sena said:

Since her father first gave me Sávitri as daughter-in-law, I don't ever remember her asking for anything unfit. So let the young wife have her wish, as she has determined. But take care, my daughter, on Sátyavat's journey.

Markandéya said:

With the permission of both, the beautiful woman went with her husband, seemingly smiling but her heart in agony.
Wide-eyed, she gazed on the surrounding woods, color- 30
ful and beautiful, the home of peacock hordes. "There are rivers, whose currents run pure, and wonderful blossoming trees—look!" said Sátyavat sweetly to Sávitri. Faultless woman, she watched her husband in every setting, for, as she remembered what the sage had said, her lord seemed dead already. But she went on following her husband, walking softly, her heart split in two, just awaiting the hour.

Markandéya said:

So, with his wife for company, the man plucked fruit, 297.1
and with his carrying strap filled, turned to splitting timber. While he was axing the wood, he started to sweat, and from this exertion his head began aching. Overcome with fatigue, he approached his dear wife and spoke:

Sátyavat said:

"Thanks to my exertion I have a headache, and my limbs and heart seem to be burning up. O Sávitri—you who are
so measured in your speech—I think I am sick. I feel as 5
though my head has been pierced with spears—I want to sleep, good lady. I don't have strength to stand."

Mārkaṇḍeya uvāca:

Sā samāsādya Sāvitrī bhartāram upagamya ca
utsaṅge 'sya śiraḥ kṛtvā niṣasāda mahītale.
Tataḥ sā Nārada|vaco vimṛśantī tapasvinī
taṃ muhūrtaṃ kṣaṇaṃ velāṃ divasaṃ ca yuyoja ha.
Muhūrtād eva c' âpaśyat puruṣaṃ rakta|vāsasam
baddha|mauliṃ vapuṣmantam āditya|sama|tejasam.
Śyām'|âvadātaṃ rakt'|âkṣaṃ pāśa|hastaṃ bhay'|āvaham
sthitaṃ Satyavataḥ pārśve nirīkṣantaṃ tam eva ca.
10 Taṃ dṛṣṭvā sahas" ôtthāya bhartur nyasya śanaiḥ śiraḥ
kṛtāñjalir uvāc' ārtā hṛdayena pravepatī.

Sāvitry uvāca:

«Daivataṃ tv" âbhijānāmi vapur etadd hy amānuṣam
kāmayā brūhi dev'|êśa kas tvaṃ? kiṃ ca cikīrṣasi?»

Yama uvāca:

«Pati|vrat" âsi Sāvitri tath" âiva ca tapo|'nvitā
atas tvām abhibhāṣāmi. viddhi māṃ tvaṃ śubhe Yamam!
Ayaṃ te Satyavān bhartā kṣīṇ'|āyuḥ pārthiv'|âtmajaḥ.
neṣyāmi tam ahaṃ baddhvā. viddhy etan me cikīrṣitam.»

Sāvitry uvāca:

«Śrūyate bhagavan dūtās tav' āgacchanti mānavān
netuṃ kila, bhavān kasmād āgato 'si svayaṃ prabho?»

MARKANDÉYA said:

Sávitri approached her husband, came close to him and sat on the ground, putting his head in her lap. Then the troubled woman, pondering Nárada's words, calculated the day, the time of day, the hour and the instant. And almost at once she saw a person dressed in red, wearing a diadem, handsome, and as radiant as the sun, pure black, red-eyed, a noose in his hand, fearsome, standing at Sátyavat's side, staring at him. Seeing him, she laid down her husband's head gently, and sprung up at once. Her hands folded in greeting, she addressed him, her heart trembling, afflicted.

SÁVITRI said:

"I know you're a god, for your form is not human. If it's your wish, tell me, great god—who are you? What do you want?"

DEATH said:

"Sávitri, because you are devoted to your husband, and because you've acquired power through ascetic practice, I shall answer: Know, good woman, that I am Death! This husband of yours, Prince Sátyavat, has used up his life; I shall bind him and take him away. This, you should know, is what I intend."

SÁVITRI said:

"I have heard, Lord, that it is your messengers who come to lead away mortal men. So why, Your Worship, have you come in person?"

MĀRKAṆḌEYA uvāca:

15 Ity uktaḥ pitṛ|rājas tāṃ bhagavān sva|cikīrṣitam
yathāvat sarvam ākhyātuṃ tat|priy'|ârthaṃ pracakrame.
«Atha ca dharma|saṃyukto rūpavān guṇa|sāgaraḥ
n' ârho mat|puruṣair netum, ato 'smi svayam āgataḥ.»
Tataḥ Satyavataḥ kāyāt pāśa|baddhaṃ vaśaṃ gatam
aṅguṣṭha|mātraṃ puruṣaṃ niścakarṣa Yamo balāt.
Tataḥ samuddhṛta|prāṇaṃ gata|śvāsaṃ hata|prabham
nirviceṣṭaṃ śarīraṃ tad babhūv' âpriya|darśanam.
Yamas tu taṃ tato baddhvā prayāto dakṣiṇā|mukhaḥ
Sāvitrī c' âiva duḥkh'|ārtā Yamam ev' ânvagacchata
niyama|vrata|saṃsiddhā mahā|bhāgā pati|vratā.

YAMA uvāca:

20 «Nivarta gaccha Sāvitri! kuruṣv' âsy' âurdhva|dehikam!
kṛtaṃ bhartus tvay" ānṛṇyaṃ. yāvad gamyaṃ gataṃ tvayā.»

SĀVITRY uvāca:

«Yatra me nīyate bhartā svayaṃ vā yatra gacchati
mayā ca tatra gantavyam, eṣa dharmaḥ sanātanaḥ.
Tapasā guru|bhaktyā ca bhartuḥ snehād vratena ca
tava c' âiva prasādena na me pratihatā gatiḥ.
Prāhuḥ sāpta padaṃ maitraṃ budhās tattv'|ârtha|darśinaḥ*
mitratāṃ ca puras|kṛtya kiṃ cid vakṣyāmi, tac chṛṇu.
Nān" ātmavantas tu vane caranti
dharmaṃ ca vāsaṃ ca pariśramaṃ ca
vijñānato dharmam udāharanti

MARKANDÉYA said:

Addressed in this way, the blessed king of the ancestors 15
duly began to tell her, as a favor, all his intentions: "Now a man so close to the law, so beautiful, such a sea of qualities, doesn't deserve to be led away by my henchmen, so I have come myself." Thereupon, bound by the noose, and subject to his power, Yama drew forcibly from Sátyavat's body a person the size of a thumb. Then the body, its life deducted, its breath stopped, its light extinguished, unmoving, became something unsightly. So Yama bound him and set out toward the south,* and Sávitri, a virtuous, devoted wife, oppressed by sorrow, skilled in self-imposed penance, followed Yama.

DEATH said:

"Sávitri, turn back! Go! Perform his funeral! You are freed 20
from your debt to your husband, you have gone as far as is possible."

SÁVITRI said:

"Wherever my husband is taken, or wherever he goes of his own accord, there I too should go—this is the eternal law. By penance, by devotion to my elders, by love for my husband, by a vow, and through your grace, my way is unimpeded. The wise, who see the truth of things, say that a friend is one who walks seven steps at one's side. On account of our friendship, I shall say something. So listen.

The self-controlled observe the law in the forest
In various ways—by living there, and by their efforts.
Through their undrestanding they exemplify the law.
Therefore the good say that the law is paramount.

tasmāt santo dharmam āhuḥ pradhānam.
25 Ekasya dharmeṇa satāṃ matena
sarve sma taṃ mārgam anuprapannāḥ.
mā vai dvitīyaṃ mā tṛtīyaṃ ca vāñche
tasmāt santo dharmam āhuḥ pradhānam.»

YAMA uvāca:

«Nivarta! tuṣṭo 'smi tav' ânayā girā
svar'|âkṣara|vyañjana|hetu|yuktayā
varaṃ vṛṇīṣv' êha vin" âsya jīvitaṃ
dadāni te sarvam anindite varam.»

SĀVITRY uvāca:

«Cyutaḥ sva|rājyād vana|vāsam āśrito|
vinaṣṭa|cakṣuḥ śvaśuro mam' āśrame.
sa labdha|cakṣur balavān bhaven nṛpas
tava prasādāj jvalan'|ârka|saṃnibhaḥ.»

YAMA uvāca:

«Dadāni te 'haṃ tam anindite varaṃ,
yathā tvay" ôktaṃ bhavitā ca tat tathā.
tav' âdhvanā glānim iv' ôpalakṣaye.
nivarta! gacchasva! na te śramo bhavet.»

By the law of the one, honored by the good,
All follow that path. I don't want a second or a third.
Therefore the wise say that the law is paramount."

Death said:

"Turn back! I am pleased with this speech of yours,
A combination of sound, vowel, consonant and reason.
Choose a gift! I will give you any gift, irreproachable woman,
Except for his life."

Sávitri said:

"My father-in-law in the hermitage—exiled from his own kingdom,
And deprived of his eyesight, he sought refuge in the forest life.
By your grace may the king regain his eyesight,
And become strong, like the fire or the sun."

Death said:

"Faultless woman, I shall give you this gift,
Just as you've asked, and that's how it will be.
I see that your journey seems to have exhausted you.
Turn back! Go! You shouldn't get tired."

SĀVITRY uvāca:

«Śramaḥ kuto bhartṛ|samīpato hi me?
yato hi bhartā mama sā gatir dhruvā.
yataḥ patiṃ neṣyasi tatra me gatiḥ,
sur'|êśa, bhūyaś ca vaco nibodha me.
30 Satāṃ sakṛt|saṅgatam īpsitaṃ paraṃ
tataḥ paraṃ mitram iti pracakṣate.
na c' âphalaṃ sat|puruṣeṇa saṅgataṃ,
tataḥ satāṃ sannivaset samāgame.»

YAMA uvāca:

«Mano|'nukūlaṃ budha|buddhi|vardhanaṃ
tvayā yad uktaṃ vacanaṃ hit'|āśrayam.
vinā punaḥ Satyavato 'sya jīvitaṃ
varaṃ dvitīyaṃ varayasva bhāmini.»

SĀVITRY uvāca:

«Hṛtaṃ purā me śvaśurasya dhīmataḥ
svam eva rājyaṃ labhatām sa pārthivaḥ.
jahyāt sva|dharmān na ca me gurur yathā
dvitīyam etad varayāmi te varam.»

YAMA uvāca:

«Svam eva rājyaṃ pratipatsyate 'cirān
na ca sva|dharmāt parihāsyate nṛpaḥ.
kṛtena kāmena mayā nṛp'|ātmaje
nivarta! gacchasva! na te śramo bhavet.»

Sávitri said:

"How can I feel fatigue in my husband's presence?
Whatever path my husband goes, that is surely mine;
Wherever you lead my husband, that is my way.
And again listen to my words, lord of the gods:
To meet just once with the good is highly desirable,
So friendship with them is considered to be better still.
A meeting with a good man is never fruitless,
So one should live in the circle of the good."

Death said:

"The speech you uttered was full of good counsel,
A contribution to scholarly insight, pleasing to the mind.
Choose a second gift, beautiful woman,
Again with the exception of Sátyavat's life."

Sávitri said:

"In the past, my wise father-in-law was deprived
Of his own kingdom—may that lord of the earth recover it,
And my superior never depart from his inherent duty.
This is the second gift I choose from you."

Death said:

"Soon the king shall regain his own kingdom,
And he will not neglect his inherent duty.
Princess, since I have granted your wish,
Turn back! Go! You shouldn't get tired."

Sāvitry uvāca:

«Prajās tvay" âitā niyamena saṃyatā
niyamya c' âitā nayase na kāmayā
tato Yamatvaṃ tava deva viśrutaṃ
nibodha c' êmāṃ giram īritāṃ mayā.
35 A|drohaḥ sarva|bhūteṣu karmaṇā manasā girā
anugrahaś ca dānaṃ ca satāṃ dharmaḥ sanātanaḥ.
Evaṃ*|prāyaś ca loko 'yaṃ: manuṣyāḥ śakti|peśalāḥ,
santas tv ev' âpy a|mitreṣu dayāṃ prāpteṣu kurvate.»

Yama uvāca:

«Pipāsitasy' êva bhaved yathā payas tathā
tvayā vākyam idaṃ samīritam.
vinā punaḥ Satyavato 'sya jīvitaṃ
varaṃ vṛṇīṣv' êha śubhe yad icchasi.»

Sāvitry uvāca:

«Mam' ân|apatyaḥ pṛthivī|patiḥ pitā.
bhavet pituḥ putra|śataṃ tath" âurasam
kulasya santāna|karaṃ ca yad bhavet
tṛtīyam etad varayāmi te varam.»

Yama uvāca:

«Kulasya santāna|karaṃ suvarcasaṃ
śataṃ sutānāṃ pitur astu te śubhe.
kṛtena kāmena nar'|âdhip'|ātmaje
nivarta! dūraṃ hi pathas tvam āgatā.»

Sávitri said:

"These creatures are restrained by you, and, having
constrained them,
You lead them away out of constraint, not willfully.
So it is, God, that your status as Yama* is
celebrated—
Hear these words I speak.

The eternal duty of the good consists of not harming any 35
creature by action, thought or speech, and of kindness and
giving. This world is generally like this: people are pleasant
according to their capabilities; but it is the good alone who,
when they meet with their enemies, take pity even on them."

Death said:

"Just as water might be to the thirsty,
So is this speech uttered by you.
Now choose what you will as a gift, fair lady,
But again with this exception—Sátyavat's life."

Sávitri said:

"My father, the king of the earth, is childless:
May he himself produce a hundred sons
To ensure the lineage. As a third gift
I choose this from you."

Death said:

"Fair lady, let your father have
One hundred splendid sons to ensure the family
lineage!
Your wish, Princess, is fulfilled.
Turn back, for you have come a long way."

SĀVITRY uvāca:

40 «Na dūram etan mama bhartr̥|saṃnidhau
mano hi me dūrataraṃ pradhāvati.
atha vrajann eva giraṃ samudyatāṃ
may" ôcyamānāṃ śr̥ṇu bhūya eva ca.
Vivasvatas tvaṃ tanayaḥ pratāpavāṃs
tato hi Vaiv«asvata ucyase budhaiḥ.
samena dharmeṇa caranti tāḥ prajās
tatas tav' êh' ēśvara dharma|rājatā.
Ātmany api na viśvāsas tathā bhavati satsu yaḥ
tasmāt satsu viśeṣeṇa sarvaḥ praṇayam icchati.
Sauhr̥dāt sarva|bhūtānāṃ viśvāso nama jāyate
tasmāt satsu viśeṣeṇa viśvāsaṃ kurute janaḥ.»

YAMA uvāca:

«Udāhr̥taṃ te vacanaṃ yad aṅgane
śubhe na tādr̥k tvad|r̥te śrutaṃ mayā.
anena tuṣṭo 'smi vin" âsya jīvitaṃ
varaṃ caturthaṃ varayasva, gaccha ca.»

SĀVITRY uvāca:

45 «Mam' ātmajaṃ Satyavatas tath" âurasaṃ
bhaved ubhābhyām iha yat kul'|ôdvaham
śataṃ sutānāṃ bala|vīrya|śālinām.
idam cáturthe vasyāmi te varam.»

Sávitri said:

"In my husband's presence it has not been far, 40
And my mind runs further forward still.
So, as you're travelling, listen again
To the ready words I have to speak.
You are the brilliant son of Vivásvat,
So the intelligent call you Vaivásvata.
These creatures behave in concord with the law,
So, Lord, yours is the sovereignty of the law on earth.

Not even in one's self does one have so much trust as in the good; therefore all want to attach themselves to the good in particular. Trust, indeed, is born from affection for all creatures; therefore people place trust in the good in particular."

Death said:

"Beautiful woman, except from you, I have never heard
The like of the words you have uttered.
I am pleased with them. Apart from his life,
Choose a fourth gift, then go."

Sávitri said:

"Then may there be, produced by Sátyavat and born from me, 45
A hundred sons, full of energy and power,
To continue the family line of both of us here.
This I choose as a fourth gift from you."

Yama uvāca:

«Śataṃ sutānāṃ bala|vīrya|śālināṃ
bhaviṣyati prītikaraṃ tav' âbale.
pariśramas te na bhaven nṛp'|ātmaje.
nivarta! dūraṃ hi pathas tvam āgatā.»

Sāvitry uvāca:

«Satāṃ sadā śāśvata|dharma|vṛttiḥ.
santo na sīdanti na ca vyathanti.
satāṃ sadbhir n' âphala|saṅgamo 'sti.
sadbhyo bhayaṃ n' ânuvartanti santaḥ.
Santo hi satyena nayanti sūryaṃ,
santo bhūmiṃ tapasā dhārayanti.
santo gatir bhūta|bhavyasya rājan.
satāṃ madhye n' âvasīdanti santaḥ.
Ārya|juṣṭam idaṃ vṛttam iti vijñāya śāśvatam
santaḥ par'|ârthaṃ kurvāṇā n' âvekṣanti parasparam.
50 Na ca prasādaḥ sat|puruṣeṣu mogho
na c' âpy artho naśyati n' âpi mānaḥ.
yasmād etan niyataṃ satsu nityaṃ
tasmāt santo rakṣitāro bhavanti.»

Yama uvāca:

«Yathā yathā bhāṣasi dharma|saṃhitam
mano|'nukūlaṃ* su|padaṃ mah''|ârthavat
tathā tathā me tvayi bhaktir uttamā.
varaṃ vṛṇīsv' âpratimaṃ pati|vrate.»

DEATH said:

"Woman, there shall be a hundred sons,
Full of energy and power for your delight.
Don't get tired, Princess.
Turn back, for you have come a long way."

SÁVITRI said:

"The good always practice the eternal law;
The good don't despair, nor do they waver;
A meeting of the good with the good is never barren;
From the good the good expect no danger.
For by truth the good govern the sun;
By asceticism the good support the earth;
The good are the way of the past and the future,
my king;
The good in midst of the good don't fail.

Knowing this is the eternal practice approved by the Nobles,* the good act for the sake of others, with no regard for benefits returned.

But no favor is fruitless among the good,
And neither profit nor honor shall be destroyed.
Since this rule is always tied to the good,
The good are therefore protectors."

DEATH said:

"As long as you utter such good words,
In accordance with the law, so pleasing to the mind,
To such great purpose, my love for you is supreme—
Choose an incomparable gift, true wife!"

Sāvitry uvāca:

«Na te 'pavargaḥ sukṛtād vinākṛtas
tathā yath" ânyeṣu vareṣu māna|da.
varaṃ vṛṇe: jīvatu Satyavān ayam,
yathā mṛtā hy evam ahaṃ patiṃ vinā.
Na kāmaye bhartṛ|vinā|kṛtā sukhaṃ,
na kāmaye bhartṛ|vinā|kṛtā divam,
na kāmaye bhartṛ|vinā|kṛtā śriyaṃ,
na bhartṛ|hīnā vyavasāmi jīvitum.
Var'|âtisargaḥ śata|putratā mama
tvay" âiva datto, hriyate ca me patiḥ.
varaṃ vṛṇe: jīvatu Satyavān ayam.
tav' âiva satyaṃ vacanaṃ bhaviṣyati.»

Mārkaṇḍeya uvāca:

55 «Tath" êty» uktvā tu taṃ pāśaṃ muktvā Vaivasvato Yama
dharma|rājaḥ prahṛṣṭ'|ātmā Sāvitrīm idam abravīt.
«Eṣa bhadre mayā mukto bhartā te kula|nandini.
arogas tava neyaś ca siddh'|ârthaḥ sa bhaviṣyati.
Catur|varṣa|śat'|āyuś ca tvayā sārdham avāpsyati
iṣṭvā yajñaiś ca dharmeṇa khyātiṃ loke gamiṣyati.
Tvayi putra|śataṃ c' âiva Satyavāñ janayiṣyati.
te c' âpi sarve rājānaḥ kṣatriyāḥ putra|pautriṇaḥ
Khyātās tvan|nāmadheyāś ca bhaviṣyant' îha śāśvatāḥ.
pituś ca te putra|śataṃ bhavitā tava mātari

SÁVITRI said:

“Since, honor-giver, you do not—as with the other gifts—
Say anything to restrict your favor,
This is the gift I choose: let Sátyavat live,
For I am dead without my husband!
Deprived of my husband, I have no wish for bliss,
Deprived of my husband, I have no wish for heaven,
Deprived of my husband, I have no wish for wealth,
Without my husband, I can’t make the effort
To go on living.
You have personally given me the gift of one hundred sons,
Yet my husband is fetched away.
This is the gift I choose: let Sátyavat live!
Then your promise shall indeed become true.”

MARKANDÉYA said:

“Let it be so,” said Yama Vaivásvata, and untied the noose. 55
Then the lord of the law, who in his heart was delighted, said this to Sávitri: “See, good woman, joy of your family, I have freed your husband. He is healthy—take him with you; he’ll be successful. Alongside you he’ll live four hundred years. Offering sacrifices, he shall, through his law, win wordly fame. And Sátyavat will beget on you a hundred sons. All will become kings and warriors and have sons and grandsons bearing your name, and shall be famous on earth forever. And your father shall beget a hundred sons on your mother,

60 Mālavyāṃ Mālavā nāma śāśvatāḥ putra|pautriṇaḥ
bhrātaras te bhaviṣyanti kṣatriyās tridaś'|ôpamāḥ.»
Evaṃ tasyai varaṃ dattvā dharma|rājaḥ pratāpavān
nivartayitvā Sāvitrīṃ svam eva bhavanaṃ yayau.
Sāvitry api Yame yāte bhartāraṃ pratilabhya ca
jagāma tatra yatr' âsyā bhartuḥ śāvaṃ kalevaram.
Sā bhūmau prekṣya bhartāram upasṛty' ôpagṛhya ca
utsaṅge śira āropya bhūmāv upaviveśa ha.
Saṃjñāṃ ca sa punar labdhvā Sāvitrīm abhyabhāṣata
proṣy'|āgata iva premṇā punaḥ punar udīkṣya vai.

SATYAVĀN uvāca:

65 «Suciraṃ bata supto 'smi! kim|arthaṃ n' âvabodhitaḥ?
kva c' âsau puruṣaḥ śyāmo yo 'sau māṃ sañcakarṣa ha?»

SĀVITRY uvāca:

«Suciraṃ tvaṃ prasupto 'si mam' âṅke puruṣa'|rṣabha.
gataḥ sa bhagavān devaḥ prajā|saṃyamano Yamaḥ.
Viśrānto 'si mahā|bhāga vinidraś ca nṛp'|ātmaja
yadi śakyaṃ samuttiṣṭha! vigāḍhāṃ paśya śarvarīm.»

MĀRKANDEYA uvāca:

Upalabhya tataḥ saṃjñāṃ sukha|supta iv' ôtthitaḥ
diśaḥ sarvā van'|ântāṃś ca nirīkṣy' ôvāca Satyavān:
«Phal'|âhāro 'smi niṣkrāntas tvayā saha su|madhyame.
tataḥ pāṭayataḥ kāṣṭhaṃ śiraso me ruj" âbhavat.
70 Śir'|âbhitāpa|santaptaḥ sthātuṃ ciram aśaknuvan
tav' ôtsaṅge prasupto 'smi, iti* sarvaṃ smare śubhe.

Málavi, whose sons and grandsons shall be called the Má- 60
lavas forever. They, your brothers, will be warriors, as good as the gods."

So, having given her the gifts, the glorious lord of the law turned Sávitri back, and went to his own home. Once Yama had gone, Sávitri, having recovered her lord, went to the place where her husband's body lay as a corpse. Seeing her husband on the ground, she approached and lifted him up, placed his head on her lap, and she sat on the earth. Becoming conscious again, he spoke to Sávitri, gazing at her ceaselessly with love, like a man back from a distant land.

SÁTYAVAT said:

"Alas, I have slept such a long time! Why didn't you wake 65
me? And where is that dark person—the one who carried me off?"

SÁVITRI said:

"You have slept a long time in my lap, bullish man. That blessed god Yama, the restrainer of creatures, has gone. Prince—fortunate man—you are rested and awake. Stand up, if you can. Look! Night has fallen."

MARKANDÉYA said:

So, having regained consciousness, Sátyavat arose, as though from a sweet sleep, and, seeing the woods stretching in all directions, said:

"Slender lady, I came out with you to gather fruit. Then,
while I was splitting wood, I got a pain in my head. Greatly 70
pained by the headache, I was unable to stand for long and fell asleep in your lap, fair lady. All this I remember. While you embraced me, my consciousness was carried off by sleep.

Tvay” ôpagūḍhasya ca me nidray” âpahṛtaṃ manaḥ.
tato ’paśyaṃ tamo ghoraṃ puruṣaṃ ca mah”|âujasam.
Tad yadi tvaṃ vijānāsi kiṃ tad brūhi su|madhyame
svapno me yadi vā dṛṣṭo yadi vā satyam eva tat.»
Tam uvāc’ âtha Sāvitrī: «rajanī vyavagāhate.
śvas te sarvaṃ yath” āvṛttam ākhyāsyāmi nṛp’|ātmaja.
Uttiṣṭh’ ôttiṣṭha, bhadraṃ te! pitarau paśya su|vrata!
vigāḍhā rajanī c’ êyaṃ nivṛttaś ca divā|karaḥ.
75 Naktaṃ|carāś caranty ete dṛṣṭāḥ krūr”|âbhibhāṣiṇaḥ.
śrūyante parṇa|śabdāś ca mṛgāṇāṃ caratāṃ vane.
Etā ghoraṃ śivā nādān diśaṃ dakṣiṇa|paścimām
āsthāya viruvanty ugrāḥ kampayantyo mano mama.»

SATYAVĀN uvāca:

«Vanaṃ pratibhay’|ākāraṃ ghanena tamasā vṛtam.
na vijñāsyasi panthānaṃ gantuṃ c’ âiva na śakṣyasi.»

SĀVITRY uvāca:

«Asminn adya vane dagdhe śuṣka|vṛkṣaḥ sthito jvalan
vāyunā dhamyamāno ’tra dṛśyate ’gniḥ kva cit kva cit.
Tato ’gnim ānayitv” êha jvālayiṣyāmi sarvataḥ.
kāṣṭhān’|îmāni sant’ îha, jahi santāpam ātmanaḥ.
80 Yadi n’ ôtsahase gantuṃ, sa|rujaṃ tvāṃ hi lakṣaye,
na ca jñāsyasi panthānaṃ tamasā saṃvṛte vane,
Śvaḥ prabhāte vane dṛśye yāsyāvo ’numate tava.
vasāv’ êha kṣapām ekāṃ rucitaṃ yadi te ’nagha.»

SATYAVĀN uvāca:

«Śiro’|rujā nivṛttā me, svasthāny aṅgāni lakṣaye.
mātā|pitṛbhyām icchāmi saṅgaṃ tvat|prasāda|jam.
Na kadā cid vikālaṃ hi gata|pūrvo may” āśramaḥ.
anāgatāyāṃ saṃdhyāyāṃ mātā me praruṇaddhi mām.

Then I saw a terrible darkness and a mighty person. If you know, then tell me, slender lady—was it my dream? Or was what I saw real?" Sávitri said to him: "The night has set in. Tomorrow, prince, I shall tell you everything, just as it happened. Stand up! Please stand up! You, whose vows are so strong, consider your parents. The night has fallen, and
the sun has set. Night animals can be seen prowling, making 75
harsh noises; you can hear the leaves rustling as beasts roam the forest. To the southwest those terrible jackals are putting up a fearful howling; they make my heart tremble."

SÁTYAVAT said:

"The forest covered by solid darkness looks daunting. You won't recognize the path and you won't be able to go on."

SÁVITRI said:

"When this forest was on fire today, a dry tree remained smoldering; fanned by the wind, the fire can be seen here, flaring up, dying down. So, once I've brought that fire here, I'll make it burn, around and about. There are these logs
here. Don't worry. I sense you have a headache—if you 80
haven't the strength to go on, and can't tell the path when the forest is covered in darkness, then, if you agree, we'll go tomorrow at first light, when the forest can be seen. If you're happy to do that, let's spend one night here, blameless man."

SÁTYAVAT said:

"My headache has disappeared, I feel my limbs are sound. If it meets with your favor, I wish to join my father and mother. Never before have I returned to the hermitage outside the normal time. My mother stops me before the onset of twilight. Even during the day, my parents worry when

Div" âpi mayi niṣkrānte saṃtapyete gurū hi mām
vicinoti hi māṃ tātaḥ sah' âiv' āśrama|vāsibhiḥ.
85 Mātrā pitrā ca subhṛśaṃ duḥkhitābhyām ahaṃ purā
upālabdhaś ca bahuśaś ‹cireṇ' āgacchas' îti› ha.
Kā tv avasthā tayor adya mad|artham iti cintaye
tayor adṛśye mayi ca mahad duḥkhaṃ bhaviṣyati.

Purā mām ūcatuś c' âiva rātrāv asrāyamāṇakau
bhṛśaṃ suduḥkhitau vṛddhau bahuśaḥ prīti|saṃyutau:
‹Tvayā hīnau na jīvāva muhūrtam api putraka.
yāvad dhariṣyase putra tāvan nau jīvitaṃ dhruvam
Vṛddhayor andhayor dṛṣṭis. tvayi vaṃśaḥ pratiṣṭhitaḥ,
tvayi piṇḍaś ca kīrtiś ca saṃtānaṃ c' āvayor iti.›
90 Mātā vṛddhā pitā vṛddhas tayor yaṣṭir ahaṃ kila
tau rātrau mām apaśyantau kām avasthāṃ gamiṣyataḥ?
Nidrāyāś c' âbhyasūyāmi yasyā hetoḥ pitā mama
mātā ca saṃśayaṃ prāptā mat|kṛte 'napakāriṇī.
Ahaṃ ca saṃśayaṃ prāptaḥ kṛcchrām āpadam āsthitaḥ
mātā|pitṛbhyāṃ hi vinā n' âhaṃ jīvitum utsahe.
Vyaktam ākulayā buddhyā prajñā|cakṣuḥ pitā mama
ek'|âikam asyāṃ velāyāṃ pṛcchaty āśrama|vāsinam.
N' ātmānam anuśocāmi yath" âhaṃ pitaraṃ śubhe
bhartāraṃ c' âpy anugatāṃ mātaraṃ paridurbalām.
95 Mat|kṛtena hi tāv adya saṃtāpaṃ param eṣyataḥ.
jīvantāv anujīvāmi, bhartavyau tau may" êti ha.
Tayoḥ priyaṃ me kartavyam iti jānāmi c' âpy aham.»

I'm out. Father searches for me together with the hermits. I 85
have before often been reproved by my overanxious mother
and father: 'You have come back very late!' But I wonder
what state they're in today on my account? Not seeing me,
they will be immensely worried.

Once before, deeply distraught at night, those two elderly
people, who have always loved me, told me through their
tears: 'Dear child, abandoned by you, we shan't live—not
even for a moment! As long as you're alive, son, our life is
secure. You are the eyes of a couple, old and blind. The line
of descent rests on you. Our fame, succession and offering
to the ancestors depend on you.' My old mother, my old 90
father—I am truly their staff. What state will they get in
if they don't see me tonight! I blame my sleep—because of
that, my innocent mother and father are afraid on my ac-
count. And I am fallen into misfortune, hit by excruciating
fear, for without my mother and father I am unable to live.
It is certain that, at this very time, my father—he whose
sight is insight—is questioning with a churning mind each
and every hermit. Fair lady, I don't grieve for myself as much
as I grieve for my father, and for my mother, who has fol-
lowed her husband, and is most weak. For now they will 95
suffer great sorrow on my account. If they are living I shall
live, and must support them. And I only know I must do
what pleases them."

Mārkaṇḍeya uvāca:

evam uktvā sa dharm'|ātmā guru|bhakto guru|priyaḥ
Ucchritya bāhū duḥkh'|ārtaḥ susvaraṃ praruroda ha.
tato 'bravīt tathā dṛṣṭvā bhartāraṃ śoka|karśitam
Pramṛjy' âśrūṇi netrābhyāṃ Sāvitrī dharma|cāriṇī:
«yadi me 'sti tapas taptaṃ, yadi dattaṃ, hutaṃ yadi,
Śvaśrū|śvaśura|bhartṝṇāṃ mama puṇy" âstu śarvarī.
na smarāmy ukta|pūrvaṃ vai svaireṣv apy anṛtāṃ giram.
Tena satyena tāv adya dhriyetāṃ śvaśurau mama.»

Satyavān uvāca:

«kāmaye darśanaṃ pitror. yāhi Sāvitri mā ciram!
Purā mātuḥ pitur v" âpi yadi paśyāmi vipriyam
na jīviṣye var'|ārohe satyen' ātmānam ālabhe.
Yadi dharme ca te buddhir, māṃ cej jīvantam icchasi
mama priyaṃ vā kartavyaṃ, gacchāv' āśramam antikāt.»

Mārkaṇḍeya uvāca:

Sāvitrī tata utthāya keśān saṃyamya bhāvinī
patim utthāpayām āsa bāhubhyāṃ parigṛhya vai.
Utthāya Satyavāṃś c' âpi pramṛjy' âṅgāni pāṇinā
sarvā diśaḥ samālokya kaṭhine dṛṣṭim ādadhe.
Tam uvāc' âtha Sāvitrī: «śvaḥ phalāni hariṣyasi.
yoga|kṣem'|ârtham etaṃ te neṣyāmi paraśuṃ tv aham.»
Kṛtvā kaṭhina|bhāraṃ sā vṛkṣa|śākh"|âvalambinam
gṛhītvā paraśuṃ bhartuḥ sakāśe punar āgamat.
Vāme skandhe tu vām'|ōrūr bhartur bāhuṃ niveśya ca
dakṣiṇena pariṣvajya jagāma gaja|gāminī.

MARKANDÉYA said:

With these words, that soul of virtue, who worshipped and loved his parents, raised his arms, and, stricken by grief, began to lament aloud. Seeing her husband so haggard with grief, Sávitri, who lived in the law, wiped the tears from her eyes and said: "If I have practiced austerities, if I have given, if I have offered sacrifices, let it be a good night for my parents-in-law and my husband. I don't remember that I've ever spoken an untrue word—even when it didn't matter. By that truth, may my parents-in-law survive today." 100

SÁTYAVAT said:

"I need to see my parents. Come, Sávitri, don't delay. If, fair-hipped woman, I discover anything dreadful has happened to my mother or father, I swear by the truth, I shall not live but kill myself! If you have a mind to the law, if you want me to go on living, or to do what pleases me, let us go to the hermitage."

MARKANDÉYA said:

Then beautiful Sávitri rose up, gathered her hair together, grasped her husband by his arms and helped him get up. Once he was up, Sátyavat wiped his limbs with his hand, looked all about him, and caught sight of the strap. Then Sá- 105
vitri said to him: "Tomorrow you'll fetch the fruit, but for your safety I'll carry this axe." Hanging the cumbersome strap on the branch of a tree, and taking up the axe, she rejoined her husband. Placing her husband's arm on her left shoulder, and encircling his body with her right arm, that woman, so shapely thighed, walked with the measured tread of an elephant.

SATYAVĀN uvāca:

«Abhyāsa|gamanād bhīru panthāno viditā mama,
vṛkṣ'|ântar'|ālokitayā jyotsnayā c' âpi lakṣaye.
Āgatau svaḥ pathā yena phalāny avacitāni ca
yath" āgataṃ śubhe gaccha panthānaṃ, mā vicāraya!
110 Palāśa|khaṇḍe c' âitasmin panthā vyāvartate dvidhā
tasy' ôttareṇa* yaḥ panthās tena gaccha tvarasva ca.
Svastho 'smi balavān asmi didṛkṣuḥ pitarāv ubhau»
bruvann eva tvarā|yuktaḥ samprāyād āśramaṃ prati.

MĀRKAṆḌEYA uvāca:

298.1 Etasminn eva kāle tu Dyumatseno mahā|balaḥ
labdha|cakṣuḥ prasannāyāṃ dṛṣṭyāṃ sarvaṃ dadarśa ha.
Sa sarvān āśramān gatvā Śaibyayā saha bhāryayā
putra|hetoḥ parām ārtiṃ jagāma Bharata'|rṣabha.
Tāv āśramān nadīś c' âiva vanāni ca sarāṃsi ca
tasyāṃ niśi vicinvantau dampatī parijagmatuḥ.
Śrutvā śabdaṃ tu yaṃ kaṃ cid unmukhau suta|śaṅkayā
«Sāvitrī|sahito 'bhyeti Satyavān ity» abhāṣatām.
5 Bhinnaiś ca paruṣaiḥ pādaiḥ savranaiḥ śonit'|ôkṣitaih
kuśa|kaṇṭaka|viddh'|âṅgāv unmattāv iva dhāvataḥ.
Tato 'bhisṛtya tair vipraiḥ sarvair āśrama|vāsibhiḥ
parivārya samāśvāsya tāv ānītau svam āsramam.
Tatra bhāryā|sahāyaḥ sa vṛto vṛddhais tapo|dhanaiḥ
āśvāsito 'pi citr'|ârthaiḥ pūrva|rājñāṃ kath"|āśrayaiḥ.
Tatas tau punar āśvastau vṛddhau putra|didṛkṣayā
bālya|vṛttāni putrasya smarantau bhṛśa|duḥkhitau.
Punar uktvā ca karuṇāṃ vācaṃ tau śoka|karśitau:

Sátyavat said:

"From frequent use I know the paths. Even in the shafts
of moonlight between the trees, I can mark them, timid
girl. The path on which we came, gathering fruit—take
that path just as we came, fair lady. Don't hesitate! Now, at 110
this gap in the foliage, the way divides in two. Take the path
to the north, and be quick. I am fit, I am strong, I want
to see both my parents." Saying this, he set off hurriedly
toward the hermitage.

Markandéya said:

And it was at this very time the mighty Dyumat·sena 298.1
regained his sight. With his sight clear he saw everything.
Once he had been with Shaibya, his wife, to all the her-
mitages, he became deeply distressed, Bhárata bull, because
of his son. Husband and wife went searching through the
night—hermitages, rivers, woods and pools; and whenever
they heard a sound they looked up, thinking it might be
their son, saying: "Sátyavat is coming with Sávitri." The two 5
of them rushed about like the mad, their bodies spiked with
thorns and *kusha* grass, their feet rough and split, blood-
stained from sores.

Then all those brahmins living in the hermitage approached and surrounded them, comforted them, took them back to their own retreat. There, surrounded by such ancient and great ascetics, the man and his wife were comforted by wonderful tales of former kings. Then, revived again, the old couple, recalling incidents out of their son's childhood from a desire to see him, were full of worry. Drawn with sorrow, lamenting, they repeated and wept «hā putra hā sādhvi vadhūḥ kv' âsi kv' âs' îty?» arodatām.

SUVARCĀ uvāca:

10 «Yath" âsya bhāryā Sāvitrī tapasā ca damena ca
ācāreṇa ca saṃyuktā tathā jīvati Satyavān.»

GAUTAMA uvāca:

«Vedāḥ s'|âṅgā may" âdhītās tapo me saṃcitaṃ mahat,
kaumāra|brahmacaryaṃ ca, guravo 'gniś ca toṣitāḥ,
Samāhitena cīrṇāni sarvāṇy eva vratāni me,
vāyu|bhakṣ'|ôpavāsaś ca kṛto me vidhivat purā.
Anena tapasā vedmi sarvaṃ para|cikīrṣitam.
satyam etan nibodhadhvaṃ: dhriyate Satyavān iti.»

ŚIṢYA uvāca:

«Upādhyāyasya me vaktrād yathā vākyaṃ viniḥsṛtam
n' âiva jātu bhaven mithyā tathā jīvati Satyavān.»

ṚSAYA ūcuḥ:

15 «Yath" âsya bhāryā Sāvitrī sarvair eva sulakṣaṇaiḥ
avaidhavya|karair yuktā tathā jīvati Satyavān.»

BHĀRADVĀJA uvāca:

«Yath" âsya bhāryā Sāvitrī tapasā ca damena ca
ācāreṇa ca saṃyuktā tathā jīvati Satyavān.»

DĀLBHYA uvāca:

«Yathā dṛṣṭiḥ pravṛttā te Sāvitryāś ca yathā vratam
gat" āhāram akṛtvā ca tathā jīvati Satyavān.»

these words: "O son, O dutiful wife, where are you? Where are you?"

Suvárcas said:

"Since his wife Sávitri is attached to asceticism, good 10
conduct, and self-control, Sátyavat's alive."

Gáutama said:

"I have meditated on the Vedas with their branches, I have built up great austerity. I am as chaste as a virgin youth, I have satisfied my elders and the fire. I have observed all my vows with concentration. By the ancient rule, I've practiced the fast that is living on air. Through this austerity I know all the intentions of others. Realize this is the truth: Sátyavat survives."

The Disciple said:

"Since no speech that springs from my preceptor's mouth may ever be false, Sátyavat's alive."

The Sages said:

"Since his wife Sávitri bears all the auspicious signs of 15
freedom from widowhood, Sátyavat's alive."

Bharad·vaja said:

"Since his wife Sávitri is attached to good conduct, asceticism and self-control, Sátyavat's alive."

Dalbhya said:

"Since your sight has been restored, and since Sávitri has completed her vow without breaking her fast, Sátyavat's alive."

ĀPASTAMBA uvāca:

«Yathā vadanti śāntāyāṃ diśi vai mṛga|pakṣiṇaḥ
pārthivī ca pravṛttis te tathā jīvati Satyavān.»

DHAUMYA uvāca:

«Sarvair guṇair upetas te yathā putro jana|priyaḥ
dīrgh'|āyur|lakṣaṇ'|ôpetas tathā jīvati Satyavān.»

MĀRKAṆḌEYA uvāca:

20 Evam āśvāsitas tais tu satya|vāgbhis tapasvibhiḥ
tāṃs tān vigaṇayan sarvāṃs tataḥ sthira iv' âbhavat.
Tato muhūrtāt Sāvitrī bhartrā Satyavatā saha
ājagām' āśramaṃ rātrau prahṛṣṭā praviveśa ha.

BRĀHMAṆĀ ūcuḥ:

«Putreṇa saṅgataṃ tvāṃ tu cakṣuṣmantaṃ nirīkṣya ca
sarve vayaṃ va pṛcchāmo vṛddhiṃ vai pṛthivī|pate.
Samāgamena putrasya Sāvitryā darśanena ca
cakṣuṣaś c' ātmano lābhāt tribhir diṣṭyā vivardhase.
Sarvair asmābhir uktaṃ yat tathā tan, n' âtra saṃśayaḥ,
bhūyo bhūyaḥ samṛddhis te kṣipram eva bhaviṣyati.»

MĀRKAṆḌEYA uvāca:

25 Tato 'gniṃ tatra saṃjvālya dvijās te sarva eva ca
upāsāṃ cakrire Pārtha Dyumatsenaṃ mahī|patim.
Śaibyā ca Satyvāṃś c' âiva Sāvitrī c' âikataḥ sthitāḥ
sarvais tair abhyanujñātā viśokāḥ samupāviśan.
Tato rājñā sah' āsīnāḥ sarve te vana|vāsinaḥ
jāta|kautūhalāḥ Pārtha papracchur nṛpateḥ sutam:

APASTÁMBA said:

"From the way in which birds and animals utter sounds from the auspicious direction, and from your activity as king, Sátyavat's alive."

DHAUMYA said:

"Since your son, loved by the people, has every virtue, and shows the signs of a long life, Satyavat's alive."

MARKANDÉYA said:

Comforted in this way by the truth-telling ascetics, and 20
esteeming them all, he seemed calm. Then, not much later, Sávitri came back to the hermitage at night, with her husband Sátyavat, and entered glad at heart.

The BRAHMINS said:

"Seeing you with your eyesight restored, and reunited with your son, all of us sincerely wish you good fortune, lord of the earth. In the meeting with your son, in the appearance of Sávitri, in the return of your sight, you are favored with a triple blessing. There can be no doubt—what we all said is so. Again, again: fortune shall swiftly be yours."

MARKANDÉYA said:

Then, Partha, when they had made the fire there blaze, all 25
those brahmins sat down respectfully with King Dyumat·sena. Shaibya, Sátyavat and Savítri had stood to one side, but, given permission by all, they happily sat down. Then, Partha, their curiosity aroused, all those forest-dwellers sitting with the king questioned the king's son.

Ṛṣaya ūcuḥ:

«Prāg eva n' āgataṃ kasmāt sabhāryeṇa tvayā vibho?
virātre c' āgataṃ kasmāt? ko 'nubandhas tav' âbhavat?
Saṃtāpitaḥ pitā mātā vayaṃ c' âiva nṛp'|ātmaja
kasmād iti na jānīmas, tat sarvaṃ vaktum arhasi.»

Satyavān uvāca:

30 «Pitr" âham abhyanujñātaḥ Sāvitrī|sahito gataḥ.
atha me 'bhūc chiro|duḥkhaṃ vane kāṣṭhāni bhindataḥ.
Suptaś c' âhaṃ vedanayā ciram ity upalakṣaye.
tāvat kālaṃ na ca mayā supta|pūrvaṃ kadā cana.
Sarveṣām eva bhavatāṃ saṃtāpo mā bhaved iti
ato virātr'|āgamanaṃ, n' ânyad ast' îha kāraṇam.»

Gautama uvāca:

«Akasmāc cakṣuṣaḥ prāptir Dyumatsenasya te pituḥ.
n' âsya tvaṃ kāraṇaṃ vetsi. Sāvitrī vaktum arhati.
Śrotum icchāmi Sāvitri, tvaṃ hi vettha par'|âvaram.
tvāṃ hi jānāmi Sāvitri Sāvitrīm iva tejasā.
35 Tvam atra hetuṃ jānīṣe tasmāt satyam nirucyatām.
rahasyaṃ yadi te n' âsti kiṃ cid atra, vadasva naḥ!»

Sāvitry uvāca:

«Evam etad yathā vettha, saṃkalpo n' ânyathā hi vaḥ,
na hi kiṃ cid rahasyaṃ me śrūyatāṃ tathyam eva yat.
Mṛtyur me patyur ākhyāto Nāradena mah"|ātmanā
sa c' âdya divasaḥ prāptas, tato n' âinaṃ jahāmy aham.
Suptaṃ c' âinaṃ Yamaḥ sākṣād upāgacchat sa|kiṃkaraḥ.

The SAGES said:

"My lord, why didn't you return earlier with your wife? Why have you come toward the end of the night? What hindered you? Prince, your mother and father, and we too were pained, but on what account we don't know. You should tell us everything."

SÁTYAVAT said:

"With father's permission, I had gone out, accompanied 30
by Sávitri. Then, while I was splitting timber in the forest,
I got a headache. Because of the pain I slept for a long
time—this much I know. I have never slept so long before.
I came back so late in the night so that you shouldn't all be
worried—that was my only reason for it."

GÁUTAMA said:

"Your father Dyumat·sena suddenly regained his sight.
Since you don't know the reason, Sávitri should speak. Sá-
vitri, I would like to hear about it, for you know the cause
and the effect. And I know, Sávitri, you are like the goddess
Sávitri in luster. You know the reason for this, so the truth 35
should be told. If there is nothing here you want to keep
secret, then tell us!"

SÁVITRI said:

"Know it just as it is, for you have no ulterior motive, nor do I have anything secret. Hear the truth about it. Great-souled Nárada had predicted the death of my husband. Today that day arrived, so I didn't leave his side. Once he was asleep, before my very eyes Yama appeared with his servants. He bound him, and led him away toward the direction

sa enam anayad baddhvā diśaṃ pitṛ|niṣevitām.
Astauṣaṃ tam ahaṃ devaṃ satyena vacasā vibhum
pañca va tena me dattā varāḥ: śṛṇuta tān mama.
40 Cakṣuṣī ca sva|rājyaṃ ca dvau varau śvaśurasya me.
labdhaṃ pituḥ putra|śataṃ, putrāṇāṃ c' ātmanaḥ śatam.
Catur|varṣa|śat'|āyur me bhartā labdhaś ca Satyavān,
bhartur hi jīvit'|ârthaṃ tu mayā cīrṇaṃ tv idaṃ vratam.
Etat sarvaṃ may" ākhyātaṃ kāraṇaṃ vistareṇa ca
yath" āvṛttaṃ sukh'|ôdarkam idaṃ duḥkhaṃ mahan mama.

ṚSAYA ūcuḥ:

«Nimajjyamānaṃ vyasanair abhidrutaṃ
kulaṃ nar'|êndrasya tamo|maye hrade
tvayā su|śīla|vrata|puṇyayā kulaṃ
samuddhṛtaṃ sādhvi punaḥ kulīnayā.»

MĀRKAṆḌEYA uvāca:

Tathā praśasya hy abhipūjya c' âiva
vara|striyaṃ tām ṛṣayaḥ samāgatāḥ
nar'|êndram āmantrya sa|putram añjasā
śivena jagmur muditāḥ svam ālayam.

MĀRKAṆḌEYA uvāca:

299.1 Tasyāṃ rātryāṃ vyatītāyām udite sūrya|maṇḍale
kṛta|paurvāhṇikāḥ sarve sameyus te tapo|dhanāḥ.
Tad eva sarvaṃ Sāvitryā mahā|bhāgyaṃ maha"|rṣayaḥ
Dyumatsenāya n' ātṛpyan kathayantaḥ punaḥ punaḥ.

where the ancestors live. I praised that omnipresent god with truthful speech. He granted me five gifts. Hear me relate them. Two gifts for my father-in-law: his eyesight 40
and his kingdom. For my father I secured a hundred sons, and a hundred sons for myself. And I gained my husband Sátyavat with a life of four hundred years: for I observed this vow for the sake of my husband's life. The entire cause of this has been told by me in detail—how this great sorrow of mine was transformed to happiness in the end."

The SEERS said:

"Overwhelmed by evils, the family of this lord
among men
Was sinking in a pool of darkness. By you, noble
lady,
Whose merit flows from vows and a good
disposition,
By you, good woman, the family line was rescued."

MARKANDÉYA said:

Then, after praising and honoring that excellent
woman,
The assembled seers took their leave of the lord
And his son, and went to their own homes quickly
And joyfully, in peace.

MARKANDÉYA said:

Once the night had passed and the sun's sphere had risen, 299.1
all those great ascetics performed their morning rites and came together. Great seers, they were not to be satisfied, except in recounting time and again to Dyumat·sena the entirety of Sávitri's great glory. Then, king, all the ministers

Tataḥ prakṛtayaḥ sarvāḥ Śālvebhyo 'bhāgatā nṛpa
ācakhyur nihitaṃ c' âiva sven' âmātyena taṃ dviṣam.
Taṃ mantriṇā hataṃ śrūtvā sasahāyaṃ sabāndhavam
nyavedayan yath" āvṛttaṃ vidrutaṃ ca dviṣad|balam
5 Eka|matyaṃ ca sarvasya janasy' âtha nṛpaṃ prati:
«sa|cakṣur v" âpy a|cakṣur vā sa no rājā bhavatv iti.
Anena niścayen' êha vayaṃ prasthāpitā nṛpa.
prāptān'|îmāni yānāni catur|aṅgaṃ ca te balam.
Prayāhi rājan! bhadraṃ te! ghuṣṭas te nagare jayaḥ.
adhyāssva cira|rātrāya pitṛ|paitā|mahaṃ padam.»

Cakṣuṣmantaṃ ca taṃ dṛṣṭvā rājānaṃ vapuṣ" ânvitam
mūrdhnā nipatitāḥ sarve vismay'|ôtphulla|locanāḥ.
Tato 'bhivādya tān vṛddhān dvijān āśrama|vāsinaḥ
taiś c' âbhipūjitaḥ sarvaiḥ prayayau nagaraṃ prati.
10 Śaibhyā ca saha Sāvitryā sv|āstīrṇena suvarcasā
nara|yuktena yānena prayayau senayā vṛtā.

Tato 'bhiṣiṣicuḥ prītyā Dyumatsenaṃ purohitāḥ
putraṃ c' âsya mah"|ātmānaṃ yauvarājye 'bhyaṣecayan.
Tataḥ kālena mahatā Sāvitryāḥ kīrti|vardhanam
tad vai putra|śataṃ jajñe śūrāṇām anivartinām.
Bhrātṝṇāṃ sodarāṇāṃ ca tath" âiv' âsy' âbhavac chatam
Madr'|âdhipasy' Âśvapater Mālavyām sumahad|balam.
Evam ātmā pitā mātā śvaśrūḥ śvaśura eva ca
bhartuḥ kulaṃ ca Sāvitryā sarvaṃ kṛcchrāt samuddhṛtam.
15 Tath" âiv' âiṣā hi kalyāṇī Draupadī śīla|sammatā
tārayiṣyati vaḥ sarvān Sāvitr" îva kul'|âṅganā.

from the land of the Shalvas arrived and told him that his enemy had been killed by his own counsellor. They related how the enemy's army scattered and fled on hearing that he, his companions and relatives had been killed by the minister, and how the entire population was single-minded toward the king:

"With or without his sight, he should be our ruler! King, it is because of this decision that we have been sent here. These carriages and your fourfold army have arrived. Set out, king! May fortune be yours! Victory has been proclaimed in your city! For countless nights to come, assume the rank that belonged to your father and grandfather."

And when they saw that the king had his eyesight, and was in beautiful shape, they all bowed their heads, wide-eyed with amazement. Then he saluted those brahmin elders who lived in the hermitage and, honored by them all, set out for the city. And Shaibya went with Sávitri in a wonderful well-fitted carriage, drawn by men, surrounded by an army.

Then joyously the priests consecrated Dyumat·sena and anointed his son, whose spirit was great, as heir presumptive. Afterwards, over a lengthy period, Sávitri gave birth to one hundred heroic and unyielding sons, who augmented her fame. And a hundred very powerful brothers of hers were born by Málavi to Ashva·pati, king of the Madras. In this way Sávitri delivered herself, her father and mother, her mother-in-law, her father-in-law, and her husband's entire family from a calamity. And just like the nobly born Sávitri, virtuous Dráupadi here, so celebrated for her character, shall rescue all of you.

VAIŚAMPĀYANA uvāca:

Evaṃ sa Pāṇḍavas tena anunīto mah"|ātmanā
viśoko vijvaro rājan Kāmyake nyavasat tadā.
Yaś c' êdaṃ śṛṇuyād bhaktyā Sāvitry|ākhyānam uttamam
sa sukhī sarva|siddh'|ârtho na duḥkhaṃ prāpnuyān naraḥ.

VAISHAM·PÁYANA said:

So, my king, the Pándava was calmed by that great-spirited man, and went on living in the Kámyaka,* without sorrow or grief. And whoever listens with devotion to the wonderful story of Sávitri, that man will be happy and successful in everything, and never know sorrow.

3.300–310
THE ROBBING OF THE EARRINGS

Janamejaya uvāca:

300.1 Yat tat tadā mahad|Brahman Lomaśo vākyam abravīt
Indrasya vacanād eva Pāṇḍu|putraṃ Yudhiṣṭhiram:
«Yac c' âpi te bhayaṃ tīvraṃ na ca kīrtayase kva cit
tat c' âpy apahariṣyāmi Dhanaṃjaya ito gate»—
Kiṃ nu taj japatāṃ śreṣṭha Karṇaṃ prati mahad|bhayam
āsīn? na ca sa dharm'|ātmā kathayām āsa kasya cit?

Vaiśampāyana uvāca:

Ahaṃ te rāja|śārdūla kathayāmi kathām imām
pṛcchato Bharata|śreṣṭha, śuśrūṣasva giraṃ mama.
5 Dvādaśe samatikrānte varṣe prāpte trayodaśe
Pāṇḍūnāṃ hita|kṛc Chakraḥ Karṇaṃ bhikṣitum udyataḥ.
Abhiprāyam atho jñātvā mah"|Êndrasya vibhā|vasuḥ
kuṇḍal'|ârthe mahā|rāja Sūryaḥ Karṇam upāgataḥ Mah"|
ârhe śayane vīraṃ spardhy"|âstaraṇa|saṃvṛte
śayānam ativiśvastaṃ brahmaṇyaṃ satya|vādinam.
Svapn'|ânte niśi rāj'|êndra darśayām āsa raśmivān
kṛpayā paray" āviṣṭaḥ putra|snehāc ca Bhārata.
Brāhmaṇo veda|vid bhūtvā Sūryo yoga'|rddhi|rūpavān*
hit'|ârtham abravīt Karṇaṃ sāntva|pūrvam idaṃ vacaḥ:
10 «Karṇa! mad|vacanaṃ tāta śṛṇu satya|bhṛtāṃ vara
bruvato 'dya mahā|bāho sauhṛdāt paramaṃ hitam.
Upāyāsyati Śakras tvāṃ Pāṇḍavānāṃ hit'|ēpsayā
brāhmaṇa|cchadmanā Karṇa kuṇḍal'|ôpajihīrṣayā.
Viditaṃ tena śīlaṃ te sarvasya jagatas tathā
yathā tvaṃ bhikṣitaḥ sadbhir dadāsy eva na yācase.
Tvaṃ hi tāta dadāsy eva brāhmaṇebhyaḥ prayācitaḥ

Janam·ejaya said:

So, great brahmin, when, at Indra's request, Lómasha 300.1
said to Pandu's son, Yudhi·shthira: "Once Dhanam·ja-
ya has gone, I shall remove that bitter fear you keep to
yourself"—what exactly was that great fear concerning Ka-
rna, best of brahmins? And was there none to whom that
spirit of the Law could tell it?

Vaisham·páyana said:

Since you ask about it, tigerish king, I shall tell that story.
Listen, best of Bháratas, to what I have to say. Twelve years 5
had passed, and the thirteenth begun, when Shakra, want-
ing the best for the Pandus, was prepared to beg from Karna.
Then, realizing what great Indra intended in the matter of
the earrings, radiant sun-god Surya came to Karna, mighty
king. The hero—confident, brahminic, true-spoken—was
lying on a splendid couch covered with a priceless throw. O
chief among kings, O Bhárata, at night in a dream the Sun
showed himself, filled with great compassion, for love of his
son. Through his yogic power, Surya became a Veda-versed
brahmin, and coaxingly uttered this speech to Karna, for
his own good.

"Karna! Son! Greatest of truth-tellers, listen to my words. 10
I speak now, Strong Arm, from love, and in your best in-
terest. Wanting to benefit the Pándavas, Shakra will come
to you, Karna, disguised as a brahmin, hoping to steal your
earrings. Like the whole world he knows your practice: that
when begged by the good, you simply give, you do not so-
licit. For they say that you, my son, when requested, give
to brahmins, refusing neither goods nor anything else from

vittaṃ yac c' ânyad apy āhur na pratyākhyāsi kasya cit.
Tvāṃ tu c' âivaṃ|vidhaṃ jñātvā svayaṃ va Pāka|śāsanaḥ
āgantā kuṇḍal'|ârthāya kavacaṃ c' âiva bhikṣitum.
15 Tasmai prayācamānāya na deye kuṇḍale tvayā.
anuneyaḥ paraṃ śaktyā śreya etadd hi te param.
Kuṇḍal'|ârthe bruvaṃs tāta kāraṇair bahubhis tvayā
anyair bahu|vidhair vittaiḥ sannivāryaḥ punaḥ punaḥ
Ratnaiḥ strībhis tathā gobhir dhanair bahuvidhair api
nidarśanaiś ca bahubhiḥ kuṇḍal'|ēpsuḥ Puraṃ|daraḥ.
Yadi dāsyasi Karṇa tvaṃ sahaje kuṇḍale śubhe
āyuṣaḥ prakṣayaṃ gatvā mṛtyor vaśam upaiṣyasi.
Kavacena samāyuktaḥ kuṇḍalābhyāṃ ca mānada
avadhyas tvaṃ raṇe 'rīṇām iti viddhi vaco mama.
20 Amṛtād utthitaṃ hy etad ubhayaṃ ratna|sambhavam,
tasmād rakṣyaṃ tvayā Karṇa jīvitaṃ cet priyaṃ tava.»

KARṆA uvāca:

«Ko mām evaṃ bhavān prāha darśayan sauhṛdaṃ param?
kāmayā bhagavan brūhi, ko bhavān dvija|veṣa|dhṛk?»

BRĀHMAṆA uvāca:

«Ahaṃ tāta sahasr'|âṃśuḥ sauhṛdāt tvāṃ nidarśaye.
kuruṣv' âitad vaco me tvam, etac chreyaḥ paraṃ hi te.»

KARṆA uvāca:

«Śreya eva mam' âtyantaṃ yasya me go|patiḥ prabhuḥ
pravakt" âdya hit'|ânveṣī śṛṇu c' êdaṃ vaco mama.

any of them. So, knowing you to be like that, the conqueror
of Paka will come himself to beg your armor and earrings.
When he begs the earrings of you, you shouldn't give them. 15
Conciliate him as best you can—that's your safest course.
When, my son, he speaks of the earrings, you should re-
peatedly fend off, with all types of reasons and many other
sorts of wealth—such as gems, women, cattle, all kinds
of riches—and with many examples—that ring-obsessed
Sacker of Cities.

If, Karna, you give up the beautiful earrings you were
born with, your life will be cut off and you will fall into the
power of death. Honor-giver, when you have the armor and
the earrings,enemies cannot kill you in battle. Remember
my words. For both these, bejewelled, have come from the 20
elixir of immortality, so guard them, Karna, if you value
your life."

KARNA said:

"Tell me, sir, who are you to show me such extraordinary friendship? Be kind enough, lord, to tell me who you are—you who look like a brahmin."

The BRAHMIN said:

"I am the thousand-rayed Sun, my son, and I instruct you because I love you. Do as I say. It's in your very best interest."

KARNA said:

"It's certainly the best thing that could have happened to me, that the powerful lord of rays should speak to me today, seeking my benefit. Now hear my reply.

Prasādaye tvāṃ varadaṃ praṇayāc ca bravīmy aham
na nivāryo vratād asmād ahaṃ yady asmi te priyaḥ.
25 Vrataṃ vai mama loko 'yaṃ
vetti kṛtsnaṃ vibhāvaso
yathā 'haṃ dvija|mukhyebhyo
dadyāṃ prāṇān api dhruvam.
Yady āgacchati māṃ Śakro brāhmaṇa|cchadmanā vṛtaḥ
hit'|ârthaṃ Pāṇḍu|putrāṇāṃ khe|car'|ôttama bhikṣitum
Dāsyāmi vibudha|śreṣṭha kuṇḍale varma c' ôttamam
na me kīrtiḥ pranaśyeta triṣu lokeṣu viśrutā.
Mad|vidhasya yaśasyaṃ hi na yuktaṃ prāṇa|rakṣaṇam,
yuktaṃ hi yaśasā yuktaṃ maraṇaṃ loka|sammatam.
So 'ham Indrāya dāsyāmi kuṇḍale saha varmaṇā.
yadi māṃ Vala|Vṛtra|ghno bhikṣ'|ârtham upayāsyati
30 Hit'|ârthe Pāṇḍu|putrāṇāṃ kuṇḍale me prayācitum
tan me kīrti|karaṃ loke tasy' âkīrtir bhaviṣyati.
Vṛṇomi kīrtiṃ loke hi jīviten' âpi bhānuman.
kīrtimān aśnute svarge hīna|kīrtis tu naśyati.
Kīrtir hi puruṣaṃ loke sañjīvayati mātṛvat
akīrtir jīvitaṃ hanti jīvato 'pi śarīriṇaḥ.
Ayaṃ purāṇaḥ śloko hi svayaṃ gīto vibhāvaso
dhātrā lok'|ēśvara yathā kīrtir āyur narasya ha:
‹Puruṣasya pare loke kīrtir eva parāyaṇam
iha loke viśuddhā ca kīrtir āyur|vivardhanī.›
35 So 'haṃ śarīra|je dattvā kīrtiṃ prāpsyāmi śāśvatīm
dattvā ca vidhivad dānaṃ brāhmaṇebhyo yathā|vidhi.
Hutvā śarīraṃ saṅgrāme kṛtvā karma suduṣkaram
vijitya ca parān ājau yaśaḥ prāpsyāmi kevalam.
Bhītānām abhayaṃ dattvā saṅgrāme jīvit'|ârthinām
vṛddhān bālān dvijātīṃś ca mokṣayitvā mahābhayāt

I propitiate you, giver of gifts, and out of love I say, if I
am dear to you, don't deflect me from this vow. O Lord of 25
boundless light, this world knows my whole vow: I would
certainly give my life itself to the first of the twice-born.
If, O greatest of those who walk the sky, Shakra comes to
me disguised as a brahmin to beg on behalf of the sons of
Pandu, I shall, greatest of gods, give him my earrings and
my excellent mail, so that my fame, which is spread across
the three worlds, may not disappear. Fame, for such a man
as me, doesn't come with saving one's life; rather, a proper
death is rewarded by the world with proper fame.

So I shall give the earrings and armor to Indra. For if the
killer of Vala and Vritra approaches me, begging, soliciting 30
my earrings for the welfare of Pandu's sons, that shall make
me famous throughout the world and redound to his in-
famy. Sun, I choose fame in the world, even at the cost of
my life. One is famous and goes to heaven, but without
fame one is lost. For fame, like a mother, gives life to a man
in the world; but infamy kills the life, even of the embodied
and living. Sun, Lord of the world, the Creator himself has
sung this ancient verse—how fame is the life of a man: 'In
the next world, fame alone is for man the final aim; in this
world, untainted fame enlarges life.'

So, by giving away what was born with my body, and 35
giving gifts properly to brahmins, just as prescribed, I shall
acquire undying fame. By offering my body in war, by doing
the difficult deed, by conquering my enemies in combat, I
shall acquire nothing but fame. By securing the safety of the
fearful who cling to their lives in battle; by liberating youths,
old men and brahmins from great danger, I shall attain the

Prāpsyāmi paramaṃ loke yaśaḥ svargyam anuttamam.
jīviten' âpi me rakṣyā kīrtis tad viddhi* me vratam.
So 'haṃ dattvā Maghavate bhikṣām etām anuttamām
brāhmaṇa|cchadmane deva loke gantā parāṃ gatim.»

SŪRYA uvāca:

301.1 «M" âhitaṃ Karṇa kārṣīs tvam ātmanaḥ suhṛdāṃ tathā
putrāṇām atha bhāryāṇām atho mātur atho pituḥ.
Śarīrasy' âvirodhena prāṇināṃ prāṇa|bhṛd|vara
iṣyate yaśasaḥ prāptiḥ kīrtiś ca tri|dive sthirā.
Yas tvaṃ prāṇa|virodhena kīrtim icchasi śāśvatīm
sā te prāṇān samādāya gamiṣyati, na saṃśayaḥ.
Jīvatāṃ kurute kāryaṃ pitā mātā sutās tathā
ye c' ânye bāndhavāḥ ke cil loke 'smin puruṣa'|rṣabha
5 Rājānaś ca nara|vyāghra pauruṣeṇa; nibodha tat.
kīrtiś ca jīvataḥ sādhvī puruṣasya mahā|dyute.
Mṛtasya kīrtyā kiṃ kāryaṃ bhasmī|bhūtasya dehinaḥ?
mṛtaḥ kīrtiṃ na jānīte jīvan kīrtiṃ samaśnute.
Mṛtasya kīrtir martyasya yathā mālā gat'|āyuṣaḥ.
ahaṃ tu tvāṃ bravīmy etad bhakto 's' îti hit'|ēpsayā.
Bhaktimanto hi me rakṣyā ity eten' âpi hetunā
bhakto 'yaṃ parayā bhaktyā mām ity eva mahā|bhuja.
Mam' âpi bhaktir utpannā. sa tvaṃ kuru vaco mama
asti c' âtra paraṃ kiṃ cid adhyātmaṃ deva|nirmitam.
ataś ca tvāṃ bravīmy etat; kriyatām aviśaṅkayā.
10 Deva|guhyaṃ tvayā jñātuṃ na śakyaṃ puruṣa'|rṣabha
tasmān n' ākhyāmi te guhyaṃ, kāle vetsyati tad bhavān.

greatest fame in the world, and highest heaven. Even at the cost of my life, my fame shall be shielded. Know that's my vow. And once I have given Indra Mághavat, disguised as a brahmin, this peerless gift, I shall attain, O god, the highest state in the world."

The Sun said:

"Karna, don't damage yourself, your friends, sons, wives, 301.1
mother and father. O best of those that breathe, the living want glory, and enduring fame in heaven, but not at the risk of their bodies. You, who desire eternal fame at the cost of your life, will lose your life pursuing it, beyond all doubt. A father, a mother, sons and any relatives, of whatever kind,
do the work of the living in this world, bull of a man—and 5
kings too, through manly valor, tigerish man. Learn from that, shining one: only the fame of the living man holds good. What's the good of fame for a mortal, whose body is ash? A dead man knows nothing of fame—fame is for the living. Fame for a dead man is like a wreath on a corpse. I'm telling you this because you are my devotee and I want to protect you.

I should protect those devoted to me, for this reason too: I think, Great Arm, that this man is devoted to me with a supreme devotion. So, if you are truly devoted to me, do as I say. There is here something profound in your inner self that has been made by a god. And so I tell you this: act
without hesitating. Bull of a man, because you haven't the 10
power to know a god's secret, I shall not tell you that secret, but in time you will come to know it.

Punar uktaṃ ca vakṣyāmi tvaṃ Rādheya; nibodha tat.
m" âsmai te kuṇḍale dadyā bhikṣite vajra|pāṇinā.
Śobhase kuṇḍalābhyāṃ ca rucirābhyāṃ mahā|dyute
Viśākhayor madhya|gataḥ śaś" îva vimale divi.
Kīrtiś ca jīvataḥ sādhvī puruṣasy' êti viddhi tat.
pratyākhyeyas tvayā tāta kuṇḍal'|ârthe sur'|ēśvaraḥ.
Śakyā bahu|vidhair vākyaiḥ kuṇḍal'|ēpsā tvay" ân|agha
vihantuṃ deva|rājasya hetu|yuktaiḥ punaḥ punaḥ.
15 Hetumad|upapann'|ârthair mādhurya|kṛta|bhūṣaṇaiḥ
Puraṃ|darasya Karṇa tvaṃ buddhim etām apānuda.
Tvaṃ hi nityaṃ nara|vyāghra spardhase savya|sācinā
savya|sācī tvayā c' êha yudhi śūraḥ sameṣyati.
Na tu tvām Arjunaḥ śaktaḥ kuṇḍalābhyāṃ samanvitam
vijetuṃ yudhi yady asya svayam Indraḥ śiro bhavet.
Tasmān na deye Śakrāya tvay" âite kuṇḍale śubhe
saṅgrāme yadi nirjetuṃ Karṇa kāmayase 'rjunam.»

KARṆA uvāca:

302.1 «Bhagavantam ahaṃ bhakto yathā māṃ vettha go|pate
tathā parama|tigm'|âṃśo n' âsty adeyam kathaṃ cana.
Na me dārā na me putrā na c' ātmā suhṛdo na ca
tath" êṣṭā vai sadā bhaktyā yathā tvaṃ go|pate mama.
Iṣṭānāṃ ca mah"|ātmāno bhaktānāṃ ca, na saṃśayaḥ,
kurvanti bhaktim iṣṭāṃ ca jānīṣe tvaṃ ca bhāskara.
‹Iṣṭo bhaktaś ca me Karṇo na c' ânyad daivataṃ divi
jānīta iti› vai kṛtvā bhagavān āha madd|hitam.
5 Bhūyaś ca śirasā yāce prasādya ca punaḥ punaḥ
iti bravīmi tigm'|âṃśo tvaṃ tu me kṣantum arhasi:

I'll repeat what I've said to you, Karna Radhéya—pay it heed: don't give your earrings to the thunderbolt-wielder when he comes begging. Great glorious man, with your lustrous earrings you shine like the moon in a clear sky between the two stars of Vishákha. Realize that fame is good only for the man alive. So, my son, refuse the lord of the gods when he comes for the earrings. Blameless one, time after time, with many arguments based on logic, you can
ward off the king of the gods' desire for the earrings. Kar- 15
na, repudiate this design of the sacker of cities with graceful figures of speech whose purport is upheld by argument. For, tigerish man, you always vie with the left-handed archer,* and here the hero, the left-handed archer, will meet you in battle. But even were Indra himself at the head of his army, Árjuna cannot defeat you in battle while the earrings are yours. So, Karna, if you want to subdue Árjuna in battle, you shouldn't give Shakra those beautiful earrings."

KARNA said:

"Lord of the rays, god of the supremely fiery rays, just as 302.1
you know I am your devotee, so you know there is nothing at all that cannot be given. Neither my wives, nor my sons, nor myself, nor my friends are as honored with my incessant devotion as you, lord of rays. You know, bright Sun, that the great-souled invariably return the devotion and honor of their dear worshippers.

Thinking, 'Karna is my chosen devotee and acknowledges no other god in heaven,' your lordship has offered
me good advice. Once more, and again, I entreat you, and 5
again, with bowed head, Lord of the fiery rays, but I say the

Bibhemi na tathā mṛtyor yathā bibhye 'nṛtād aham.
viśeṣeṇa dvi|jātīnāṃ sarveṣāṃ sarvadā satām
Pradāne jīvitasy' âpi na me 'tr' âsti vicāraṇā.
yac ca māṃ āttha deva tvaṃ Pāṇḍavaṃ Phālgunaṃ prati
Vyetu saṃtāpajaṃ duḥkhaṃ tava bhāskara mānasam
Arjunaṃ prati māṃ c' âiva; vijeṣyāmi raṇe 'rjunam.
Tav' âpi viditaṃ deva mam' âsty astra|balaṃ mahat
Jāmadagnyād upāttaṃ yat tathā Droṇān mah"|ātmanaḥ.
10 Idaṃ tvam anujānīhi sura|śreṣṭha vrataṃ mama:
bhikṣate vajriṇe dadyām api jīvitam ātmanaḥ.»

SŪRYA uvāca:

«Yadi tāta dadāsy ete vajriṇe kuṇḍale śubhe
tvam apy enam atho brūyā vijay'|ârthaṃ mahā|balam:
‹Niyamena pradadyāṃ te kuṇḍale vai śata|krato
avadhyo hy asi bhūtānāṃ kuṇḍalābhyāṃ samanvitaḥ.›
Arjunena vināśaṃ hi tava dānava|sūdanaḥ
prārthayāno raṇe vatsa kuṇḍale te jihīrṣati.
Sa tvam apy enam ārādhya sūnṛtābhiḥ punaḥ punaḥ
abhyarthayethā dev'|ēśam amogh'|ârthaṃ puraṃ|daram:
15 ‹Amoghāṃ dehi me śaktim amitra|vinibarhiṇīm.
dāsyāmi te sahasr'|âkṣa kuṇḍale varma c' ôttamam.›
Ity eva niyamena tvaṃ dadyāḥ śakrāya kuṇḍale,
tayā tvaṃ Karṇa saṃgrāme haniṣyasi raṇe ripūn.
N' âhatvā hi mahā|bāho śatrūn eti karaṃ punaḥ
sā śaktir deva|rājasya śataśo 'tha sahasraśaḥ.»

same thing—you must forgive me—I fear death nowhere near as much as I fear the lie. To all good people at any time, and especially to brahmins,I have no hesitation in giving even my life. And what you have said to me, god, concerning Phálguna Pándava—dispel, light-maker, your burning inner sorrow concerning Árjuna and myself: I shall overcome Árjuna in battle. You know, god, that I have a great power of weapons obtained from Jamad·agnya and
great-souled Drona. Allow this vow of mine, best of gods: 10
that I may even give my own life to the thunderbolt-wielder, if he comes begging."

The SUN said:

"My son, if you give these bright earrings to the thunderbolt-wielder, in order to secure victory, you, whose strength is so great, should tell him: "God of a hundred sacrifices, I give you the earrings on condition, for no creatures can kill you while you are wearing the earrings." So the killer of the Dánavas, wanting Árjuna to destroy you in battle, wishes to appropriate your earrings, dear son. You should repeatedly propitiate him with pleasant and truthful words, you should beseech the lord of the gods, the destroyer of
citadels, whose purpose is unerring: "Give me an infallible 15
spear that will crush my enemies, and I will give you, god of a thousand eyes, my earrings and incomparable armor." This is the condition on which you should give Shakra the earrings; with that spear, Karna, you will kill your enemies in battle. For the lord of the gods' spear does not return to one's hand, Great Arm, before it has killed enemies in their hundreds and thousands."

VAIŚAMPĀYANA uvāca:

Evam uktvā sahasr'|âṃśuḥ sahas" ântaradhīyata.
tataḥ Sūryāya japy'|ânte Karṇaḥ svapnaṃ nyavedayat,
Yathā dṛṣṭaṃ yathā tattvaṃ yath" ôktam ubhayor niśi
tat sarvam ānupūrvyeṇa śaśaṃs' âsmai Vṛṣas tadā.
20 Tac chrutvā bhagavān devo bhānuḥ Svarbhānu|sūdanaḥ
uvāca taṃ «tath" êty» eva Karṇaṃ Sūryaḥ smayann iva.
Tatas «tattvam» iti jñātvā Rādheyaḥ para|vīra|hā
śaktim ev' âbhikāṅkṣan vai Vāsavaṃ pratyapālayat.

JANAMEJAYA uvāca:

303.1 Kiṃ tad guhyaṃ na c' ākhyātaṃ
Karṇāy' êh' ôṣṇa|raśminā,
kīdṛśe kuṇḍale te ca
kavacaṃ c' âiva kīdṛśam?
Kutaś ca kavacaṃ tasya kuṇḍale c' âiva sattama?
etad icchāmy ahaṃ śrotuṃ; tan me brūhi tapo|dhana.

VAIŚAMPĀYANA uvāca:

Ayaṃ rājan bravīmy etat tasya guhyaṃ vibhā|vasoḥ:
yādṛśe kuṇḍale te ca kavacaṃ c' âiva yādṛśam.
Kuntibhojaṃ purā rājan brāhmaṇaḥ paryupasthitaḥ
tigma|tejā mahā prāṃśuḥ śmaśru|daṇḍa|jaṭā|dharaḥ
5 Darśanīyo 'navady'|âṅgas tejasā prajvalann iva
madhu|piṅgo madhura|vāk tapaḥ|svādhyāya|bhūṣaṇaḥ.
Sa rājānaṃ Kuntibhojam abravīt sumahā|tapāḥ:
«bhikṣām icchāmi vai bhoktuṃ tava gehe vimatsara.
Na me vyalīkaṃ kartavyaṃ tvayā vā tava c' ânugaiḥ.
evaṃ vatsyāmi te gehe yadi te rocate 'nagha.

VAISHAM·PÁYANA said:

Having spoken thus, the thousand-rayed one suddenly disappeared. Then, after he had finished reciting his prayers, Karna told the Sun his dream. Karna Vrisha recited to him everything that had happened between the two of them in sequence: just as it had been seen, happened, and said.
Having heard that, the revered lord Sun, Surya, Svar·bha- 20
nu's killer, said to Karna, with something like a smile, "So it is." So, knowing it to be the truth, Radhéya, the killer of hostile heroes, wanting only that spear, waited for Vásava.

JANAM·EJAYA said:

And what was that secret the fierce-beamed Sun didn't 303.1
tell Karna? What kind were the earrings? What kind the armor? And whence came his earrings and armor, foremost among men? This is what I want to hear—tell me about it, you who are rich in asceticism.

VAISHAM·PÁYANA said:

King, I shall tell you this—this secret of his, the bright lord's—and what kind the earrings were, and what kind the armor. In the past there appeared to Kunti·bhoja a brahmin, sharply lustrous, large, tall, with matted locks, and bearded,
carrying a staff. He was good to look at, perfectly propor- 5
tioned, and seemed to blaze with luster; honey-yellow, a sweet speaker, bejewelled with asceticism and Vedic study.

That prodigious ascetic said to King Kunti·bhoja: "I wish for alms—to eat in your house, unselfish man. Neither you nor your followers should do me wrong in that way, blameless one. I shall live in your house, if you are agreeable. I must come and go as I please, king, and whether I'm in

Yathā|kāmaṃ ca gaccheyam āgaccheyaṃ tath" âiva ca
śayy"|āsane ca me rājan n' âparādhyeta kaś cana.»
Tam abravīt Kuntibhojaḥ prīti|yuktam idaṃ vacaḥ:
«evam astu paraṃ c' êti» punaś c' âinam ath' âbravīt:
10 «Mama kanyā mahā|prājña Pṛthā nāma yaśasvinī
śīla|vṛtt'|ânvitā sādhvī niyatā na c' âiva bhāvinī.
Upasthāsyati sā tvāṃ vai pūjay' ânavamanya ca
tasyāś ca śīla|vṛttena tuṣṭiṃ samupayāsyasi.»

Evam uktvā tu taṃ vipram abhipūjya yathā|vidhi
uvāca kanyām abhyetya Pṛthāṃ pṛthula|locanām.

«Ayaṃ vatse mahā|bhāgo brāhmaṇo vastum icchati
mama gehe mayā c' âsya ‹tath" êty› evaṃ pratiśrutam.
Tvayi vatse parāśvasya brāhmaṇasy'|âbhirādhanam
tan me vākyaṃ na mithyā tvaṃ kartum arhasi karhi cit.
15 Ayaṃ tapasvī bhagavān svādhyāya|niyato dvijaḥ
yad yad brūyān mahā|tejās tat tad deyam amatsarāt.
Brāhmaṇo hi paraṃ tejo, brāhmaṇo hi paraṃ tapaḥ,
brāhmaṇānāṃ namaskāraiḥ sūryo divi virājate.
Amānayan hi mān'|ârhān Vātāpiś ca mah"|âsuraḥ
nihato Brahma|daṇḍena Tālajaṅghas tath" âiva ca.
So 'yaṃ vatse mahā|bhāra āhitas tvayi sāṃpratam
tvaṃ sadā niyatā kuryā brāhmaṇasy' âbhirādhanam.

Jānāmi praṇidhānaṃ te bālyāt prabhṛti nandini
brāhmaṇeṣv iha sarveṣu guru|bandhuṣu c' âiva ha.
20 Tathā preṣyeṣu sarveṣu mitra|saṃbandhi|mātṛṣu
mayi caiva yathāvat tvaṃ sarvam āvṛtya vartase.
Na hy atuṣṭo jano 'st' îha pure c' ântaḥpure ca te
samyag|vṛtty" ânavady'|âṅgi tava bhṛtya|janeṣv api.

bed or seated, no one must offend me." Kunti·bhoja addressed this friendly speech to him: "Let that and more be so!" And again he said to him: "O you of great wisdom, I have a beautiful daughter called Pritha; she is noble, chaste and temperate, of good conduct and character. She shall wait on you, honoring you without disrespect, and you will come to be satisfied with her conduct and character."

Having said this to the brahmin, and having suitably honored him, he addressed Pritha, his wide-eyed daughter, who had now come in:

"Darling, this eminent brahmin wishes to live in my house, and I have promised that it can be so. Having expressed my confidence that you, my dear, can propitiate a brahmin, don't at any time make my words ring falsely. This revered brahmin is an ascetic and wedded to Vedic study. A man of great luster, whatever he may ask for, you should, disinterestedly, give it to him. For a brahmin is the supreme energy, the supreme austerity. It is because of brahmins' greetings that the sun shines in the sky. The great *ásura* Vatápi, failing to honor those deserving of honor, was killed by Brahma's staff, as was Tala·jangha. This is a great weight that has been fitly placed on you, my dear, that you should be ever intent on propitiating the brahmin.

Daughter, I know that ever since your childhood you have been most attentive here to brahmins, and to all your elders and relatives. Likewise, attentive to everything, you have conducted yourself properly toward all the servants, to friends, relations and mothers, and to me. And because, faultless beauty, you discharge your duties so well—even toward the serving people—there is not a person here, in

Saṃdeṣṭavyāṃ tu manye tvāṃ dvi|jātiṃ kopanaṃ prati
Pṛthe bāl" êti kṛtvā vai sutā c' âsi mam' eti ca.
Vṛṣṇīnāṃ tvaṃ kule jātā Śūrasya dayitā sutā
dattā prītimatā mahyaṃ pitrā bālā purā svayam.
Vasudevasya bhaginī sutānāṃ pravarā mama
agryam agre pratijñāya ten' âsi duhitā mama.
25 Tādṛśe hi kule jātā kule c' âiva vivardhitā
sukhāt sukham anuprāptā hradādd hradam iv' āgatā.
Dauṣkuleyā viśeṣeṇa kathaṃ cit pragrahaṃ gatāḥ
bāla|bhāvād vikurvanti prāyaśaḥ pramadāḥ śubhe.
Pṛthe rāja|kule janma rūpaṃ c' âpi tav' âdbhutam
tena ten' âsi saṃpannā* samupetā ca bhāvinī.
Sā tvaṃ darpaṃ parityajya dambhaṃ mānaṃ ca bhāvini
ārādhya varadaṃ vipraṃ śreyasā yokṣyase Pṛthe.
Evaṃ prāpsyasi kalyāṇi kalyāṇam anaghe dhruvam,
kopite tu dvija|śreṣṭhe kṛtsnaṃ dahyeta me kulam.»

KUNTY uvāca:

304.1 «Brāhmaṇaṃ yantritā rājann upasthāsyāmi pūjayā
yathā|pratijñaṃ rāj'|êndra, na ca mithyā bravīmy aham.
Eṣa c' âiva sva|bhāvo me pūjayeyaṃ dvi|jān iti
tava c' âiva priyaṃ kāryaṃ śreyaś ca paraṃ mama.
Yady ev'|âiṣyati sāy' âhne yadi prātar atho niśi
yady ardha|rātre bhagavān na me kopaṃ kariṣyati.

the city, or in the palace, dissatisfied with you. So I think you should be briefed to deal with an angry brahmin. Pritha, as an infant, you were adopted by me as a daughter; you were born into the family of the Vrishnis, the beloved daughter of Shura. Shortly after, your father himself, out of affection for me, gave me you, an infant girl.

Since he promised me the first of his children, you are
my daughter—the sister of Vasu·deva, and the first of my
daughters. Born to such a family, and reared in such an- 25
other, you have attained happiness in the wake of happiness,
as though you had come from a lake to a lake. Lowborn women, in particular, although somehow kept on a tight rein throughout out of foolishness, generally alter for the worse, radiant girl. But Pritha, your birth into a royal family and your beauty are extraordinary. Furnished with both these, beautiful woman, you have turned out well. Beautiful woman, Pritha, renounce arrogance, hypocrisy and pride. Conciliate the brahmin gift-giver, and you shall yoke yourself to fortune. In that way, blameless and virtuous girl, you will certainly be fortunate, but if that best of brahmins is angered my whole family will burn."

KUNTÍ said:

"Restrained, I shall attend on the brahmin with rever- 304.1
ence, king, according to your promise, and I shall utter no falsehood, Indra among kings. For it is my nature to honor the twice-born, and the greatest good for me is to do what pleases you. If the blessed lord comes in the evening, in the morning, or at night—even in the middle of the night—he will not anger me. Indra among kings, this is my profit: that

Lābho mam' âiṣa rāj'|êndra yad vai pūjayatī dvi|jān
ādeśe tava tiṣṭhantī hitaṃ kuryāṃ nar'|ôttama.
5 Visrabdho bhava rāj'|êndra; na vyalīkaṃ dvij'|ôttamaḥ
vasan prāpsyati te gehe, satyam etad bravīmi te.
Yat priyaṃ ca dvi|jasy' âsya hitaṃ c' âiva tav' ânagha
yatiṣyāmi tathā rājan; vyetu te mānaso jvaraḥ.
Brāhmaṇā hi mahā|bhāgāḥ pūjitāḥ pṛthivī|pate
tāraṇāya samarthāḥ syur viparīte vadhāya ca.
S" âham etad vijānantī toṣayiṣye dvij'|ôttamam;
na mat|kṛte vyathāṃ rājan prāpsyasi dvija|sattamāt.
Aparādhe 'pi rāj'|êndra rājñām aśreyase dvijāḥ
bhavanti Cyavano yadvat Sukanyāyāḥ kṛte purā.
10 Niyamena pareṇ' âham upasthāsye dvij'|ôttamam
yathā tvayā nar'|êndr' êdaṃ bhāṣitaṃ brāhmaṇaṃ prati.»
Evaṃ bruvantīṃ bhṛśaṃ pariṣvajya samarthya ca
iti c' êti ca kartavyaṃ rājā sarvam ath' âdiśat:

RĀJ" ôvāca

«Evam etat tvayā bhadre
kartavyam aviśaṅkayā
madd|hit'|ârthaṃ tath" ātm'|ârthaṃ
kul'|ârthaṃ c' âpy anindite.»
Evam uktvā tu tāṃ kanyāṃ Kuntibhojo mahā|yaśāḥ
Pṛthāṃ paridadau tasmai dvijāya dvija|vatsalaḥ:
«Iyaṃ Brahman mama sutā bālā sukha|vivardhitā
aparādhyeta yat* kiṃ cin na kāryaṃ hṛdi tat tvayā.
15 Dvijātayo mahā|bhāgā vṛddha|bāla|tapasviṣu
bhavanty akrodhanāḥ prāyo viruddheṣv api nityadā.

by adhering to your command and honoring the twice-born
I may do what is beneficial, foremost of men. Be confident, 5
Indra among kings, while he's living in your house, the fore-
most of brahmins shall suffer no offense. This is the truth
I'm telling you. And what is pleasing for him, the brahmin,
and what is beneficial for you, blameless man, that shall
I strive to do. Therefore, king, banish your mind's fever.
For when very eminent brahmins are honored, lord of the
earth, they are able to save, but in the reverse circumstances
they may destroy. Knowing this, I shall satisfy that foremost
brahmin; the preeminent brahmin will not, king, cause you
anguish on account of me. For, when offended, Indra of
kings, brahmins are bad fortune for rulers, as Chyávana
was, on account of Sukánya in the past.* I shall wait on 10
the superior brahmin with great self-control, just as you
described it to the brahmin, Indra among men."

So she spoke at length, and earned the embraces and the
support of the king, who then pointed out all she should do.

The King said:

"So you should do this without hesitation, my dear, for
my benefit, for the family's, and for yours as well, virtu-
ous girl."

Having spoken in that way to the girl, renowned Kun-
ti·bhoja, devoted to the twice-born, gave Pritha to that
brahmin:

"Brahmin, this is my young daughter, brought up in com-
fort. If she offends you in some way, don't take it to heart. As 15
a rule, eminent brahmins feel no anger toward the elderly,
children or ascetics, even when these are frequent offend-

Sumahaty aparādhe 'pi kṣāntiḥ kāryā dvijātibhiḥ
yathā|śakti yath"|ôtsāhaṃ pūjā grāhyā dvij'|ôttama.»
«Tath" êti» brāhmaṇen' ôkte* sa rājā prīta|mānasaḥ
haṃsa|candr'|âṃśu|saṃkāśaṃ gṛham asya* nyavedayat.
Tatr' âgni|śaraṇe kḷptam āsanaṃ tasya bhānumat
āhār'|ādi ca sarvaṃ tat tath" âiva pratyavedayat.
Nikṣipya rāja|putrī tu tandrīṃ mānaṃ tath" âiva ca
ātasthe paramaṃ yatnaṃ brāhmaṇasy' âbhirādhane.
20 Tatra sā brāhmaṇaṃ gatvā Pṛthā śauca|parā satī
vidhivat paricār'|ârhaṃ devavat paryatoṣayat.

VAIŚAMPĀYANA uvāca:

305.1 Sā tu kanyā mahā|rāja brāhmaṇaṃ saṃśita|vratam
toṣayām āsa śuddhena manasā saṃśita|vratā.
«Prātar eṣyāmy ath' êty» uktvā kadā cid dvija|sattamaḥ
tata āyāti rāj'|êndra sāyaṃ rātrāv atho punaḥ.
Taṃ ca sarvāsu velāsu bhakṣya|bhojya|pratiśrayaiḥ
pūjayām āsa sā kanyā vardhamānais tu sarvadā.
Ann'|ādi|samudācāraḥ śayy"|āsana|kṛtas tathā
divase divase tasya vardhate na tu hīyate.
5 Nirbhartsan'|âpavādaiś ca tath"|âiv' âpriyayā girā
brāhmaṇasya Pṛthā rājan na cakār' âpriyaṃ tadā.
Vyaste kāle punaś c' âiti na c' âiti bahuśo dvijaḥ
sudurlabham api hy annaṃ «dīyatām» iti so 'bravīt.
«Kṛtam eva ca tat sarvaṃ yathā» tasmai nyavedayat
śiṣyavat putravac c' âiva svasṛvac ca susaṃyatā.
Yath"|ôpajoṣaṃ rāj'|êndra dvijāti|pravarasya sā

ers. And even if the offense is very great, brahmins should practice forgiveness. Accept her worship, best of brahmins, in the light of her power and exertion."

"So be it!" said the brahmin. Then the king, in a happy mood, gave him a house as white as a moonbeam or a goose. In the place where the sacrificial fire was kept, he prepared a brilliant seat for him, and gave him food and everything else of a similar kind. Then, casting off lassitude as well as pride, the princess, thereafter, was devoted to making
an exceptional effort to propitiate the brahmin. Intent on 20
purity, virtuous Pritha duly went to the brahmin, so worthy of service, and satisfied him entirely, as though he were a god.

VAISHAM·PÁYANA said:

So, great king, with a pure heart that girl of meticulous 305.1
vows looked after the brahmin, whose vows were punctilious. Sometimes, Indra among kings, the eminent brahmin, having said, "I'll be back in the morning," would return again in the evening or at night. But at all times of day that girl honored him with ever more food, drink and assistance.

Day after day, her hospitality to him, whether with food or other things, as well as in respect of bed and seat, did
not diminish at all, but only increased. In spite of his blam- 5
ing and reproaching her with disagreeable words, O king, Pritha didn't do anything displeasing to the brahmin. The brahmin came back late, and at odd times, and frequently he didn't come back at all. And he ordered her to serve food, even when it was difficult to come by. But, well composed, like a pupil, a son or a sister, she reported to him, "All is

prītim utpādayām āsa kanyā ratnam aninditā.
Tasyās tu śīla|vṛttena tutoṣa dvija|sattamaḥ;
avadhānena bhūyo 'syāḥ paraṃ yatnam ath' âkarot.
10 Tāṃ prabhāte ca sāyaṃ ca pitā papraccha Bhārata:
«api tuṣyati te putri brāhmaṇaḥ paricaryayā?»
Taṃ sā: «paramam ity» eva pratyuvāca yaśasvinī
tataḥ prītim avāp' âgryāṃ Kuntibhojo mahā|manāḥ.
Tataḥ saṃvatsare pūrṇe yad" âsau japatāṃ varaḥ
n' âpaśyad duṣkṛtaṃ kiṃ cit Pṛthāyāḥ sauhṛde rataḥ.
Tataḥ prīta|manā bhūtvā sa enāṃ brāhmaṇo 'bravīt:
«prīto 'smi paramaṃ bhadre paricāreṇa te śubhe.
Varān vṛṇīṣva kalyāṇi dur|āpān mānuṣair iha
yais tvaṃ sīmantinīḥ sarvā yaśas" âbhibhaviṣyasi.»

KUNTY uvāca:

15 «Kṛtāni mama sarvāṇi yasyā me Veda|vittama
tvaṃ prasannaḥ pitā c' âiva kṛtaṃ vipra varair mama.»

BRĀHMAṆA uvāca:

«Yadi n' êcchasi mattas tvaṃ varaṃ bhadre śuci|smite
imaṃ mantraṃ gṛhāṇa tvam āhvānāya divaukasām.
Yaṃ yaṃ devaṃ tvam etena mantreṇ' āvāhayiṣyasi
tena tena vaśe bhadre sthātavyaṃ te bhaviṣyati.
Akāmo vā sakāmo vā sa sameṣyati te vaśe
vibudho mantra|saṃśānto vākye bhṛtya iv' ānataḥ.»

ready." And by such means, Indra of a king, that blame-
less girl—a jewel—generated the brahmin's satisfaction and
enjoyment. As she made her supreme effort, full of atten-
tiveness, the best of the twice-born was satisfied with her
conduct and character. Bhárata, in the morning and during 10
the evening her father asked her: "Daughter, is the brah-
min satisfied with your service?" The beautiful girl replied:
"Completely!," and the high-minded Kunti·bhoja experi-
enced the greatest delight. Then, when a year had passed,
that best of mantra-reciters had grown fond of Pritha and
had not seen any fault in her. So, being joyous-minded, the
brahmin said to her: "Beautiful girl, I am entirely delighted
with your service. Choose some gift, my beauty, that people
here find difficult to obtain, by which you shall surpass all
women in glory."

KUNTÍ said:

"If you and father are pleased with me, greatest of Veda 15
knowers, everything I need has been given to me; I have my
gifts already, brahmin."

The BRAHMIN said:

"If you don't want a gift from me, brightly smiling girl, accept this mantra for the invocation of the gods. Whichever god you invoke with this spell, he shall be brought under your control. Tranquillized by the mantra, willing or unwilling, the god shall come under your control, like a genuflecting servant."

VAIŚAMPĀYANA uvāca:

Na śaśāka dvitīyaṃ sā pratyākhyātum aninditā
taṃ vai dvijāti|pravaraṃ tadā śāpa|bhayān nṛpa.
20 Tatas tām anavady'|âṅgīṃ grāhayām āsa vai dvijaḥ
mantra|grāmaṃ tadā rājann Atharvaśirasi śrutam.
Taṃ pradāya tu rāj'|êndra Kuntibhojam uvāca ha:
«uṣito 'smi sukhaṃ rājan kanyayā paritoṣitaḥ.
Tava geheṣu vihitaḥ sadā supratipūjitaḥ
sādhayiṣyāmahe tāvad ity» uktv" ântaradhīyata.
Sa tu rājā dvijaṃ dṛṣṭvā tatr' âiv' ântarhitaṃ tadā
babhūva vismay'|āviṣṭaḥ Pṛthāṃ ca samapūjayat.

VAIŚAṂPĀYANA uvāca:

306.1 Gate tasmin dvija|śreṣṭhe kasmiṃś cit kāraṇ'|ântare
cintayām āsa sā kanyā mantra|grāma|bal'|âbalam:
«Ayaṃ vai kīdṛśas tena mama datto mah"|ātmanā
mantra|grāmo? balaṃ tasya jñāsye n' âticirād iti.»
Evaṃ saṃcintayantī sā dadarśa rtuṃ yadṛcchayā.
vrīḍitā s" âbhavad bālā kanyā|bhāve rajasvalā.

Tato harmya|tala|sthā sā mah"|ârha|śayan'|ôcitā
prācyāṃ diśi samudyantaṃ dadarś' āditya|maṇḍalam.
5 Tatra baddha|mano|dṛṣṭir abhavat sā sumadhyamā
na c' âtapyata rūpeṇa bhānoḥ sandhyā|gatasya sā.

Tasyā dṛṣṭir abhūd divyā: s" âpaśyad divya|darśanam
āmukta|kavacaṃ devaṃ kuṇḍalābhyāṃ vibhūṣitam.
Tasyāḥ kautūhalaṃ tv āsīn mantraṃ prati nar'|âdhipa
āhvānam akarot s" âtha tasya devasya bhāminī.

VAISHAM·PÁYANA said:

From fear of his curse, the virtuous girl could not refuse
that best of brahmins more than once, O king. So then, O 20
king, the brahmin taught her—she whose body was without
blemish—a collection of mantras revealed in the Athárva·
shiras. And when he had given it, Indra among kings, he
said to Kunti·bhoja: "I have had a happy stay, king, and
I am very pleased with your daughter. I have always been
well served and honored in your dwellings. I shall now set
out!" So saying, he disappeared. And the king, having seen
the brahmin there one moment and gone the next, was
overcome with astonishment, and commended Pritha.

VAISHAM·PÁYANA said:

When that best of the twice-born had gone off on some 306.1
other business, the girl wondered about the strength and
the weakness of her collection of mantras: "What kind of
mantra collection is this that the great-soul has given me?
I shall know its power before long." Thus preoccupied, she
saw that her period had started unexpectedly, and she was
ashamed to be young and menstruating and not yet married.

Then, seated in her palace on her usual magnificent bed,
she saw the solar disk rising in the eastern sky. And there 5
the woman with the wonderful waist was riveted, sight and
mind, but not consumed by the beauty of the sun in the
twilight of dawn.

Her sight became divine—she saw the god who seemed divine, dressed in armor, adorned with earrings. Yet, lord of men, she was curious about the mantra, and so, radiant woman, she invoked the god. Having cleansed her vital

Prāṇān upaspṛśya tadā hy ājuhāva divā|karam
ājagāma tato rājaṃs tvaramāṇo divā|karaḥ
Madhu|piṅgo mahā|bāhuḥ kambu|grīvo hasann iva
aṅgadī baddha|mukuṭo diśaḥ prajvālayann iva.
10 Yogāt kṛtvā dvidh'|ātmānam ājagāma tatāpa ca.
ābabhāṣe tataḥ Kuntīṃ sāmnā parama|valgunā:
«Āgato 'smi vaśaṃ bhadre tava mantra|balāt kṛtaḥ.
kiṃ karomy avaśo rājñi? brūhi! kartā tad asmi te.»

KUNTY uvāca:

«Gamyatāṃ bhagavaṃs tatra yata ev' âgato hy asi
kautūhalāt samāhūtaḥ prasīda bhagavann iti.»

SŪRYA uvāca:

«Gamiṣye 'haṃ yathā māṃ tvaṃ bravīṣi tanu|madhyame,
na tu devaṃ samāhūya nyāyyaṃ preṣayituṃ vṛthā.
Tav' âbhisaṃdhiḥ subhage sūryāt putro bhaved iti
vīryeṇ' âpratimo loke kavacī kuṇḍal" îti ca.
15 Sā tvam ātma|pradānaṃ vai kuruṣva gaja|gāmini,
utpatsyati hi putras te yathā|saṃkalpam aṅgane.
Atha gacchāmy ahaṃ bhadre tvayā saṃgamya susmite.
yadi tvaṃ vacanaṃ n' âdya kariṣyasi mama priyam
Śapiṣye tvām ahaṃ kruddho brāhmaṇaṃ pitaraṃ ca te.
tvat|kṛte tān pradhakṣyāmi sarvān api na saṃśayaḥ.
Pitaraṃ c' âiva te mūḍhaṃ yo na vetti tav' ânayam
tasya ca brāhmaṇasy' âdya yo 'sau mantram adāt tava
Śīla|vṛttam avijñāya dhāsyāmi vinayaṃ param.

breaths, she summoned the day-maker, and there, O king,
the Sun came, hurrying, honey-yellow, mighty-armed, neck
grooved like a conch, as though laughing; arm-braceleted,
crowned, as though kindling space. Since he had split him- 10
self in two through yoga, he both appeared there and went
on radiating; then he spoke to Kuntí in an extraordinarily
beautiful tone: "Through the power of your mantra, I have
come under your control, good lady. What wish, queen,
shall I make happen? Tell me, I shall do it for you willy-
nilly."

KUNTÍ said:

"Go back, lord, there from whence you came. Out of curiosity I invoked you. Be gracious, lord!"

The SUN said:

"I shall go, just as you have asked me, slender-waisted
woman. But, having invoked a god, it's not proper to dismiss
him in vain. Your purpose, pretty girl, was by the Sun to
have a son, peerless in the world for his heroism, wearing
armor and earrings. So, girl who sways like an elephant, give 15
yourself to me, and just as you wished, shapely woman, you
shall have a son.

Once I have lain with you, then I shall go, sweet-smiling girl. If today you don't graciously do what I ask, enraged, I shall curse you, your father and the brahmin. Be in no doubt, on your account I shall incinerate them all. And on your foolish father, who doesn't know of your bad behavior, and on the brahmin who gave you that spell today, ignorant of your character and conduct, I shall impose the severest discipline. For, led by Puran·dara, all these gods in heaven

ete hi vibudhāḥ sarve Puraṃdara|mukhā divi
20 Tvayā pralabdhaṃ paśyanti smayanta iva bhāmini.
paśya c' âinān sura|gaṇān, divyaṃ cakṣur idaṃ hi te
pūrvam eva mayā dattaṃ, dṛṣṭavaty asi yena mām.»

VAIŚAMPĀYANA uvāca:

Tato 'paśyat tridaśān rāja|putrī
sarvān eva sveṣu dhiṣṇyeṣu kha|sthān
prabhāvantaṃ bhānumantaṃ mahāntaṃ
yath" ādityaṃ rocamānāṃs tath" âiva ca.
Sā tān dṛṣṭvā vrīḍamān" âiva bālā
sūryaṃ devī vacanaṃ prāha bhītā:
«gaccha tvaṃ vai go|pate svaṃ vimānaṃ!
kanyā|bhāvād duḥkha ev' âpacāraḥ.
Pitā mātā guravaś c' âiva ye 'nye
dehasy' âsya prabhavanti pradāne.
n' âhaṃ dharmaṃ lopayiṣyāmi loke.
strīṇāṃ vṛttaṃ pūjyate deha|rakṣā.
Mayā mantra|balaṃ jñātum āhūtas tvaṃ vibhāvaso
bālyād. bāl" êti tat kṛtvā kṣantum arhasi me vibho.»

SŪRYA uvāca:

25 «Bāl" êti kṛtv" ânunayaṃ tav' âhaṃ
dadāni. n' âny" ânunayaṃ labheta.
ātma|pradānaṃ kuru Kunti kanye,
śāntis tav' âivaṃ hi bhavec ca bhīru.

see you deceive me, and they seem to be smiling, lady. Since 20
your eyesight is divine—I gave it you before, that's how you're seeing me—look at those troops of gods!"

VAISHAM·PÁYANA said:

Then the princess saw the gods,
All in their own orbs, standing in the sky,
Shining like the luminous, radiant, and eminent sun itself.
Seeing them, the girl, a goddess, was frightened
And, feeling ashamed, she spoke to the Sun: "Go,
Lord of rays, to your own carriage; because of my virginity,
Such impropriety is misery indeed.
Only my father, mother and other elders
Have the power to bestow this body.
In this world I shall not violate the law: the protection
Of women's bodies is an honored practice.

I invoked you who are bursting with light to learn the power of the spell. I am a young girl, I did it from childishness. Please, lord, forgive me."

The SUN said:

"It's because you did it like a child that I am kind to you. 25
Let me tell you: another would not be treated so kindly.
Make a gift of yourself, child Kuntí,
For in that way bliss may be yours, timid girl.

Na c' âpi yuktaṃ gantuṃ hi mayā mithyā|kṛtena vai
asametya tvayā bhīru mantr'|āhūtena bhāvini.
Gamiṣyāmy anavady'|âṅgi loke samavahāsyatām
sarveṣāṃ vibudhānāṃ ca vaktavyaḥ syāṃ tathā śubhe.
Sā tvaṃ mayā samāgaccha. putraṃ lapsyasi mā|dṛśam;
viśiṣṭā sarva|lokeṣu bhaviṣyasi, na saṃśayaḥ.»

VAIŚAMPĀYANA uvāca:

307.1 Sā tu kanyā bahu|vidhaṃ bruvantī madhuraṃ vacaḥ
anunetuṃ sahasr'|âṃśuṃ na śaśāka manasvinī.
Na śaśāka yadā bālā pratyākhyātuṃ tamo|nudam
bhītā śāpāt tato rājan dadhyau dīrgham ath' ântaram:
«An|āgasaḥ pituḥ śāpo brāhmaṇasya tath" âiva ca
man|nimittaḥ kathaṃ na syāt kruddhād asmād vibhāvasoḥ?
Bālen' âpi satā mohād bhṛśaṃ pāpa|kṛtāny api
n' âbhyāsādayitavyāni tejāṃsi ca tapāṃsi ca.
5 S" âham adya bhṛśaṃ bhītā gṛhītvā ca kare bhṛśam
kathaṃ tv akāryaṃ kuryāṃ vai pradānaṃ hy ātmanaḥ svaya

VAIŚAMPĀYANA uvāca:

Sā vai śāpa|paritrastā bahu cintayatī hṛdā
mohen' âbhiparīt'|âṅgī smayamānā punaḥ punaḥ
Taṃ devam abravīd bhītā bandhūnāṃ rāja|sattama
vrīḍā|vihvalayā vācā śāpa|trastā viśāṃ pate:

KUNTY uvāca:

«Pitā me dhriyate deva mātā c' ânye ca bāndhavāḥ
na teṣu dhriyamāṇeṣu vidhi|lopo bhaved ayam.
Tvayā me saṃgamo deva yadi syād vidhi|varjitaḥ
man|nimittaṃ kulasy' âsya loke kīrtir naśet tataḥ.

Beautiful, bashful woman, invoked by you with spells, it would be wrong of me to go without lying with you, with nothing achieved. Girl with a perfect body, in this world I shall be laughed at, and then, beautiful girl, I would be the talk of all the gods. So couple with me, and you will get a son just like me. You will be distinguished in every world; don't doubt it."

VAISHAM·PÁYANA said:

Although her words were sweet and many, that clever girl 307.1
could not sway the thousand-rayed Sun. And when the girl
could not dissuade the darkness-dispeller, she pondered,
for a long time, my king, afraid of the curse: "How can
my blameless father and the brahmin avoid the curse of
the angry Sun, brought on by me? Energies and powers, let
alone evil deeds, shouldn't be rashly entertained by someone
good, child or not. I have been grasped by the hand with 5
ardor, and now I am terribly afraid: how can I do what
shouldn't be done—give myself away?"

VAISHAM·PÁYANA continued:

Terrified by the curse, her body racked by confusion, her thoughts were racing, but she kept on smiling. Afraid for her relatives, scared by the curse, she addressed that god in a voice distorted by shame, best of kings, lord of the people.

KUNTÍ said:

"God, my father survives, as does my mother, and other relatives too. This violation of the rule should not occur while they are alive. If, god, you lie with me, against the rule, then this family's name throughout the world will be

10 Atha vā dharmam etaṃ tvaṃ manyase tapatāṃ vara
ṛte pradānād bandhubhyas tava kāmaṃ karomy aham.
Ātma|pradānaṃ durdharṣa tava kṛtvā satī tv aham.
tvayi dharmo yaśaś c' âiva kīrtir āyuś ca dehinām.»

Sūrya uvāca:

«Na te pitā na te mātā guravo vā śuci|smite
prabhavanti var'|ārohe, bhadraṃ te! śṛṇu me vacaḥ.
Sarvān kāmayate yasmāt kaner dhātoś ca bhāvini
tasmāt kany" êha suśroṇi sva|tantrā vara|varṇini.
N' âdharmaś caritaḥ kaś cit tvayā bhavati bhāvini.
adharmaṃ kuta ev' âhaṃ careyaṃ loka|kāmyayā?
15 Anāvṛtāḥ striyaḥ sarvā narāś ca varavarṇini,
svabhāva eṣa lokānāṃ vikāro 'nya iti smṛtaḥ.
Sā mayā saha saṃgamya punaḥ kanyā bhaviṣyasi
putraś ca te mahā|bāhur bhaviṣyati mahā|yaśāḥ.»

Kunty uvāca:

«Yadi putro mama bhavet tvattaḥ sarva|tamo|nuda
kuṇḍalī kavacī śūro mahā|bāhur mahā|balaḥ.»

Sūrya uvāca:

«Bhaviṣyati mahā|bāhuḥ kuṇḍalī divya|varma|bhṛt
ubhayaṃ c' âmṛta|mayaṃ tasya bhadre bhaviṣyati.»

destroyed because of me. But if you think this is the Law, 10
best of those that burn, I shall do as you desire, without being bestowed by my relatives. Making you the gift of myself, dreadful being, I shall be virtuous still. The Law, fame, reputation, and the life span of the embodied—they are in you."

The SUN said:

"Neither your father, nor your mother, nor elders, sweet-smiling, fair-hipped girl, have such power. Good fortune be yours! Listen to me: beautiful, fair-hipped girl, in this world an independent girl, a virgin, is called *"kanyā,"* from the verbal root *kan*,* because she desires them all. Beautiful girl, you do nothing unlawful at all; and how can I, out
of love for the world, transgress? All men and women are 15
free, fair-hipped girl; such is the nature of things: anything else is a perversion of nature. Once you have lain with me, you'll be a virgin still, and your son will be mighty-armed and most glorious."

KUNTÍ said:

"If I have a son from you, dispeller of darkness, may he be earringed and armored, a great-armed hugely strong hero!"

The SUN said:

"Mighty-armed he shall be, dear lady, earringed and wearing divine armor, and both made of the essence of immortality."

KUNTY uvāca:

«Yady etad amṛtād asti kuṇḍale varma c' ôttamam
mama putrasya yaṃ vai tvaṃ matta utpādayiṣyasi
20 Astu me saṃgamo deva yath"|ôktaṃ bhagavaṃs tvayā,
tvadvīrya|rūpa|sattv'|âujā dharma|yukto bhavet sa ca.»

SŪRYA uvāca:

«Adityā kuṇḍale rājñi datte me matta|kāśini
te âsya dāsyāmi vai bhīru varma c' âiv' êdam uttamam.»

PṚTHĀ uvāca:

«Paramaṃ bhagavann evaṃ saṃgamiṣye tvayā saha
yadi putro bhaved evaṃ yathā vadasi go|pate.»

VAIŚAMPĀYANA uvāca:

«Tath" êty» uktvā tu tāṃ Kuntīm āviveśa vihaṃ|gamaḥ
svarbhānu|śatrur yog'|ātmā nābhyāṃ pasparśa c' âiva tām.
Tataḥ sā vihval" êv' āsīt kanyā sūryasya tejasā
papāt' âtha ca sā devī śayane mūḍha|cetanā.

SŪRYA uvāca:

25 «Sādhayiṣyāmi suśroṇi. putraṃ vai janayiṣyasi
sarva|śastra|bhṛtāṃ śreṣṭhaṃ, kanyā c' âiva bhaviṣyasi.»

VAIŚAMPĀYANA uvāca:

Tataḥ sā vrīḍitā bālā tadā sūryam ath' âbravīt:
«evam astv iti» rāj'|êndra prasthitaṃ bhūri|varcasam.

Kuntí said:

"If the earrings and ultimate armor of the son you father on me are made from the essence of immortality, then let me lie with you, god, as your lordship suggests. May he, like you, be heroic and handsome, powerful, energetic and inseparable from the Law."

The Sun said:

"Áditi gave me these earrings, Queen, and I shall give them to him, shy enchantress, along with this supreme armor."

Pritha said:

"In that case, lord, if my son shall turn out just as you say, I shall lie with you, Lord of rays."

Vaisham·páyana said:

With a cry of "So be it!," the sky-goer, yoga personified, Svar·bhanu's enemy, entered Kuntí and touched her to the navel. And that girl-queen, convulsed, it seemed, by the Sun's energy, fell stupefied on her bed.

The Sun said:

"I shall leave now, fair-hipped woman. You shall give birth to a son, of all weapon-wielders the foremost, and you shall remain a virgin."

Vaisham·páyana said:

Then, Indra of kings, the girl called bashfully, to the Sun, so splendid, as he departed: "May it be so!"

Iti sm' ôktā Kunti|rāj'|ātma|jā
sā vivasvantaṃ yācamānā salajjā
tasmin puṇye śayanīye papāta
moh'|āviṣṭā bhajyamānā lat" êva.
Tigm'|âṃśus tāṃ tejasā mohayitvā
yogen' āviśy' ātma|saṃsthāṃ cakāra.
na c' âiv' âināṃ dūṣayām āsa bhānuḥ
saṃjñāṃ lebhe bhūya ev' âtha bālā.

VAIŚAṂPĀYANA uvāca:

308.1 Tato garbhaḥ samabhavat Pṛthāyāḥ pṛthivī|pate
śukle daś'|ôttare pakṣe tārā|patir iv' âmbare.
Sā bāndhava|bhayād bālā garbhaṃ taṃ vinigūhatī
dhārayām āsa suśroṇī na c' âināṃ bubudhe janaḥ.
Na hi tāṃ veda nāry anyā kā cid dhātreyikām ṛte
kanyā|pura|gatāṃ bālāṃ nipuṇāṃ parirakṣaṇe.
Tataḥ kālena sā garbhaṃ suṣuve vara|varṇinī
kany" âiva tasya devasya prasādād amara|prabham.
5 Tath" âiv' ābaddha|kavacaṃ kanak'|ôjjvala|kuṇḍalam
hary|akṣaṃ vṛṣabha|skandhaṃ yath" âsya pitaraṃ tathā.
Jāta|mātraṃ ca taṃ garbhaṃ dhātryā saṃmantrya bhāvin
mañjūṣāyām samādhāya svāstīrṇāyāṃ samantataḥ
Madh'|ûcchiṣṭa|sthitāyāṃ sā sukhāyāṃ rudatī tathā
ślakṣṇāyāṃ supidhānāyām Aśva|nadyām avāsṛjat.
Jānatī c' âpy akartavyaṃ kanyāyā garbha|dhāraṇam
putra|snehena sā rājan karuṇaṃ paryadevayat.
Samutsṛjantī mañjūṣām Aśva|nadyās tadā jale
uvāca rudatī Kuntī yāni vākyāni tac chṛṇu!

Addressed in that way when, bashfully, she solicited
the Sun,
The daughter of King Kunti, full of confusion,
Flopped on that fair bed, like a broken shoot.
Hot-rayed, the Sun, stupefied her with his luster,
Entered her by yoga, and gave her a child.
But the Sun did not defile her, and the girl became
conscious again.

VAISHAM·PÁYANA said:

Then, as the moon grows in the sky in the bright half 308.1
of the tenth month, so, lord of the earth, a child grew in
Pritha. From fear of her relatives, that fair-hipped girl hid
her pregnancy—she carried it secretly. For apart from the
wet nurse, no other women knew about that girl, protecting
herself cleverly, living in the quarters allocated to virgins.

Then, in time, that beautiful, unmarried girl gave birth,
by the grace of the god, to a child like an immortal. He was 5
strapped into a coat of mail, his earrings were luminous gold,
he was as yellow-eyed and bull-shouldered as his father.

And as soon as that child had been born, the beautiful girl, having talked with her nurse, placed him in a roomy basket, comfortable and soft, sealed with beeswax, securely fastened; and, weeping, she launched it on the River Ashva. And although she knew it was proscribed for an unmarried girl to bear a child, she wept pitifully, O king, for love of her son. Then, pushing the basket out onto the waters of the Ashva, Kuntí spoke these words through her tears—listen!

10 «Svasti te c' ântarikṣebhyaḥ pārthivebhyaś ca putraka
divyebhyaś c' âiva bhūtebhyas tathā toyacarāś ca ye.
Śivās te santu panthāno mā ca te pari|panthinaḥ,
āgatāś ca tathā putra bhavantv adroha|cetasaḥ.
Pātu tvāṃ Varuṇo rājā salile salil'|êśvaraḥ
antarikṣe 'ntarikṣa|sthaḥ pavanaḥ sarvagas tathā.
Pitā tvāṃ pātu sarvatra tapanas tapatāṃ varaḥ
yena datto 'si me putra divyena vidhinā kila.
Ādityā Vasavo Rudrāḥ Sādhyā viśve ca devatāḥ
Marutaś ca sah' Êndreṇa diśaś ca sa|dig|īśvarāḥ
15 Rakṣantu tvāṃ surāḥ sarve sameṣu viṣameṣu ca.
vetsyāmi tvāṃ videśe 'pi kavacen' âbhisūcitam.

Dhanyas te putra janako devo bhānur vibhāvasuḥ
yas tvāṃ drakṣyati divyena cakṣuṣā vāhinī|gatam.
Dhanyā sā pramadā yā tvāṃ putratve kalpayiṣyati.
yasyās tvaṃ tṛṣitaḥ putra stanaṃ pāsyasi deva|ja.
Ko nu svapnas tayā dṛṣṭo yā tvām āditya|varcasam
divya|varma|samāyuktaṃ divya|kuṇḍala|bhūṣitam
Padmā'|āyata|viśāl'|âkṣaṃ padma|tāmra|dal'|ôjjvalam
su|lalāṭaṃ su|keś'|ântaṃ putratve kalpayiṣyati?
20 Dhanyā drakṣyanti putra tvāṃ bhūmau saṃsarpamāṇakam
avyakta|kala|vākyāni vadantaṃ reṇu|guṇṭhitam.
Dhanyā drakṣyanti putra tvāṃ punar yauvana|gocaram
Himavad|vana|saṃbhūtaṃ siṃhaṃ kesariṇaṃ yathā.»

"May the creatures of sky, earth and heaven, and those that live in the water, protect you, my little boy. May your roads be auspicious, and nothing stand in your path. And let those who encounter you, my son, have minds without malice. King Váruna, lord of the waters, protect you in water; so, in the sky, may the airy wind, which goes to all quarters, protect you. And may the Sun, best of burners, your father—who certainly gave me you by the will of the gods—protect you, my son. May the Adítyas, Vasus, Rudras, Sadhyas, the All-Gods, the Maruts with Indra, and the directions with their lords, and all the celestials protect you, through the rough and the smooth. By your singular armor I shall know you, even in a foreign land.

Happy your father, the wide-shining sun-god, who, with his divine eye, shall follow you, my son, floating downriver. Happy that woman who shall adopt you as son, from whose breast, thirsting, you, a god's son, shall drink. What vision has she dreamed, she who shall adopt you her child—you as bright as the sun, dressed in armor and earrings from heaven, eyes wide and lotus-long—you who are as beautiful as the copper-petalled lotus, and have a fine brow and beautiful hair? Happy they who shall see you, my son, crawling on the earth, uttering sweet, garbled words, and covered in dust. Happy again those who shall see you, my son, in the prime of your youth, like a maned lion from the Himálayan forest."

Evaṃ bahu|vidhaṃ rājan vilapya karuṇaṃ Pṛthā
avāsṛjata mañjūṣām Aśva|nadyāṃ tadā jale
Rudatī putra|śok'|ārtā niśīthe kamal"|ēkṣaṇā
dhātryā saha Pṛthā rājan putra|darśana|lālasā.
Visarjayitvā mañjūṣāṃ saṃbodhana|bhayāt pituḥ
viveśa rāja|bhavanaṃ punaḥ śok'|āturā tataḥ.
25 Mañjūṣā tv Aśva|nadyāḥ sā yayau Carmaṇvatīṃ nadīm
Carmaṇvatyāś ca Yamunāṃ tato Gaṅgāṃ jagāma ha.
Gaṅgāyāḥ sūta|viṣayaṃ Campām anuyayau purīm
sa mañjūṣā|gato garbhas taraṅgair uhyamānakaḥ.
Amṛtād utthitaṃ divyaṃ tanu|varma sa|kuṇḍalam
dhārayām āsa taṃ garbhaṃ daivaṃ ca vidhi|nirmitam.

VAIŚAMPĀYANA uvāca:

309.1 Etasminn eva kāle tu Dhṛtarāṣṭrasya vai sakhā
Sūto 'dhiratha ity eva sadāro Jāhnavīṃ yayau.
Tasya bhāry" âbhavad rājan rūpeṇ' âsadṛśī bhuvi
Rādhā nāma mahā|bhāgā; na sā putram avindata.
Apaty'|ârthe paraṃ yatnam akaroc ca viśeṣataḥ.
sā dadarś' âtha mañjūṣām uhyamānāṃ yad|ṛcchayā
Datta|rakṣā|pratisarām anvālambhana|śobhitām
ūrmī|taraṅgair Jāhnavyāḥ samānītām upahvaram.
5 Sā tāṃ kautūhalāt prāptāṃ grāhayām āsa bhāminī,
tato nivedayām āsa sūtasy' Adhirathasya vai.
Sa tām uddhṛtya mañjūṣām utsārya jalam antikāt
yantrair udghāṭayām āsa; so 'paśyat tatra bālakam
Taruṇ'|âditya|saṃkāśaṃ hema|varma|dharaṃ tathā

So, king, lamenting pitifully in all kinds of ways, Pritha, with her nurse, launched the basket onto the waters of the Ashva River, in the middle of the night—Pritha, sick with grief for her son, weeping from lotus eyes, yearning for a glimpse of her boy.

Once the basket was launched, fearful of awakening her father, and sick with sorrow, she reentered the royal palace.
But the basket floated from the River Ashva into the River 25
Charmánvati, and from the Charmánvati into the Yámuna, and so down to the Ganga. Borne by the waves of the Ganga, the child in the basket journeyed on to the city of Champa, the home of the *suta**—so that child was preserved, with his godly armor and earrings sprung from the heavenly elixir, by his preordained fate.

VAISHAM·PÁYANA said:

At that very time, a friend of Dhrita·rashtra, a *suta* called 309.1
Ádhiratha, went with his wife to the Jáhnavi River. His wife, a noble lady called Radha, had no earthly equal in beauty, my king; but even though she had tried her utmost to have children, she had never had a son. Then, by chance, she saw the floating basket, protected by amulets and fitted with a handle: erratically, the motion of the Jáhnavi's waves carried it toward her.

Curious, the beautiful woman had it caught and secured, 5
and then informed the *suta* Ádhiratha. He lifted the basket and removed it from the water; using tools, he opened it and saw the little boy, like the new-risen sun, in golden armor, with a face framed by polished earrings, most royal. Together with his wife, the *suta*'s eyes widened in wonder, and, lifting that child onto his lap, said to his wife:

mṛṣṭa|kuṇḍala|yuktena vadanena virājatā.
Sa Sūto bhāryayā sārdhaṃ vismay'|ôtphulla|locanaḥ
aṅkam āropya taṃ bālaṃ bhāryāṃ vacanam abravīt:
«Idam atyadbhutaṃ bhīru yato jāto 'smi bhāvini
dṛṣṭavān; deva|garbho 'yaṃ manye 'smān samupāgataḥ.
10 Anapatyasya putro 'yaṃ devair datto dhruvaṃ mama»
ity uktvā taṃ dadau putraṃ Rādhāyai sa mahī|pate.
Pratijagrāha taṃ Rādhā vidhivad divya|rūpiṇam
putraṃ kamala|garbh'|ābhaṃ deva|garbhaṃ śriyā vṛtam.
Puposa c' âinaṃ vidhivad vavṛdhe sa ca vīryavān,
tataḥ prabhṛti c' âpy anye prābhavann aurasāḥ sutāḥ.
Vasu|varma|dharaṃ dṛṣṭvā taṃ bālaṃ hema|kuṇḍalam
nāmāsya Vasuṣeṇ' êti tataś cakrur dvi|jātayaḥ.
Evaṃ sa sūta|putratvaṃ jagām' âmita|vikramaḥ
Vasuṣeṇa iti khyāto Vṛṣa ity eva ca prabhuḥ.
15 Sūtasya vavṛdhe 'ṅgeṣu śreṣṭha|putraḥ sa vīryavān.
cāreṇa viditaś c' āsīt Pṛthayā divya|varma|bhṛt.
Sūtas tv Adhirathaḥ putraṃ vivṛddhaṃ samayena tam
dṛṣṭvā prasthāpayām āsa puraṃ vāraṇa|s'|āhvayam.
Tatr' ôpasadanaṃ cakre Droṇasy' êṣv|astra|karmaṇi
sakhyaṃ Duryodhanen' âivam agacchat sa ca vīryavān.
Droṇāt Kṛpāc ca Rāmāc ca so 'stra|grāmaṃ catur|vidham
labdhvā loke 'bhavat khyātaḥ param'|êṣv|āsatāṃ gataḥ.
Saṃdhāya Dhārtarāṣṭreṇa Pārthānāṃ vipriye sthitaḥ
yoddhum āśaṃsate nityaṃ Phalgunena mah"|ātmanā.
20 Sadā hi tasya spardh" āsīd Arjunena viśāṃ pate
Arjunasya ca Karṇena yato dṛṣṭo babhūva saḥ.

"Shy beauty, in my whole life this is the greatest wonder I have seen; I think this is the child of a god that has come to us. Surely this son was given to me, who am childless, by the gods." With these words, lord of the earth, he gave the child to Radha.

As ordained, Radha adopted that divine-looking child, bright as a lotus cup, the child of a god, covered with fortune. She duly raised him, and he grew up strong. And from then on she had further sons of her own. Seeing that child wearing valuable armor and golden earrings, the twice-born called him "Vasu·shena".* Thus one whose strength was boundless became the son of a *suta*, and came to be called Vasu·shena, as well as Vrisha. The first son of the *suta* grew up with power in his limbs; and through a spy, Pritha learned that he was wearing divine armor.

And the *suta* Ádhiratha, having, in time, seen his son grow up, sent him to the city named after the elephant.* There he approached Drona to learn archery, and in this way the powerful man became friendly with Duryódhana. Obtaining the fourfold weapons' collection from Drona, Kripa and Rama, he became famous in this world as a great bowman. Having allied himself with Dhrita·rashtra's son, he was intent on being hostile to the Parthas; he always hoped to fight with great-souled Phálguna. For, lord of the people, he was always in competition with Árjuna, as was Árjuna with Karna, from the moment he saw him.

Etad guhyaṃ mahā|rāja sūryasy' āsin, na saṃśayaḥ:
yaḥ sūrya|sambhavaḥ Karṇaḥ Kuntyāṃ sūta|kule tathā.
Taṃ tu kuṇḍalinaṃ dṛṣṭvā varmaṇā ca samanvitam
avadhyaṃ samare matvā paryatapyad Yudhiṣṭhiraḥ.
Yadā tu Karṇo rājendra bhānumantaṃ divā|karam
stauti madhyaṃ|dine prāpte prāñjaliḥ salil'|ôtthitaḥ
Tatr' âinam upatiṣṭhanti brāhmaṇā dhana|hetunā
n' âdeyaṃ tasya tat|kāle kiṃ cid asti dvi|jātiṣu.
25 Tam Indro brāhmaṇo bhūtvā «bhikṣāṃ deh' îty» upasthitaḥ
«svāgataṃ c' êti» Rādheyas tam atha pratyabhāṣata.

VAIŚAMPĀYANA uvāca:

310.1 Deva|rājam anuprāptaṃ brāhmaṇa|cchadmanā Vṛtaṃ*
dṛṣṭvā: «svāgatam ity» āha; na bubodh' âsya mānasam.
«Hiraṇya|kaṇṭhīḥ pramadā grāmān vā bahu|go|kulān
kiṃ dadān' îti»? taṃ vipram uvāc' Adhirathis tataḥ.

BRĀHMAṆA uvāca:

«Hiraṇya|kaṇṭhyaḥ pramadā yac cānyat prīti|vardhanam
n' âhaṃ dattam ih' êcchāmi: tad|arthibhyaḥ pradīyatām.
Yad etat saha|jaṃ varma kuṇḍale ca tav' ânagha
etad utkṛtya me dehi yadi satya|vrato bhavān.
5 Etad icchāmy ahaṃ kṣipraṃ tvayā dattaṃ paraṃ|tapa.
eṣa me sarva|lābhānāṃ lābhaḥ paramako mataḥ.»

Without a doubt, this was the Sun's secret, great king: Karna, begotten by the Sun on Kuntí, was now in the *suta*'s family. And seeing him wearing earrings and in armor, Yudhi·shthira supposed him invincible in battle, and he was very troubled. And, king of kings, when Karna praised the radiant sun at midday, risen from the water with folded hands, brahmins came up to him there, in pursuit of wealth, since at that time there was nothing he would not give to the
twice-born. So Indra became a brahmin and approached 25
him saying: "Give me alms!," and Radhéya replied: "You are welcome."

VAISHAM·PÁYANA said:

On seeing the king of the gods concealed by disguise as 310.1
a brahmin, he said "Welcome;" he did not know what was in his mind. Ádhiratha's son asked the brahmin: "What am I to give? Beautiful women with golden necklaces? Or villages with many herds of cattle?"

The BRAHMIN said:

"I don't want a gift of beautiful women with golden necklaces, or anything else to enhance pleasure. Give them to those who want such things. If you are a man of your word, cut off your earrings and the armor you were born with,
and give them to me, blameless man. I want you to give me 5
this quickly, incinerator of the foe; I think it the greatest gift among gifts."

KARṆA uvāca:

«Avaniṃ pramadā gāś ca nirvāpaṃ bahu|vārṣikam
tat te vipra pradāsyāmi na tu varma sa|kuṇḍalam.»

VAIŚAMPĀYANA uvāca:

Evaṃ bahu|vidhair vākyair yācyamānaḥ sa tu dvijaḥ
Karṇena Bharata|śreṣṭha n' ânyaṃ varam ayācata.
Sāntvitaś ca yathā|śakti pūjitaś ca yathā|vidhi
na c' ânyaṃ sa dvija|śreṣṭhaḥ kāmayām āsa vai varam.
Yadā n' ânyaṃ pravṛṇute varaṃ vai dvija|sattamaḥ
tad" âinam abravīd bhūyo Rādheyaḥ prahasann iva:
10 «Saha|jaṃ varma me vipra kuṇḍale c' âmṛt'|ôdbhave,
ten' âvadhyo 'smi lokeṣu, tato n' âitaj jahāmy aham.
Viśālaṃ pṛthivī|rājyaṃ kṣemaṃ nihata|kaṇṭakam
pratigṛhṇīṣva mattas tvaṃ sādhu brāhmaṇa|puṃgava.
Kuṇḍalābhyāṃ vimukto 'haṃ varmaṇā saha|jena ca
gamanīyo bhaviṣyāmi śatrūṇāṃ dvija|sattama.»

VAIŚAMPĀYANA uvāca:

Yad" ânyaṃ na varaṃ vavre bhagavān Pāka|śāsanaḥ
tataḥ prahasya Karṇas taṃ punar ity abravīd vacaḥ:
«Vidito deva|dev'|ēśa prāg ev' āsi mama prabho.
na tu nyāyyaṃ mayā dātuṃ tava śakyaṃ vṛthā varam.
15 Tvaṃ hi dev'|ēśvaraḥ sākṣāt tvayā deyo varo mama
anyeṣāṃ c' âiva bhūtānām īśvaro hy asi bhūta|kṛt.
Yadi dāsyāmi te deva kuṇḍale kavacaṃ tathā
vadhyatām upayāsyāmi tvaṃ ca Śakr' âvahāsyatām.
Tasmād vinimayaṃ kṛtvā kuṇḍale varma c' ôttamam
harasva Śakra kāmaṃ me; na dadyām aham anyathā.»

KARNA said:

"I will give you land, women, cattle and offerings for many years, but not earrings and armor, brahmin."

VAISHAM·PÁYANA said:

In this way Karna appealed to the brahmin with many kinds of words, best of the Bharatas, but he chose no other gift. Although appeased as much as possible, and honored in line with the rules, that best of brahmins desired no other gift. Since the foremost brahmin chose no other gift, Radhéya, smiling, spoke to him again:

"Brahmin, the armor I was born with, and the earrings, 10
came from the essence of immortality. For that reason, there is nowhere in the universe where I can be killed, so I will not give them up. Good bull of a brahmin, take from me my wide kingdom on earth, safe and cleared of foes. Parted from my earrings and the armor that was born with me, I shall be vulnerable to my enemies, best of brahmins."

VAISHAM·PÁYANA said:

When the lord, the punisher of Paka, did not choose another gift, smiling, Karna addressed him again:

"Lord! Lord god of gods, you were already known to me. But it would not be right for me to give you a gift for
nothing. Since you are manifestly the lord of the gods, the 15
creator of creatures, and the lord of all beings, you should give me a gift. If, god, I give you the earrings and armor, I shall become vulnerable, and you, Shakra, will be laughed at. Therefore reciprocate first, Shakra, and then take my earrings and supreme armor, as you wish. Otherwise, I cannot give."

Śakra uvāca:

«Vidito 'haṃ raveḥ pūrvam āyann* eva tav' ântikam,
tena te sarvam ākhyātam, evam etan na saṃśayaḥ.
Kāmam astu tathā tāta tava Karṇa yath' êcchasi.
varjayitvā tu me vajraṃ pravṛṇīṣva yath' êcchasi!»

Vaiśaṃpāyana uvāca:

20 Tataḥ Karṇaḥ prahṛṣṭas tu upasaṃgamya Vāsavam
amoghāṃ śaktim abhyetya vavre sampūrṇa|mānasaḥ.

Karṇa uvāca:

«Varmaṇā kuṇḍalābhyāṃ ca śaktiṃ me dehi Vāsava
amoghāṃ śatru|saṃghānāṃ ghātanīṃ pṛtanā|mukhe.»
Tataḥ saṃcintya manasā muhūrtam iva Vāsavaḥ
śakty|arthaṃ pṛthivī|pāla Karṇaṃ vākyam ath" âbravīt:
«Kuṇḍale me prayacchasva varma c' âiva śarīra|jam
gṛhāṇa Karṇa śaktiṃ tvam anena samayena me.
Amoghā hanti śataśaḥ śatrūn mama kara|cyutā
punaś ca pāṇim abhyeti mama daityān vinighnataḥ.
25 S" êyaṃ tava kara|prāptā hatv" âikaṃ ripum ūrjitam
garjantaṃ pratapantaṃ ca mām ev' âiṣyati sūta|ja.»

Karṇa uvāca:

«Ekam ev' âham icchāmi ripuṃ hantuṃ mahā|have
garjantaṃ pratapantaṃ ca yato mama bhayaṃ bhavet.»

SHAKRA said:

"From the Sun you knew that I was coming in advance—without a doubt, he told you everything. So, young Karna, wish according to your desire: with the exception of my thunderbolt, choose what you want."

VAISHAM·PÁYANA said:

Thrilled, Karna then approached Vásava, and 20
with a full heart chose the unerring spear.

KARNA said:

"Vásava, for the armor and the earrings, give me the unerring spear that kills hosts of enemies on the battlefield."

Then, ruler of the earth, as though considering in his mind for a moment, Vásava said this to Karna with regard to the spear:

"Give me the earrings and the armor that was born with you, and you, Karna, take the spear—on this condition: Flung from my hand, my unerring spear kills enemies by the hundreds, as I demolish the *daityas*; then it returns to my
hand. From your hand, once it has killed a single powerful, 25
roaring and burning enemy, it will come back to me, son of the *suta*."

KARNA said:

"All I want is to kill in a great battle just the one roaring and burning enemy, who would endanger me."

INDRA uvāca:

«Ekaṃ haniṣyasi ripuṃ garjantaṃ balinaṃ raṇe
tvaṃ tu yaṃ prārthayasy ekaṃ rakṣyate sa mah"|ātmanā.
Yam āhur Veda|vidvāṃso varāham aparājitaṃ
Nārāyaṇam acintyaṃ ca, tena Kṛṣṇena rakṣyate.»

KARṆA uvāca:

«Evam apy astu bhagavann eka|vīra|vadhe mama
amoghā. dehi me śaktiṃ yathā hanyāṃ pratāpinam.
30 Utkṛtya tu pradāsyāmi kuṇḍale kavacaṃ ca te
nikṛtteṣu tu gātreṣu na me bībhatsatā bhavet.»

INDRA uvāca:

«Na te bībhatsatā Karṇa bhaviṣyati kathaṃ cana
vraṇaś c' âiva na gātreṣu yas tvaṃ n' ânṛtam icchasi.
Yādṛśas te pitur varṇas tejaś ca vadatāṃ vara
tādṛśen' âiva varṇena tvaṃ Karṇa bhavitā punaḥ.
Vidyamāneṣu śastreṣu yady amoghām asaṃśaye
pramatto mokṣyase c' âpi tvayy ev' âiṣā patiṣyati.»

KARṆA uvāca:

«Saṃśayaṃ paramaṃ prāpya vimokṣye Vāsavīm imām
yathā māṃ āttha Śakra tvaṃ; satyam etad bravīmi te.»

VAIŚAṂPĀYANA uvāca:

35 Tataḥ śaktiṃ prajvalitāṃ pratigṛhya viśāṃ pate
śastraṃ gṛhītvā niśitaṃ sarva|gātrāṇy akṛntata.

INDRA said:

"You shall kill one roaring, powerful enemy in battle, but the very one you want* is protected by the great soul, whom those who know the Veda call invincible Boar, and inconceivable Naráyana—he is protected by him, by Krishna."

KARNA said:

"Even so, lord, let it unerringly kill a single hero for me.
Give me the spear so I may destroy the burning one. I shall 30
cut off the earrings and armor, and give them to you. But when I have flayed my limbs, save me from being repulsive."

INDRA said:

"Karna, you, who want nothing to do with lies, will not be in the least repulsive, and your limbs will show no blemish. The color and energy of your father shall again be your color, Karna, greatest of orators. But if, when you can make do with other weapons, you carelessly release the unerring spear, it will for certain fall on you."

KARNA said:

"Just as you instruct me, Shakra, I shall release Indra's spear only when facing the greatest danger. I am telling you the truth."

VAISHAM·PÁYANA said:

Then, lord of the people, having accepted the blazing 35
spear, he took his sharpened sword and flayed all of his limbs.

Tato devā mānavā dānavāś ca
nikṛntantaṃ Karṇam ātmānam evam
dṛṣṭvā sarve siṃha|nādān praṇedur,
na hy asy' āsīn muḥkhajo vai vikāraḥ.
Tato divyā dundubhayaḥ praṇeduḥ
papāt' ôccaiḥ puṣpa|varṣaṃ ca divyam
dṛṣṭvā Karṇaṃ śastra|saṃkṛtta|gātraṃ
muhuś c' âpi smayamānaṃ nṛ|vīram.
Tataś chitvā kavacaṃ divyam aṅgāt
tath" âiv" ārdraṃ pradadau Vāsavāya
tath" ôtkṛtya pradadau kuṇḍale te
karṇāt tasmāt karmaṇā tena «Karṇaḥ»
Tataḥ Śakraḥ prahasan vañcayitvā
Karṇaṃ loke yaśasā yojayitvā,
kṛtaṃ kāryaṃ Pāṇḍavānāṃ hi mene,
tataḥ paścād divam ev' ôtpapāta.
40 Śrutvā Karṇaṃ muṣitaṃ Dhārtarāṣṭrā dīnāḥ
sarve bhagna|darpā iv' âsan.
tāṃ c' âvasthāṃ gamitaṃ sūta|putraṃ
śrutvā Pārthā jahṛṣuḥ kānana|sthāḥ.

JANAMEJAYA uvāca:

Kva|sthā vīrāḥ Pāṇḍavās te babhūvuḥ?
kutaś c' âite śrutavantaḥ priyaṃ tat?
kiṃ v" âkārṣur dvādaśe 'bde vyatīte?
tan me sarvaṃ bhagavān vyākarotu.

And when the gods, men and *dánava*s
Saw Karna flaying himself in that way,
They roared a lion's roar,
For the expression of his face did not change.
Then at the sight of Karna,
Whose limbs had been flayed by his own sword,
Still smiling incessantly, a hero among men,
Celestial drums were beaten,
And a celestial rain of flowers poured from above.
His divine armor cut from his body,
He gave it still wet to Vásava;
And cutting off his earrings, he gave those too.
And from this deed involving his ear, He is "Karna."*
So Shakra, having made Karna famous throughout the world,
But having deceived him, smiled since he thought
He had saved the Pándavas.
And so he flew back to heaven.
Hearing that Karna had been robbed,
The sons of Dhrita·rashtra
All became depressed, as though their pride had been broken.
And hearing of that state the son of the *suta* had been reduced to,
The sons of Pritha, living in the forest, rejoiced.

JANAM·EJAYA said:

Where were those Pándava heroes living,
And from whom did they hear this good news?
What did they do once the twelfth year had passed?
Tell me all of it, lord.

Vaiśaṃpāyana uvāca:
Labdhvā Kṛṣṇāṃ Saindhavaṃ drāvayitvā
vipraiḥ sārdhaṃ Kāmyakād* āśramāt te
Mārkaṇḍeyāc chrutavantaḥ purāṇaṃ
deva'|rṣīṇāṃ caritaṃ vistareṇa
Pratyājagmuḥ sarathāḥ sānuyātrāḥ
sarvaiḥ sārdhaṃ sūda|paurogavaiś ca
tataḥ puṇyaṃ Dvaitavanaṃ nṛ|vīrā
nistīry' ôgraṃ vanavāsaṃ samagram.*

VAISHAM·PÁYANA said:

Once the Sáindhava had been put to flight
And they had rescued Krishná;
Once they had heard in detail from Markandéya
About the ancient deeds of gods and seers,
Those heroes among men, with their priests,
Their chariots, their retinue,
With all their cooks and kitchen inspectors,
Returned from the Kámyaka hermitage to fair
  Dvaita·vana,*
Their cruel term in the forest entirely discharged.

3.311–315
ABOUT THE DRILLING STICKS

JANAMEJAYA uvāca:

311.1 EVAṂ HṚTĀYĀṂ BHĀRYĀYĀṂ prāpya kleśam anuttamam
pratipadya tataḥ Kṛṣṇāṃ kim akurvata Pāṇḍavāḥ?

VAIŚAṂPĀYANA uvāca:

Evaṃ hṛtāyāṃ Kṛṣṇāyāṃ prāpya kleśam anuttamam
vihāya Kāmyakaṃ rājā saha bhrātṛbhir Acyutaḥ
Punar Dvaitavanaṃ ramyam ājagāma Yudhiṣṭhiraḥ
svādu|mūla|phalaṃ ramyaṃ vicitrabahupādapam.
Anubhukta|phal'|āhārāḥ sarva eva mit'|âśanāḥ
nyavasan Pāṇḍavās tatra Kṛṣṇayā saha bhāryayā.
5 Vasan Dvaitavane rājā Kuntī|putro Yudhiṣṭhiraḥ
Bhīmaseno 'rjunaś c' âiva Mādrī|putrau ca Pāṇḍavau
Brāhmaṇ'|ârthe parākrāntā dharm'|ātmāno yata|vratāḥ
kleśam ārcchanta vipulaṃ sukh'|ôdarkaṃ paraṃ|tapāḥ.
Tasmin prativasantas te yat prāpuḥ Kuru|sattamāḥ
vane kleśaṃ sukh'|ôdarkaṃ tat pravakṣyāmi te; śṛṇu!
Araṇī|sahitaṃ manthaṃ brāhmaṇasya tapasvinaḥ
mṛgasya gharṣamānasya viṣāṇe samasajjata.
Tad ādāya gato rājaṃs tvaramāṇo mahā|mṛgaḥ
āśram'|ântaritaḥ śīghraṃ plavamāno mahā|javaḥ.
10 Hriyamāṇaṃ tu taṃ dṛṣṭvā sa vipraḥ Kuru|sattama
tvārito 'bhyāgamat tatra agni|hotra|parīpsayā.
Ajātaśatrum āsīnaṃ bhrātṛbhiḥ sahitaṃ vane
āgamya brāhmaṇas tūrṇaṃ saṃtaptaś c' êdam abravīt:

JANAM·EJAYA said:

AFTER THEY HAD SUFFERED the terrible affliction of 311.1
their wife's abduction, and had then recovered Kri-
shná, what did the Pándavas do next?

VAISHAM·PÁYANA said:

After they had suffered the terrible affliction of Krishná's
abduction, King Áchyuta and his brothers left Kámyaka.
Yudhi·shthira went again to delightful and pleasant Dvai-
ta·vana, with its sweet fruit and roots, its many and various
trees. All the Pándavas lived there with Krishná their wife,
eating sparingly, living on a diet of fruit. While staying in 5
Dvaita·vana, Kuntí's son, King Yudhi·shthira, Bhima·sena,
Árjuna and Madri's Pándava twin sons, law-spirited keepers
of strict vows, incinerators of the foe, took action on behalf
of a brahmin, and so fell into a great trouble that was to end
in happiness. I shall tell you about that trouble which was
to end in joy, which the best of Kurus suffered while living
in that wood—listen!

When a deer was rubbing itself, the two pieces of wood an
ascetic brahmin used for drilling his fire stuck to its antlers.
Moving at speed, the great deer, so very fleet, carried them
away, king—leaping swiftly, it vanished from the hermitage.
That brahmin, seeing them being carried off, best of Kurus, 10
approached there quickly, worrying about his *agni·hotra*.*
Coming up quickly on Ajáta·shatru, sitting with his broth-
ers in the forest, the agitated brahmin said this:

«Araṇī|sahitaṃ manthaṃ samāsaktaṃ vanas|patau
mṛgasya gharṣamāṇasya viṣāṇe samasajjata.
Tam ādāya gato rājaṃs tvaramāṇo mahā|mṛgaḥ
āśramāt tvaritaḥ śīghraṃ plavamāno mahā|javaḥ.
Tasya gatvā padaṃ rajann āsādya ca mahā|mṛgam
agni|hotraṃ na lupyeta tad ānayata Pāṇḍavāḥ.»
15 Brāhmaṇasya vacaḥ śrutvā saṃtapto 'tha Yudhiṣṭhiraḥ
dhanur ādāya Kaunteyaḥ prādravad bhrātṛbhiḥ saha.
Sannaddhā dhanvinaḥ sarve prādravan nara|puṃgavāḥ
brāhmaṇ'|ârthe yatantas te śīghram anvagaman mṛgam.
Karṇi|nālīka|nārācān utsṛjanto mahā|rathāḥ
n' âvidhyan Pāṇḍavās tatra paśyanto mṛgam antikāt.
Teṣāṃ prayatamānānāṃ n' âdṛśyata mahā|mṛgaḥ.
apaśyanto mṛgaṃ śrāntā duḥkhaṃ prāptā manasvinaḥ.
Śītala|cchāyam āgamya nyagrodhaṃ gahane vane
kṣut|pipāsā|parīt'|âṅgāḥ Pāṇḍavāḥ samupāviśan.
20 Teṣāṃ samupaviṣṭānāṃ Nakulo duḥkhitas tadā
abravīd bhrātaraṃ śreṣṭham amarṣāt Kuru|nandanam.
«N' âsmin kule jātu mamajja dharmo
na c' ālasyād artha|lopo babhūva ha.
anuttarāḥ sarva|bhūteṣu bhūyaḥ
saṃprāptāḥ smaḥ saṃśayaṃ kena rājan?»

Yudhiṣṭhira uvāca:

312.1 «N' āpadām asti maryādā na nimittaṃ na kāraṇam
dharmas tu vibhajaty artham ubhayoḥ puṇya|pāpayoḥ.»

"When a deer was rubbing itself, the two pieces of wood used for drilling the fire, which were attached to a tree, stuck to its antlers. Moving at speed, the great deer, so very fleet, carried them away, king—leaping swiftly, it rushed from the hermitage. Track the great deer, attack it, and bring them back, king, so that the agni·hotra, Pándavas, may not be destroyed."

At the brahmin's words, Yudhi·shthira was greatly agi- 15
tated; the son of Kunti took up his bow, and rushed out together with his brothers. All the archers—bulls among men—equipped themselves and ran off, striving in the brahmin's cause, swiftly following the deer. Seeing the deer nearby, the great warriors, the Pándavas, shot eared and iron arrows, and spears, but could not hit it. While they were trying, the great deer became invisible. Unable to see the beast, the clever men became tired and depressed. In the depths of the forest, the Pándavas reached the cool shade of a banyan tree. They sat down together, their bodies racked by hunger and thirst.

Then, while they were sitting, Nákula, depressed and in- 20
dignant, said to his senior brother, the descendant of Kuru:

"In our house the Law never sets,
Nor does our purpose fail because of idleness.
Then why do we, so superior to all creatures,
Suffer such difficulty, king?"

YUDHI·SHTHIRA said:

"Misfortunes have no limit, ground or cause. But the law 312.1
apportions them to the good and the bad alike."

BHĪMA uvāca:

«Prātikāmy anayat Kṛṣṇāṃ sabhāyāṃ preṣyavat tadā
na mayā nihatas tatra, tena prāptāḥ sma saṃśayam.»

ARJUNA uvāca:

«Vācas tīkṣṇ" âsthi|bhedinyaḥ sūta|putreṇa bhāṣitāḥ
atitīkṣṇā mayā kṣāntās, tena prāptāḥ sma saṃśayam.»

SAHADEVA uvāca:

«Śakunis tvāṃ yad" âjaiṣīd akṣa|dyūtena Bhārata
sa mayā na hatas tatra, tena prāptāḥ sma saṃśayam.»

VAIŚAṂPĀYANA uvāca:

5 Tato Yudhiṣṭhiro rājā Nakulaṃ vākyam abravīt:
«āruhya vṛkṣaṃ Mādreya nirīkṣasva diśo daśa.
Pānīyam antike paśya vṛkṣāṃś c' âpy udak'|āśritān
ete hi bhrātaraḥ śrāntās tava tāta pipāsitāḥ.»
Nakulas tu «tath" êty» uktvā śīghram āruhya pādapam
abravīd bhrātaraṃ jyeṣṭham abhivīkṣya samantataḥ:
«Paśyāmi bahulān rājan vṛkṣān udaka|saṃśrayān
sārasānāṃ ca nirhrādam; atr' ôdakam asaṃśayam.»
Tato 'bravīt satya|dhṛtiḥ Kuntī|putro Yudhiṣṭhiraḥ:
«gaccha saumya tataḥ śīghraṃ tūrṇaṃ pānīyam ānaya.»
10 Nakulas tu «tath" êty» uktvā bhrātur jyeṣṭhasya śāsanāt
prādravad yatra pānīyaṃ śīghraṃ c' âiv' ânvapadyata.
Sa dṛṣṭvā vimalaṃ toyaṃ sārasaiḥ parivāritam
pātu|kāmas tato vācam antarikṣāt sa śuśruve:

BHIMA said:

"We are in difficulty because, when that servant brought Krishná like a slave to the assembly, I did not kill him on the spot."

ÁRJUNA said:

"We are in difficulty because I tolerated the acid-sharp, bone-piercing words uttered by the *suta*'s son.*"

SAHA·DEVA said:

"We are in difficulty because, when Shákuni defeated you at dice, Bhárata, I did not kill him on the spot."

VAISHAM·PÁYANA said:

Then King Yudhi·shthira said to Nákula: "Climb a tree, 5
Madréya, and scan the ten directions. Look for water nearby, or even for trees that grow near water, for these brothers of yours, dear man, are tired and thirsty."

Agreeing, Nákula quickly climbed a tree, looked all around, and said to his eldest brother: "King, I can see plenty of trees that grow near water, and there's the screeching of cranes. There has to be water here."

Then Kuntí's son, Yudhi·shthira, fixed in truth, said: "So, gentle brother, go swiftly, swiftly, and fetch water to drink."

"So be it," said Nákula to his elder brother's instructions, 10
and ran toward the water, coming upon it swiftly. At the sight of the unpolluted water, surrounded by cranes, he wanted to drink, but then, from above, he heard a voice:

YAKṢA uvāca:

«Mā tāta sāhasaṃ kārṣīr. mama pūrva|parigrahaḥ.
praśnān uktvā tu Mādreya tataḥ piba harasva ca.»
Anādṛtya tu tad vākyaṃ Nakulaḥ su|pipāsitaḥ
apibac chītalaṃ toyaṃ, pītvā ca nipapāta ha.
Cirāyamāṇe Nakule Kuntī|putro Yudhiṣṭhiraḥ
abravīd bhrātaraṃ vīraṃ Sahadevam ariṃ|damam:
15 «Bhrātā hi cirāyati naḥ Sahadeva tav' âgra|jaḥ
tath" âiv' ānaya sodaryaṃ, pānīyaṃ ca tvam ānaya.»
Sahadevas tath" êty uktvā tāṃ diśaṃ pratyapadyata,
dadarśa ca hataṃ bhūmau bhrātaraṃ Nakulaṃ tadā.
Bhrātṛ|śok'|âbhisaṃtaptas tṛṣayā ca prapīḍitaḥ
abhidudrāva pānīyaṃ. tato vāg abhyabhāṣata:
«Mā tāta sāhasaṃ kārṣīr. mama pūrva|parigrahaḥ.
praśnān uktvā yathā kāmaṃ pibasva ca harasva ca.»
Anādṛtya tu tad vākyaṃ Sahadevaḥ pipāsitaḥ
apibac chītalaṃ toyaṃ, pītvā ca nipapāta ha.
20 Ath' âbravīt sa Vijayaṃ Kuntī|putro Yudhiṣṭhiraḥ:
«bhrātarau te cira|gatau Bībhatso śatru|karśana.
Tau c' âiv' ānaya, bhadraṃ te! pānīyaṃ ca tvam ānaya.
tvaṃ hi nas tāta sarveṣāṃ duḥkhitānāṃ apāśrayaḥ.»
Evam ukto Guḍākeśaḥ pragṛhya sa|śaraṃ dhanuḥ
āmukta|khaḍgo medhāvī tat saraḥ pratyapadyata.
Tataḥ puruṣa|śārdūlau pānīya|haraṇe gatau
tau dadarśa hatau tatra bhrātarau śveta|vāhanaḥ.

The *yaksha* said:

"Don't act too hastily, friend. This has been mine from ancient times. When you have answered my questions, Madréya, then you can drink and carry." But Nákula was very thirsty and ignored those words. He drank the cool water, and having drunk he dropped down dead.

When Nákula took a long time, Kuntí's son, Yudhi·shthira, said to his heroic brother, Saha·deva, the enemy conqueror: "Saha·deva, our brother, who was born just before 15
you, has been gone for a long time. So go and fetch your twin, and bring back some water."

Saha·deva agreed and set out in that direction; and then he saw his brother Nákula dead on the ground. Burning with grief for his brother, and tortured by thirst, he rushed toward the water. Then the voice spoke: "Don't act too hastily, friend. This has been mine from ancient times. When you have answered my questions, then you can drink and carry as you wish." But Saha·deva was thirsty and ignored those words. He drank the cool water, and having drunk he dropped down dead.

Then Kuntí's son, Yudhi·shthira, said to Víjaya: "Árjuna, 20
harasser of your enemies, your brothers have been gone for a long time. If you will, go and fetch them, and bring back some water. For you, dear brother, are the refuge of us all in affliction."

At this request, judicious Guda·kesha took his bow and arrows, and with his sword unsheathed set out for the lake. So the one whose horses are white saw the two brothers who had gone to fetch water, tigers among men, lying there stricken. Seeing them as though asleep, Kuntí's son, a lion of

Prasuptāv iva tau dṛṣṭvā nara|siṃhaḥ su|duḥkhitaḥ
dhanur udyamya Kaunteyo vyalokayata tad vanam.
25 N' âpaśyat tatra kiṃ cit sa bhūtam asmin mahā|vane.
savya|sācī tataḥ śrāntaḥ pānīyaṃ so 'bhyadhāvata.
Abhidhāvaṃs tato vākyam antarikṣāt sa śuśruve:
«kim āsīdasi? pānīyaṃ n' âitac chakyaṃ balāt tvayā.
Kaunteya yadi praśnāṃs tān may" ôktān pratipatsyase
tataḥ pāsyasi pānīyaṃ hariṣyasi ca Bhārata.»
Vāritas tv abravīt Pārtho: «dṛśyamāno nivāraya
yāvad bāṇair vinirbhinnaḥ punar n' âivaṃ vadiṣyasi!»
Evam uktvā tataḥ Pārthaḥ śarair astr'|ânumantritaiḥ
pravavarṣa diśaṃ kṛtsnāṃ śabda|vedhaṃ ca darśayan.
30 Karṇi|nālīka|nārācān utsṛjan Bharata'|rṣabha
sa tv amoghān iṣūn muktvā tṛṣṇay" âbhiprapīḍitaḥ
Anekair iṣu|saṃghātair antarikṣaṃ vavarṣa ha.

YAKṢA uvāca:

«kiṃ vighātena te Pārtha? praśnān uktvā tataḥ piba.
Anuktvā ca piban praśnān pītv" âiva na bhaviṣyasi.»
evam uktas tataḥ Pārthaḥ savya|sācī Dhanaṃjayaḥ
Avijñāy' âiva tān vācaṃ pītv" âiva nipapāta ha.
ath' âbravīd Bhīmasenaṃ Kuntī|putro Yudhiṣṭhiraḥ:
«Nakulaḥ Sahadevaś ca Bībhatsuś ca paraṃ|tapa
ciraṃ gatās toya|hetor na c' āgacchanti Bhārata.
35 Tāṃś c' âiv' ānaya, bhadraṃ te! pānīyaṃ ca tvam ānaya.»

a man, was greatly grieved. Raising his bow, he looked about
the forest. In this great forest he did not see a single creature. 25
Then, tired, the left-handed archer ran toward the water.

As he ran he heard words from the sky: "Why do you approach? You won't be able to take this water by force. If, son of Kuntí, you answer these questions I'll ask, then, Bhárata, you shall drink and fetch the water."

Impeded, Partha said: "Stop me by showing yourself! So, shot through by my arrows, you won't speak such words again!" So saying, Partha sprayed the entire area with magic
arrows, showing his ability to target by sound alone. Shoo- 30
ting eared and iron arrows, and spears, bull of the Bharatas, releasing his unerring arrows, he was tortured by thirst. He had sprayed the sky with many swarms of arrows.

The *yaksha* said:

"Why strike back, Partha? Answer the questions and then you can drink. But if you drink and haven't answered the questions, as soon as you touch so much as a drop, you'll die." Addressed in this way, Partha Dhanam·jaya, the left-handed archer, ignored such words, drank and dropped down dead.

Then Kuntí's son, Yudhi·shthira, said to Bhima·sena: "Nákula, Saha·deva and Árjuna, have been gone a long time looking for water, and are not coming back, Bhárata, incin-
erator of the foe. If you will, go and fetch them, and bring 35
back some water."

Bhīmasenas «tath" êty» uktvā tāṃ diśaṃ pratyapadyata
Yatra te puruṣa|vyāghrā bhrātaro 'sya nipātitāḥ.
tān dṛṣṭvā duḥkhito Bhīmas tṛṣayā ca prapīḍitaḥ
Amanyata mahā|bāhuḥ: «karma tad yakṣa|rakṣasām.
sa cintayām āsa tadā: yoddhavyaṃ dhruvam adya vai.»
«Pāsyāmi tāvat pānīyam iti». Pārtho vṛk'|ôdaraḥ
tato 'bhyadhāvat pānīyaṃ pipāsuḥ puruṣa'|rṣabhaḥ.

YAKṢA uvāca:

«Mā tāta sāhasaṃ kārṣīr. mama pūrva|parigrahaḥ.
praśnān uktvā tu Kaunteya tataḥ piba harasva ca.»
40 Evam uktas tadā Bhīmo yakṣeṇ' âmita|tejasā
avijñāy' âiva* tān praśnān pītv" âiva nipapāta ha.
Tataḥ Kuntī|suto rājā vicintya puruṣa'|rṣabhaḥ
samutthāya mahā|bāhur dahyamānena cetasā
Vyapeta|jana|nirghoṣaṃ praviveśa mahā|vanam
rurubhiś ca varāhaiś ca pakṣibhiś ca niṣevitam
Nīla|bhāsvara|varṇaiś ca pādapair upaśobhitam
bhramarair upagītaṃ ca pakṣibhiś ca mahā|yaśāḥ.
Sa gacchan kānane tasmin hema|jāla|pariṣkṛtam
dadarśa tat saraḥ śrīmān Viśvakarma|kṛtaṃ yathā
45 Upetaṃ nalinī|jālaiḥ sindhuvāraiś ca vetasaiḥ*
ketakaiḥ karavīraiś ca pippalaiś c' âiva saṃvṛtam.
śram'|ārtas tad upāgamya saro dṛṣṭv" âtha vismitaḥ.

VAIŚAṂPĀYANA uvāca:

313.1 Sa dadarśa hatān bhrātṝn loka|pālān iva cyutān
yugānte samanuprāpte Sakra|pratima|gauravān.
Vinikīrṇa|dhanur|bāṇaṃ dṛṣṭvā nihatam Arjunam
Bhīmasenaṃ yamau c' âiva nirviceṣṭān gat'|āyuṣaḥ

Bhima·sena agreed, and set out for that place where those tigerish men, his brothers, had fallen. Seeing them, Bhima was distressed, and tortured by thirst. Great Arm thought: "This is the work of *yaksha*s or *rákshasa*s." He realized then that he would certainly have to fight that day. "But before that I shall drink the water." So thinking, wolf-bellied Partha, bull of a man, ran thirstily to the water.

The *yaksha* said:

"Don't act too hastily, friend. This has been mine from ancient times. When you have answered my questions, son
of Kuntí, then you can drink and carry." Thus addressed 40
by the *yaksha*, whose energy was measureless, Bhima then ignored those questions, drank and dropped down dead.

Then Kuntí's son, the strong-armed king, deliberated, and arose with his mind on fire. He entered the great forest, inhabited by deer and boar and birds, where human sound had ceased. It was made beautiful by trees the color of light and dark; the celebrated man was sung to by bees and birds. Walking in that forest, he saw the beautiful lake, surrounded
by nets of gold, as though made by Vishva·karman. It was 45
covered with interlaced lotuses, Negundo lilies, reeds, *kétakas*, oleanders and fig trees. He had approached the lake wearily, but once he had seen it he was amazed.

VAISHAM·PÁYANA said:

He saw his dead brothers, as weighty as Shakra, fallen 313.1
like the world's guardians at the end of a world age. Seeing Árjuna, his bow and arrows scattered, Bhima·sena and the twins motionless and lifeless, he sighed long and hot, bathed in tears of grief. Seeing all those brothers lying dead,

Sa dīrgham uṣṇaṃ niḥśvasya śoka|bāṣpa|pariplutaḥ
tān dṛṣṭvā patitān bhrātṝn sarvāṃś cintā|samanvitaḥ
Dharma|putro mahā|bāhur vilalāpa suvistaram:
«nanu tvayā mahā|bāho pratijñātaṃ Vṛkodara:
5 ‹Suyodhanasya bhetsyāmi gadayā sakthinī raṇe!›
vyarthaṃ tad adya me sarvaṃ tvayi vīre nipātite
Mah"|ātmani mahā|bāho Kurūṇāṃ kīrti|vardhane.
manuṣya|sambhavā vāco vidharmiṇyaḥ pratiśrutāḥ.
Bhavatāṃ, divya|vācas tu tā bhavantu kathaṃ mṛṣā?
devāś c' âpi yad" âvocan sūtake tvāṃ Dhanaṃjaya:
‹Sahasr'|âkṣād an|avaraḥ Kunti putras tav' êti› vai
uttare Pāriyātre ca jagur bhūtāni sarvaśaḥ:
‹Vipranaṣṭāṃ śriyaṃ c' âiṣām āhartā punar añjasā
n' âsya jetā raṇe kaś cid, ajetā n' âiṣa kasya cit.›
10 So 'yaṃ mṛtyu|vaśaṃ yātaḥ kathaṃ Jiṣṇur mahā|balaḥ?
ayaṃ mam' āśāṃ saṃhatya śete bhūmau Dhanaṃjaya
Āśritya yaṃ vayaṃ nāthaṃ duḥkhāny etāni sehima.
raṇe pramattau vīrau ca sadā śatrūṇi barhaṇau
Kathaṃ ripu|vaśaṃ yātau Kuntī|putrau mahā|balau
yau sarv'|âstr'|âpratihatāu Bhīmasena|Dhanaṃjayau?
Aśma|sāra|mayaṃ nūnaṃ hṛdayaṃ mama durhṛdaḥ
yamau yad etau dṛṣṭv" âdya patitau n' âvadīryate.
Śāstra|jñā deśa|kāla|jñās tapo|yuktāḥ kriy"|ânvitāḥ
akṛtvā sadṛśaṃ karma kiṃ śedhvaṃ puruṣa'|rṣabhāḥ?
15 Avikṣata|śarīrāś| c' âpy apramṛṣṭa|śarāsanāḥ
asaṃjñā bhuvi saṅgamya kiṃ śedhvam aparājitāḥ?»

Great Arm, the son of Dharma, was full of care; vehemently, he lamented:

"Surely, Great Arm Vrikódara, you vowed: 'With a mace I shall smash Suyódhana's thighs in battle!' All that is now useless for me, Great Arm, booster of the fame of the Kurus, since you, the great-souled hero, have fallen. The promises that men produce may transgress the Law. Very well, how can divine utterances be in vain? Even when the gods said of you at your birth, Dhanam·jaya: 'Your son, Kuntí, is not inferior to Indra of a thousand eyes!' And in the northern Pariyátra mountains, all beings sang: 'And he shall quickly restore these people's lost glory. No one shall beat him in battle, and there is no one he shall not beat.'

Then how has Jishnu, whose power is so great, fallen into the power of death? Dhanam·jaya lies on the ground, killing my hope—the protector on whom we depended while enduring such miseries. How have those heroes, the mighty sons of Kuntí, Bhima·sena and Dhanam·jaya, reckless in battle, ever tearing their enemies, who repelled every weapon, fallen into the power of the enemy? Surely my wicked heart is made of iron, since, seeing these two prone, it does not split.

Bulls among men, you know scripture, time and place, you are wedded to asceticism, and practice ritual—what's the good of lying down when you haven't performed the required action? What's the good of coming together unconquered, and lying senseless on the earth, with your bows unbroken, and your bodies unhurt?"

Sānūn iv' âdreḥ saṃsuptān dṛṣṭvā bhrātṝn mahā|matiḥ
sukhaṃ prasuptān prasvinnaḥ khinnaḥ kaṣṭāṃ daśāṃ gataḥ
«Evam ev' êdam ity» uktvā dharm|ātmā sa nar'|ēśvaraḥ
śoka|sāgara|madhya|stho dadhyau kāraṇam ākulaḥ.
Iti|kartavyatāṃ c' êti deśa|kāla|vibhāga|vit
n' âbhipede mahā|bāhuś cintayāno mahā|matiḥ.
Atha saṃstabhya dharm'|ātmā tad" ātmānaṃ tapaḥ|sutaḥ
evaṃ vilapya bahudhā dharma|putro Yudhiṣṭhiraḥ
Buddhyā vicintayām āsa vīrāḥ kena nipātitāḥ:
«N' âiṣāṃ śastra|prahāro 'sti. padaṃ n' êh' âsti kasya cit.
bhūtaṃ mahad idaṃ manye bhrātaro yena me hatāḥ.
Ek'|âgraṃ cintayiṣyāmi, pītvā vetsyāmi vā jalam.
syāt tu Duryodhanen' êdam upāṃśu|vihitaṃ kṛtam,
Gāndhāra|rāja|racitaṃ satataṃ jihma|buddhinā
yasya kāryam akāryaṃ vā samam eva bhavaty uta.
Kas tasya viśvased vīro duṣ|kṛter akṛt'|ātmanaḥ
atha vā puruṣair gūḍhaiḥ prayogo 'yaṃ dur|ātmanaḥ?
Bhaved iti» mahā|buddhir bahudhā tad acintayat.
tasy' âsīn na viṣeṇ' êdam udakaṃ dūṣitaṃ yathā.
«Mṛtānām api c' âiteṣāṃ vikṛtaṃ n' âiva jāyate
mukha|varṇāḥ prasannā me bhrātṝṇām ity» acintayat.
«Ek'|âikaśaś c' âugha|balān imān puruṣa|sattamān
ko 'nyaḥ pratisamāseta kāl'|ântaka|Yamād ṛte?»
Etena vyavasāyena tat toyam vyavagāḍhavān,
gāhamānaś ca tat toyam antarikṣāt sa śuśruve:

Seeing his brothers sleeping happily, like slumbering mountain ridges, high-minded Yudhi·shthira, sweating, was filled with pain. Saying, "So that's the way it is. . . ," the soul of the Law, the lord of men, confounded, and marooned on an ocean of grief, sought to establish the cause. And so reflecting, the mighty-armed and clever man, who knew the divisions of time and place, could not decide what was to be done. Then, the son of the Law, the soul of the Law, Yudhi·shthira, the son of austerity, who had lamented in many ways, rallied himself, and reflected in his mind on who had felled the heroes.

"There is no mark of a weapon upon them, and no trace of anyone else. I suppose this is a mighty being that has slain my brothers. I shall ponder this intently—or I shall drink the water and know. But it may be that what has been done was arranged secretly by Duryódhana, and produced, as always, by the Gandhára king* with the crooked mind. What hero would put his trust in that man of unfashioned soul and wicked behavior, for whom right and wrong are one and the same? Or this may be a device of that wicked soul employing hidden henchmen. So it was that that most 25
intelligent man thought about it in many ways. It seemed to him that the water was not fouled with poison, since, although they were dead, there was no sign of disfigurement: "My brothers' complexions are clear," he thought. "Who else except Yama—all-destroying time—could be a match, one by one, for these supreme men, who had the power of a flood?" With this decided, he plunged into the water; and while he was immersing himself, he heard a voice from the sky:

YAKṢA uvāca:

«Ahaṃ bakaḥ śaivala|matsya|bhakṣo.
nītā mayā preta|vaśaṃ tav' ânujāḥ.
tvaṃ pañcamo bhavitā rāja|putra
na cet praśnān pṛcchato vyākaroṣi.
30 Mā tāta sāhasaṃ kārṣīr. mama pūrva|parigrahaḥ.
praśnān uktvā tu Kaunteya tataḥ piba harasva ca.»

YUDHIṢṬHIRA uvāca:

«Rudrāṇāṃ vā Vasūnāṃ vā Marutāṃ vā pradhāna|bhāk,
pṛcchāmi, ko bhavān devo? n' âitac chakuninā kṛtam.
Himavān Pāriyātraś ca Vindhyo Malaya eva ca
catvāraḥ parvatāḥ kena pātitā bhuri|tejasāḥ?
Atīva te mahat karma kṛtaṃ ca balināṃ vara.
yān na devā na gandharvā n' âsurāś ca na rākṣasāḥ
Viṣaheran mahā|yuddhe kṛtaṃ te tan mah"|âdbhutam.
na te jānāmi yat kāryaṃ n' âbhijānāmi kāṅkṣitam.
35 Kautūhalaṃ mahaj jātaṃ sādhvasaṃ c' āgataṃ mama
yen' âsmy udvigna|hṛdayaḥ samutpanna|śiro|jvaraḥ.
Pṛcchāmi bhagavaṃs tasmāt: ko bhavān iha tiṣṭhati?»

YAKṢA uvāca:

«yakṣo 'ham asmi, bhadraṃ te! n' âsmi pakṣī jale|caraḥ.
May" âite nihatāḥ sarve bhrātaras te mah"|âujasaḥ.»

The *yaksha* said:

"I am a crane living on duckweed and fish.
It is I who have brought your brothers
Under the power of death.
You'll make a fifth, prince,
If you don't answer the questions I ask.

Don't act too hastily, friend. This has been mine from 30
ancient times. When you have answered my questions, son of Kuntí, then you can drink and carry."

YUDHI·SHTHIRA said:

"Who are you, I ask? A god? The greatest of the Rudras, Vasus or Maruts? A bird could not have done this. By whom have the four most glorious mountains—Himálaya, Pariyátra, Vindhya and Málaya*—been overthrown? You have done a very great deed, mightiest of the mighty! You have performed a great wonder on those whom neither gods, *gandhárvas*, anti-gods nor demons could overcome in mighty battle. I don't know your business, and I don't know your intention. I am full of a great curiosity, and I am very afraid. 35
I ask you therefore, respectfully, you, who have sorrowed my heart, and given me a feverish headache, who are you, standing here?"

The *yaksha* said:

"I am, dear sir, a *yaksha*, and not a water bird. I felled all your mighty brothers."

VAIŚAMPĀYANA uvāca:

tatas tām aśivāṃ śrutvā vācaṃ sa paruṣ'|âkṣarām
Yakṣasya bruvato rājann upakramya tadā sthitaḥ.
virūp'|âkṣaṃ mahā|kāyaṃ yakṣaṃ tāla|samucchrayam
Jvalan'|ârka|pratīkāśam adhṛṣyaṃ parvat'|ôpamam
vṛkṣam āśritya tiṣṭhantaṃ dadarśa Bharata'|rṣabhaḥ
40 Megha|gambhīra|nādena tarjayantaṃ mahā|svanam.

YAKṢA uvāca:

«ime te bhrātaro rājan vāryamāṇā may" âsakṛt
Balāt toyaṃ jihīrṣantas tato vai mṛditā mayā.
na peyam udakaṃ rājan prāṇān iha parīpsatā.
Pārtha mā sāhasaṃ kārṣīr. mama pūrva|parigrahaḥ.
praśnān uktvā tu Kaunteya tataḥ piba harasva ca.»

YUDHIṢṬHIRA uvāca:

«Na c' âhaṃ kāmaye yakṣa tava pūrva|parigraham.
kāmaṃ n' âitat praśaṃsanti santo hi puruṣāḥ sadā.
Yad" ātmanā svam ātmānaṃ praśaṃset puruṣaḥ prabho*
yathā|prajñaṃ tu te praśnān prativakṣyāmi. pṛccha mām!»

YAKṢA uvāca:

45 «Kiṃ svid ādityam unnayati? ke ca tasy' âbhitaś carāḥ?
kaś c' âinam astaṃ nayati? kasmiṃś ca pratitiṣṭhati?»

YUDHIṢṬHIRA uvāca:

«Brahm" ādityam unnayati. devās tasy' âbhitaś carāḥ.
dharmaś c' âstaṃ nayati ca. satye ca pratitiṣṭhati.»

VAISHAM·PÁYANA said:

So, king, hearing the harsh and pernicious words spoken by the *yaksha*, he approached and stood there. The bull of the Bharatas saw the *yaksha* settled on a tree, standing like a mountain, unassailable, like fire or the sun, as high as a palm
tree, big-bodied, with deformed eyes, making a threatening 40
noise, deep as the rumbling of a thundercloud.

The *yaksha* said:

"I repeatedly stopped these, your brothers, king, as they tried to remove the water by force: I killed them. Those here who wish to live should not drink this water, king! Don't act too hastily, Partha. This has been mine from ancient times. When you have answered my questions, son of Kuntí, then you can drink and carry."

YUDHI·SHTHIRA said:

"*Yaksha*, I don't covet your ancient property; in any case, people never approve of that. As a person esteems himself through himself, so I shall answer your questions, my lord, according to my insight. Ask me!"

The *yaksha* said:

"What makes the sun rise? And what moves about him? 45
What makes him set? And on what is he founded?"

YUDHI·SHTHIRA said:

"Brahman makes the sun rise. The gods move about him. The Law makes him set. And he is founded on truth."

YAKṢA uvāca:

«Kena svic chrotriyo bhavati? kena svid vindate mahat?
kena svid dvitīyavān bhavati rājan? kena ca buddhimān?»

YUDHIṢṬHIRA uvāca:

«Śrutena śrotriyo bhavati. tapasā vindate mahat.
dhṛtyā dvitīyavān bhavati. buddhimān vṛddha|sevayā.»

YAKṢA uvāca:

«Kiṃ brāhmaṇānāṃ devatvaṃ?
kaś ca dharmaḥ satām iva?
kaś c' âiṣāṃ mānuṣo bhāvaḥ?
kim eṣām asatām iva?»

YUDHIṢṬHIRA uvāca:

50 «Svādhyāya eṣāṃ devatvaṃ. tapa eṣāṃ satām iva.
maraṇaṃ mānuṣo bhāvaḥ. parivādo 'satām iva.»

YAKṢA uvāca:

«Kiṃ kṣatriyāṇāṃ devatvaṃ? kaś ca dharmaḥ satām iva?
kaś c' âiṣāṃ mānuṣo bhāvaḥ? kim eṣām asatām iva?»

YUDHIṢṬHIRA uvāca:

«Iṣv|astram eṣāṃ devatvaṃ. yajña eṣāṃ satām iva.
bhayaṃ vai mānuṣo bhāvaḥ. parityāgo 'satām iva.»

The *yaksha* said:

"By what does one become learned? By what does one attain the great? Through what, king, can one have a second? And by what does one acquire judgment?"

YUDHI·SHTHIRA said:

"By instruction one becomes learned. By asceticism one attains the great. Through resolution one can have a second. By serving the elders one acquires judgment."

The *yaksha* said:

"What is the divinity of brahmins? What way of life do they share with the good? What is their human nature? What do they share with the bad?"

YUDHI·SHTHIRA said:

"Vedic study is their divinity, asceticism what they share 50
with the good; being mortal is their human nature, slander what they share with the bad."

The *yaksha* said:

"What is the divinity of warriors? What way of life do they share with the good? What is their human nature? What do they share with the bad?"

YUDHI·SHTHIRA said:

"The bow is their divinity, sacrifice what they share with the good; fear is their human nature, desertion what they share with the bad."

Yakṣa uvāca:

«Kim ekaṃ yajñiyaṃ sāma? kim ekaṃ yajñiyaṃ yajuḥ?
kā c' âikā vṛṇute yajñaṃ? kāṃ yajño n' âtivartate?»

Yudhiṣṭhira uvāca:

«Prāṇo vai yajñiyaṃ sāma. mano vai yajñiyaṃ yajuḥ.
vāg ekā vṛṇute yajñaṃ. tāṃ yajño n' âtivartate.»

Yakṣa uvāca:

55 «Kiṃ svid āvapatāṃ śreṣṭhaṃ?
kiṃ|svin nivapatāṃ varam?
kiṃ svit pratiṣṭhamānānāṃ,
kiṃ|svit prasavatāṃ varam?»

Yudhiṣṭhira uvāca:

«Varṣam āvapatāṃ śreṣṭhaṃ. bījaṃ nivapatāṃ varam.
gāvaḥ pratiṣṭhamānānāṃ, putraḥ prasavatāṃ varaḥ.»

Yakṣa uvāca:

«Indriy'|ârthān anubhavan buddhimān loka|pūjitaḥ
saṃmataḥ sarva|bhūtānām ucchvasan ko na jīvati?»

The *yaksha* said:

"What is the one sacrificial chant? What is the one sacrificial formula? What one thing covers the sacrifice? What one thing does the sacrifice not exceed?"

YUDHI·SHTHIRA said:

"Breath is the sacrificial chant, mind the sacrificial formula. Speech is the one thing that covers the sacrifice, and that is the thing the sacrifice does not exceed."

The *yaksha* said:

"What is the best for those cultivating? What is the best 55
for those sowing? What is best for those dwelling, for those
begetting?"

YUDHI·SHTHIRA said:

"Rain is the best for the cultivating; seed is the best for the sowing. Cows are the best for those dwelling, a son for those begetting."

The *yaksha* said:

"Who experiences the objects of the senses, is intelligent, honored in the world, respected by all beings, breathing, but not alive?"

Yudhiṣṭhira uvāca:

«Devat”|âtithi|bhṛtyānāṃ pitṝṇām ātmanaś ca yaḥ
na nirvapati pañcānām ucchvasan na sa jīvati.»

Yakṣa uvāca:

«Kiṃ svid gurutaraṃ bhūmeḥ?
kiṃ svid uccataraṃ ca khāt?
kiṃ svic chīghrataraṃ vāyoḥ?
kiṃ svid bahutaraṃ tṛṇāt?»

Yudhiṣṭhira uvāca:

60 «Mātā gurutarā bhūmeḥ. khāt pit” ôccataras tathā.
manaḥ śīghrataraṃ vātāc. cintā bahutarī tṛṇāt.»

Yakṣa uvāca:

«Kiṃ svit suptaṃ na nimiṣati? kiṃ svij jātaṃ na copati?
kasya svidd hṛdayaṃ n' âsti? kiṃ svid vegena vardhate?»

Yudhiṣṭhira uvāca:

«Matsyaḥ supto na nimiṣaty. aṇḍaṃ jātaṃ na copati.
aśmano hṛdayaṃ n' âsti. nadī vegena vardhate.»

Yakṣa uvāca:

«Kiṃ svit pravasato mitraṃ? kiṃ svin mitraṃ gṛhe sataḥ?
āturasya ca kiṃ mitraṃ? kiṃ svin mitraṃ mariṣyataḥ?»

Yudhiṣṭhira uvāca:

«Sārthaḥ pravasato mitraṃ. bhāryā mitraṃ gṛhe sataḥ.
āturasya bhiṣaṅ mitraṃ. dānaṃ mitraṃ mariṣyataḥ.»

Yudhi·shthira said:

"One who makes no offering to the five—gods, guests, dependents, ancestors, himself—is breathing but not alive."

The *yaksha* said:

"What is heavier than the earth, higher than heaven, faster than the wind, more numerous than grass?"

Yudhi·shthira said:

"The mother is weightier than the earth, and the father 60
higher than heaven; the mind is faster than the wind, and cares more numerous than grass."

The *yaksha* said:

"What does not shut its eyes when asleep? What does not stir when born? What has no heart? What increases by rushing?"

Yudhi·shthira said:

"A fish does not shut its eyes when asleep. An egg doesn't stir when born. A stone has no heart. A river increases by rushing."

The *yaksha* said:

"What is the friend of the traveller? What is the friend of the one at home? What is the friend of the sick? What is the friend of the dying?"

Yudhi·shthira said:

"A caravan is the friend of the traveller. A wife is the friend of the one at home. A doctor the friend of the sick. Charity is the friend of the dying."

YAKṢA uvāca:

65 «Ko 'tithiḥ sarva|bhūtānāṃ?
kiṃ svid dharmaṃ sanātanam?
amṛtaṃ kiṃ svid rāj'|êndra?
kiṃ svit sarvam idaṃ jagat?»

YUDHIṢṬHIRA uvāca:

«Atithiḥ sarva|bhūtānām agniḥ. somo gav"|âmṛtam.
sanātano 'mṛto dharmo. vāyuḥ sarvam idaṃ jagat.»

YAKṢA uvāca:

Kiṃ svid eko vicarate? jātaḥ ko jāyate punaḥ?
kiṃ svidd himasya bhaiṣajyaṃ? kiṃ svid āvapanaṃ mahat?

YUDHIṢṬHIRA uvāca:

«Sūrya eko vicarati. candramā jāyate punaḥ.
agnir himasya bhaiṣajyaṃ. bhūmir āvapanaṃ mahat.»

YAKṢA uvāca:

«Kiṃ svid eka|padaṃ dharmyaṃ?
kiṃ svid eka|padaṃ yaśaḥ?
kiṃ svid eka|padaṃ svargyaṃ?
kiṃ svid eka|padaṃ sukham?»

YUDHIṢṬHIRA uvāca:

70 «Dākṣyam eka|padaṃ dharmyaṃ.
dānam eka|padaṃ yaśaḥ.
satyam eka|padaṃ svargyaṃ.
śīlam eka|padaṃ sukham.»

YAKṢA uvāca:

«Kiṃ svid ātmā manuṣyasya? kiṃ svid daiva|kṛtaḥ sakhā?
upajīvanaṃ kiṃ svid asya? kiṃ svid asya parāyaṇam?»

The *yaksha* said:

"Who is the guest of all beings? What is the Eternal Law? 65
What is the nectar of immortality, king of kings? What is this whole universe?"

YUDHI·SHTHIRA said:

"Fire is the guest of all beings. Soma is immortal cow-milk. The Eternal Law is immortality. Wind is the whole universe."

The *yaksha* said:

What travels alone? Who is born again? What is the remedy against snow? What is the great vessel?

YUDHI·SHTHIRA said:

"The sun travels alone. The moon is born again. Fire is the remedy against snow. The earth is the great vessel."

The *yaksha* said:

"What in a word is virtuous? What in a word is fame? What in a word leads to heaven? What in a word is happiness?"

YUDHI·SHTHIRA said:

"In a word, industry is virtuous. In a word, giving is fame. 70
In a word, truth leads to heaven. In a word, good conduct is happiness."

The *yaksha* said:

"What is the self of a man? What is the friend made by fate? What supports his life? What is his final resort?"

Yudhiṣṭhira uvāca:

«Putra ātmā manuṣyasya. bhāryā daiva|kṛtaḥ sakhā.
upajīvanaṃ ca parjanyo. dānam asya parāyaṇam.»

Yakṣa uvāca:

«Dhanyānām uttamaṃ kiṃ svid
dhanānāṃ syāt kiṃ uttamam?
lābhānām uttamaṃ kiṃ syāt?
sukhānāṃ syāt kim uttamam?»

Yudhiṣṭhira uvāca:

«Dhanyānām uttamaṃ dākṣyaṃ.
dhanānām uttamaṃ śrutam.
lābhānāṃ śreya ārogyaṃ.
sukhānāṃ tuṣṭir uttamā.»

Yakṣa uvāca:

75 «Kaś ca dharmaḥ paro loke? kaś ca dharmaḥ sadā|phalaḥ?
kiṃ niyamya na śocanti? kaiś ca saṃdhir na jīryate?»

Yudhiṣṭhira uvāca:

«Ānṛśaṃsyaṃ paro dharmas. trayī|dharmaḥ sadā|phalaḥ.
mano yamya na śocanti. saṃdhiḥ sadbhir na jīryate.»

Yakṣa uvāca:

«Kiṃ nu hitvā priyo bhavati? kiṃ nu hitvā na śocati?
kiṃ nu hitv" ârthavān bhavati? kiṃ nu hitvā sukhī bhavet?»

YUDHI·SHTHIRA said:

"A son is the self of a man. A wife is the friend made by fate. The rain cloud supports his life. Charity is his final resort."

The *yaksha* said:

"What is the greatest of riches? What is the greatest of possessions? What is the greatest of profitable things? What is the greatest of agreeable things?"

YUDHI·SHTHIRA said:

"Skill is the greatest of riches. Learning is the greatest of possessions. Being healthy is the greatest of profitable things. Contentment is the greatest of agreeable things."

The *yaksha* said:

"What is the highest Law in the world? What Law always 75
bears fruit? What doesn't cause them grief when controlled?
The bond with whom cannot decay?"

YUDHI·SHTHIRA said:

"Absence of cruelty is the highest Law in the world. The Vedic law always bears fruit. The mind doesn't cause them grief when controlled. The bond with the good cannot decay."

The *yaksha* said:

"One becomes friendly through renouncing what? One does not grieve through renouncing what? One becomes wealthy through renouncing what? One may become happy through renouncing what?"

YUDHIṢṬHIRA uvāca:
«Mānaṃ hitvā priyo bhavati. krodhaṃ hitvā na śocati.
kāmaṃ hitv" ârthavān bhavati. lobhaṃ hitvā sukhī bhavet.»

YAKṢA uvāca:
Kim|arthaṃ brāhmaṇe dānaṃ? kim|arthaṃ naṭa|nartake?
kim|arthaṃ c' âiva bhṛtyeṣu? kim|arthaṃ c' âiva rājasu?

YUDHIṢṬHIRA uvāca:
80 Dharm'|ârthaṃ brāhmaṇe dānaṃ,
yaśo|'rthaṃ naṭa|nartake.
bhṛtyeṣu bharaṇ'|ârthaṃ vai.
bhay'|ârthaṃ c' âiva rājasu.

YAKṢA uvāca:
«Kena svid āvṛto lokaḥ? kena svin na prakāśate?
kena tyajati mitrāṇi? kena svargaṃ na gacchati?»

YUDHIṢṬHIRA uvāca:
«Ajñānen' āvṛto lokas tamasā na prakāśate.
lobhāt tyajati mitrāṇi. saṅgāt svargaṃ na gacchati.»

YAKṢA uvāca:
«Mṛtaḥ kathaṃ syāt puruṣaḥ?
kathaṃ rāṣṭraṃ mṛtaṃ bhavet?
śrāddhaṃ mṛtaṃ kathaṃ ca syāt?
kathaṃ yajño mṛto bhavet?»

YUDHI·SHTHIRA said:

"By renouncing pride one becomes friendly. By renouncing anger one does not grieve. By renouncing desire one becomes wealthy. By renouncing greed one becomes happy."

The *yaksha* said:

What is the purpose of giving to brahmins? To dancers and actors? To servants? And to kings?

YUDHI·SHTHIRA said:

One gives to brahmins for religious merit; to dancers and 80
actors for fame; to servants to support them; to kings out of fear.

The *yaksha* said:

"Because of what is the world hidden? Because of what does it not become visible? Because of what are friends abandoned? Because of what does one not go to heaven?"

YUDHI·SHTHIRA said:

"Because of ignorance the world is hidden. Because of the constituent of darkness it does not appear. Because of greed friends are abandoned. Because of wordly attachment one does not go to heaven."

The *yaksha* said:

"How can a man be dead? How can a kingdom be dead? How can a ritual for the dead be dead? How can a sacrifice be dead?"

YUDHIṢṬHIRA uvāca:

«Mṛto daridraḥ puruṣo. mṛtaṃ rāṣṭram arājakam.
mṛtam aśrotriyaṃ śrāddhaṃ. mṛto yajñas tv adakṣiṇaḥ.»

YAKṢA uvāca:

85 «Kā dik? kim udakaṃ proktaṃ?
kim annaṃ? kiṃ ca vai viṣam?
śrāddhasya kālam ākhyāhi,
tataḥ piba harasva ca.»

YUDHIṢṬHIRA uvāca:

«Santo dig. jalam ākāśaṃ. gaur annaṃ. prārthanā viṣam.
śrāddhasya brāhmaṇaḥ kālaḥ. kathaṃ vā yakṣa manyase?»

YAKṢA uvāca:

«Tapaḥ kiṃ|lakṣaṇaṃ proktaṃ? ko damaś ca prakīrtitaḥ?
kṣamā ca kā parā proktā? kā ca hrīḥ parikīrtitā?»

YUDHIṢṬHIRA uvāca:

«Tapaḥ svadharma|vartitvaṃ. manaso damanaṃ damaḥ.
kṣamā dvandva|sahiṣṇutvaṃ. hrīr akārya|nivartanam.»

YAKṢA uvāca:

«Kiṃ jñānaṃ procyate rājan? kaḥ śamaś ca prakīrtitaḥ?
dayā ca kā parā proktā? kiṃ c' ārjavam* udāhṛtam?»

YUDHI·SHTHIRA said:

"A poor man is dead. A kingdom without a king is dead. A ritual for the dead without a learned brahmin is dead. And a sacrifice without a fee for the priests is dead."

The *yaksha* said:

"What is the right direction? What is called water? What 85
food, and what poison? Tell me the time for the ritual for the dead. Then you can drink and carry."

YUDHI·SHTHIRA said:

"The good are the right direction. Space is water, the cow is food, begging is poison. A brahmin is the time for the ritual for the dead.* Or what do you think, *yaksha*?"

The *yaksha* said:

"What is said to be the distinguishing characteristic of asceticism? What is called self-restraint? What is known as the highest forbearance? And what is called shame?"

YUDHI·SHTHIRA said:

"Living according to your inherent duty is asceticism. Subduing the mind is self-restraint. Forbearance is the ability to support opposites. Shame is giving up improperly."

The *yaksha* said:

"What is said to be knowledge, king? What is called peace? What is said to be the highest compassion? What is called rectitude?"

YUDHIṢṬHIRA uvāca:

90 «Jñānaṃ tattv'|ârtha|sambodhaḥ. śamaś citta|praśāntatā.
dayā sarva|sukh'|âiṣitvam. ārjavaṃ sama|cittatā.»

YAKṢA uvāca:

«Kaḥ śatrur durjayaḥ? puṃsāṃ kaś ca vyādhir anantakaḥ?
kīdṛśaś ca smṛtaḥ sādhur? asādhuḥ kīdṛśaḥ smṛtaḥ?»

YUDHIṢṬHIRA uvāca:

«Krodhaḥ sudurjayaḥ śatrur. lobho vyādhir anantakaḥ.
sarva|bhūta|hitaḥ sādhur. asādhur nirdayaḥ smṛtaḥ.»

YAKṢA uvāca:

«Ko moho procyate rājan? kaś ca mānaḥ prakīrtitaḥ?
kim ālasyaṃ ca vijñeyaṃ? kaś ca śokaḥ prakīrtitaḥ?»

YUDHIṢṬHIRA uvāca:

«Moho hi dharma|mūḍhatvaṃ.
mānas tv ātm'|âbhimānitā.
dharma|niṣkriyat" ālasyaṃ.
śokas tv ajñānam ucyate.»

YAKṢA uvāca:

95 «Kiṃ sthairyam ṛṣibhiḥ proktaṃ?
kiṃ ca dhairyam udāhṛtam?
snānaṃ ca kiṃ paraṃ proktaṃ?
dānaṃ ca kim ih' ôcyate?»

YUDHIṢṬHIRA uvāca:

«Sva|dharme sthiratā sthairyam. dhairyam indriya|nigrahaḥ
snānaṃ mano|mala|tyāgo. dānaṃ vai bhūta|rakṣaṇam.»

Yudhi·shthira said:

"Knowledge is understanding of the nature of reality. 90
Peace is a composed mind. Compassion is wishing well in all directions. Rectitude is a balanced mind."

The *yaksha* said:

"What enemy is invincible? And what is an unending disease for man? What kind of person is recalled as honest? What kind as dishonest?"

Yudhi·shthira said:

"Anger is a most invincible enemy, greed is an unending disease. An honest person is recalled as one well disposed toward all beings, a dishonest person as cruel."

The *yaksha* said:

"What is called delusion, king? And what is called pride? What is known as idleness? And what is called grief?"

Yudhi·shthira said:

"Delusion is confusion concerning the Law. Pride is self-conceitedness; idleness neglect of duties. Grief is called ignorance."

The *yaksha* said:

"What do the seers call stability? What is fortitude called? 95
What is the unsurpassed bath? What is liberality?"

Yudhi·shthira said:

"Stability is sticking to one's inherent duty, fortitude is controlling the senses, the unsurpassed bath is washing away the mind's impurities, and liberality is protecting creatures."

YAKṢA uvāca:

«Kaḥ paṇḍitaḥ pumāñ jñeyo? nāstikaḥ kaś ca ucyate?
ko mūrkhaḥ? kaś ca kāmaḥ syāt? ko matsara iti smṛtaḥ?»

YUDHIṢṬHIRA uvāca:

«Dharma|jñaḥ paṇḍito jñeyo. nāstiko mūrkha ucyate.
kāmaḥ saṃsāra|hetuś ca. hṛt|tāpo matsaraḥ smṛtaḥ.»

YAKṢA uvāca:

«Ko 'haṅkāra iti proktaḥ. kaś ca dambhaḥ prakīrtitaḥ?
kiṃ tad daivaṃ paraṃ proktaṃ. kiṃ tat paiśunyam ucyate?»

YUDHIṢṬHIRA uvāca:

100 «Mah"|âjñānam ahaṅkāro.
dambho dharmo dhvaj'|ôcchrayaḥ.
daivaṃ dāna|phalaṃ proktaṃ.
paiśunyaṃ para|dūṣaṇam.»

YAKṢA uvāca:

«Dharmaś c' ârthaś ca kāmaś ca paras|para|virodhinaḥ.
eṣām nitya|viruddhānāṃ katham ekatra saṅgamaḥ?»

YUDHIṢṬHIRA uvāca:

«Yadā dharmaś ca bhāryā ca paras|para|vaś'|ânugau
tadā dharm'|ârtha|kāmānāṃ trayāṇām api saṅgamaḥ.»

YAKṢA uvāca:

«Akṣayo narakaḥ kena prāpyate Bharata'|rṣabha?
etaṃ me pṛcchataḥ praśnaṃ tac chīghraṃ vaktum arhasi!»

The *yaksha* said:

"What man should be thought learned? Who is called an atheist? Who is called stupid? What causes desire? What is envy?"

YUDHI·SHTHIRA said:

"One who knows the Law is thought learned. A stupid person* is called an atheist, an atheist is called stupid. Desire is caused by the cycle of rebirth, and heart's anguish is envy."

The *yaksha* said:

"What is called egoism? What is called hypocrisy? What is the best thing to come from the gods? What is calumny?"

YUDHI·SHTHIRA said:

"Great ignorance is egoism. Hypocrisy is the raising of a 100
religious banner. The fruit of giving is said to come from the gods. Calumny is disparaging others."

The *yaksha* said:

"Law, profit and desire are opposed to one another. How can these perpetual opposites come together in the same place?"

YUDHI·SHTHIRA said:

"When Law and a wife are submissive to each other, then the triad of Law, profit and desire come together."

The *yaksha* said:

"Bull of the Bharatas, who goes to imperishable hell? Answer my question swiftly!"

YUDHIṢṬHIRA uvāca:

«Brāhmaṇaṃ svayam āhūya yācamānam akiñcanam
paścān ‹n' âst' îti› yo brūyāt so 'kṣayaṃ narakaṃ vrajet.
105 Vedeṣu dharma|śāstreṣu mithyā yo vai dvi|jātiṣu
deveṣu pitṛ|dharmeṣu so 'kṣayaṃ narakaṃ vrajet.
Vidyamāne dhane lobhād dāna|bhoga|vivarjitaḥ
paścān ‹n' âst' îti› yo brūyāt so 'kṣayaṃ narakaṃ vrajet.»

YAKṢA uvāca:

«Rājan kulena vṛttena svādhyāyena śrutena vā
brāhmaṇyaṃ kena bhavati? prabrūhy etat suniścitam!»

YUDHIṢṬHIRA uvāca:

«Śṛṇu yakṣa! kulaṃ tāta na svādhyāyo na ca śrutam
kāraṇaṃ hi dvi|jatve ca; vṛttam eva, na saṃśayaḥ.
Vṛttaṃ yatnena saṃrakṣyaṃ brāhmaṇena viśeṣataḥ.
akṣīṇa|vṛtto na kṣīṇo vṛttatas tu hato hataḥ.
110 Paṭhakāḥ pāṭhakāś c' âiva ye c' ânye śāstra|cintakāḥ
sarve vyasanino mūrkhā; yaḥ kriyāvān sa paṇḍitaḥ.
Catur|vedo 'pi dur|vṛttaḥ sa śūdrād atiricyate.
yo 'gnihotra|paro dāntaḥ sa brāhmaṇa iti smṛtaḥ.»

YUDHI·SHTHIRA said:

“He who voluntarily summons a destitute brahmin ask-
ing for a gift, and then tells him there is nothing for him, is
cast into an imperishable hell. He who acts improperly with 105
regard to the Vedas, the Law Manuals, the twice-born, gods
and the rites due to the fathers is cast into an imperishable
hell. He who has wealth but, because of his greed, doesn't
give or enjoy it, and then denies that he has anything, is cast
into an imperishable hell.”

The *yaksha* said:

“By what, king, does one become a brahmin—birth, behavior, study or learning? Say for certain!”

YUDHI·SHTHIRA said:

“Listen, dear *yaksha*, neither birth, study nor learning
make one a brahmin. It's behavior alone, without a doubt!
A brahmin, especially, should take pains to guard his be-
haviour. The man whose conduct does not fail is not cor-
rupted, but one can be undone again and again in line with
one's behavior. Teachers and taught, and others who study 110
the texts, all work hard at being stupid; it's the man who
performs religious rites who is a learned authority. Even a
man who knows the four Vedas is inferior to a servant* if his
behavior is bad. It is the restrained man, who concentrates
on the offering into the fire, who is designated a brahmin.”

YAKṢA uvāca:

«Priya|vacana|vādī kiṃ labhate?
vimṛśita|kārya|karaḥ kiṃ labhate?
bahu|mitra|karaḥ kiṃ labhate?
dharme rataḥ kiṃ labhate? kathaya!»

YUDHIṢṬHIRA uvāca:

«Priya|vacana|vādī priyo bhavati.
vimṛśita|kārya|karo 'dhikaṃ jayati.
bahu|mitra|karaḥ sukhaṃ vasate.
yaś ca dharma|rataḥ sa gatiṃ labhate.»

YAKṢA uvāca:

«Ko modate? kim āścaryaṃ? kaḥ panthāḥ? kā ca vārttikā?
vada me caturaḥ praśnān, mṛtā jīvantu bāndhavāḥ.»

YUDHIṢṬHIRA uvāca:

115 «Pañcame 'hani ṣaṣṭe vā śākaṃ pacati sve gṛhe
an|ṛṇī c' âpravāsī ca sa vāri|cara modate.
Ahany ahani bhūtāni gacchant' îha Yam'|ālayam
śeṣāḥ sthāvaram icchanti. kim āścaryam ataḥ param?
Tarko 'pratiṣṭhaḥ, śrutayo vibhinnā,
n' âika ṛṣir yasya mataṃ pramāṇam,
dharmasya tattvaṃ nihitaṃ guhāyāṃ.
mahā|jano yena gataḥ sa panthāḥ.
Asmin mahā|moha|maye kaṭāhe

The *yaksha* said:

What does the utterer of pleasant words attain?
What is to be gained by the man who performs his actions after consideration?
What does the man who has made many friends obtain?
What does the man devoted to the Law attain? Speak!

YUDHI·SHTHIRA said:

The utterer of pleasant words becomes popular;
The man who performs his actions after consideration acquires an abundance;
The man who has made many friends lives happily;
And the man devoted to the Law attains a good rebirth.

The *yaksha* said:

"Who is happy? What is quite extraordinary? What is the path? And what is the news? Answer my four questions, and your dead brothers shall live."

YUDHI·SHTHIRA said:

"The man who, O water-goer, on the fifth or sixth day, 115
cooks vegetables in his own home, who has no debts and is not in exile, is truly happy. Day after day creatures here go to Yama's realm; the rest go on wanting something permanent. What could be more extraordinary than that?

Reasoning has no foundation,
The revealed texts contradict one another,
There is not one sage whose opinion is authoritative,
The truth concerning the Law is hidden in a cave.
The way the great have gone—that is the path.
In this boiler made from delusion,

sūry'|âgninā rātri|div'|êndhanena
māsa'|rtu|darvī|parighaṭṭanena
bhūtāni kālaḥ pacat' îti vārttā.»

YAKṢA uvāca:

«Vyākhyātā me tvayā praśnā yathā tathyaṃ paraṃ|tapa.
puruṣaṃ tv idānīm vyākhyāhi yaś ca sarva|dhanī naraḥ.»

YUDHIṢṬHIRA uvāca:

120 «Divaṃ spṛśati bhūmiṃ ca śabdaḥ puṇyena karmaṇā.
yāvat sa śabdo bhavati tāvat puruṣa ucyate.
Tulye priy'|âpriye yasya sukha|duḥkhe tath' âiva ca
atīt'|ânāgate c' ôbhe sa vai sarva|dhanī naraḥ.»

YAKṢA uvāca:

«Vyākhyātaḥ puruṣo rājan yaś ca sarva|dhanī naraḥ
tasmāt tvam ekaṃ bhrātṝṇāṃ yam icchasi sa jīvatu.»

YUDHIṢṬHIRA uvāca:

«Śyāmo ya eṣa rakt'|âkṣo bṛhac|chāla iv' ôtthitaḥ
vyūḍh'|ôrasko mahā|bāhur Nakulo yakṣa jīvatu.»

YAKṢA uvāca:

«Priyas te Bhīmaseno 'yam, Arjuno vaḥ parāyaṇam.
sa kasmān Nakulo rājan sāpatnaṃ jīvam icchasi?
125 Yasya nāga|sahasreṇa daśa|saṃkhyena vai balam
tulyaṃ taṃ Bhīmam utsṛjya Nakulaṃ jīvam icchasi?

With the sun as its fire,
and days and nights as its kindling,
With the months and seasons as its stirring ladle,
Time cooks beings—that is the news."

The *yaksha* said:

"You have answered my questions correctly, incinerator of the foe. Tell me now, who is a man, and what man possesses all riches?"

YUDHI·SHTHIRA said:

"The report of a good action touches heaven and earth: 120
as long as that report lasts one is called a man. The man for whom pleasure and pain are the same, and happiness and misery, and both the past and the future, possesses all riches."

The *yaksha* said:

"King, you have told me who is a man, and what man possesses all riches. So one of your brothers will live—you choose."

YUDHI·SHTHIRA said:

"The dark one with red eyes, shot up like a great *shala* tree, broad-chested and mighty-armed—Nákula. Let him live, *yaksha*."

The *yaksha* said:

"Bhima·sena is dear to you, this Árjuna is the support of you all; why, king, do you want Nákula, a half brother, to
live? Giving up Bhima, whose strength is equal to a herd 125
of ten thousand elephants, you want Nákula to live? People say that he, Bhima·sena, is dear to you. Then what kind of

Tath' âinaṃ manujāḥ prāhur Bhīmasenaṃ priyaṃ tava
atha ken' ânubhāvena sāpatnaṃ jīvam icchasi?
Yasya bāhu|balaṃ sarve Pāṇḍavāḥ samupāsate
Arjunaṃ tam apāhāya Nakulaṃ jīvam icchasi?»

YUDHIṢṬHIRA uvāca:

«Dharma eva hato hanti, dharmo rakṣati rakṣitaḥ.
tasmād dharme na tyajāmi, mā no dharmo hato 'vadhīt.
Ānṛśaṃsyaṃ paro dharmaḥ param'|ârthāc ca me matam.
ānṛśaṃsyaṃ cikīrṣāmi: Nakulo yakṣa jīvatu.
130 Dharma|śīlaḥ sadā rājā iti māṃ mānavā viduḥ.
sva|dharmān na caliṣyāmi; Nakulo yakṣa jīvatu.
Kuntī c' âiva tu Mādrī ca dve bhārye tu pitur mama
ubhe saputre syātāṃ vai iti me dhīyate matiḥ.
Yathā Kuntī tathā Mādrī, viśeṣo n' âsti me tayoḥ
mātṛbhyāṃ samam icchāmi: Nakulo yakṣa jīvatu.»

YAKṢA uvāca:

«Tasya te 'rthāc ca kāmāc ca ānṛśaṃsyaṃ paraṃ matam
tasmāt te bhrātaraḥ sarve jīvantu Bharata'|rṣabha.»

VAIŚAṂPĀYANA uvāca:

314.1 Tatas te yakṣa|vacanād udatiṣṭhanta Pāṇḍavāḥ
kṣut|pipāse ca sarveṣāṃ kṣaṇena vyagacchatām.

YUDHIṢṬHIRA uvāca:

«Sarasy ekena pādena tiṣṭhantam aparājitam
pṛcchāmi ko bhavān devo? na me yakṣo mato bhavān.
Vasūnāṃ vā bhavān eko Rudrāṇām atha vā bhavān
atha vā Marutāṃ śreṣṭho vajrī vā tridaś'|ēśvaraḥ?

feeling is it that makes you want your half brother alive? Abandoning Árjuna, on the strength of whose arms all the Pándavas depend, you want Nákula to live?"

YUDHI·SHTHIRA said:

"The Law hurt, the Law hurts: protected, it protects. Therefore, that the Law may not abandon us, I don't abandon the Law. Compassion I consider the highest Law, superior even to the highest goal. My wish is to practice compas-
sion: *yaksha*, let Nákula live! People know this of me: that 130
the king is ever the Law personified. I shall not stray from my inherent duty: *yaksha*, let Nákula live! Kuntí and Madri were my father's two wives: my wish is that they should both have sons. As is Kuntí, so is Madri: for me there is no difference between them. I want the same for both my mothers: *yaksha*, let Nákula live!"

The *yaksha* said:

"Since you regard compassion as superior to profit or pleasure, all your brothers shall live, bull of a Bharata."

VAISHAM·PÁYANA said:

Then, because of the *yaksha*'s words, the Pándavas stood 314.1
up, and the hunger and thirst of them all disappeared in an instant.

YUDHI·SHTHIRA said:

"What god are you, I ask, standing on one leg in a pool, unconquerable? I can't think you're a *yaksha*. Are you one of the Vasus or Rudras, or the best of the Maruts, or the lord of the gods, the thunderbolt-wielder*? My brothers here are the conquerors of hundreds and thousands—I don't see

Mama hi bhrātara ime sahasra|śata|yodhinaḥ
taṃ yodhaṃ na prapaśyāmi yena sarve nipātitāḥ.
5 Sukhaṃ pratiprabuddhānām indriyāṇy upalakṣaye.
sa bhavān suhṛdo 'smākam atha vā naḥ pitā bhavān?»

Yakṣa uvāca:

«Ahaṃ te janakas tāta Dharmo mṛdu|parākrama
tvāṃ didṛkṣur anuprāpto; viddhi māṃ Bharata'|rṣabha.
Yaśaḥ satyaṃ damaḥ śaucam ārjavaṃ hrīr acāpalam
dānaṃ tapo brahmacaryam ity etās tanavo mama.
Ahiṃsā samatā śāntis tapaḥ śaucam amatsaraḥ
dvārāṇy etāni me viddhi, priyo hy asi sadā mama.
Diṣṭyā pañcasu rakto 'si, diṣṭyā te ṣaṭ|padī jitā,
dve pūrve madhyame dve ca dve c' ânte sāṃparāyike.
10 Dharmo 'ham iti bhadraṃ te! jijñāsus tvām ih' âgataḥ.
ānṛśaṃsyena tuṣṭo 'smi varaṃ dāsyāmi te 'nagha.
Varaṃ vṛṇīṣva rāj'|êndra dātā hy asmi tav' ânagha
ye hi me puruṣā bhaktā na teṣām asti durgatiḥ.»

Yudhiṣṭhira uvāca:

«Araṇī|sahitaṃ yasya mṛgo hy ādāya gacchati
tasy' âgnayo na lupyeran, prathamo 'stu varo mama.»

Dharma uvāca:

«Araṇī|sahitaṃ tasya brāhmaṇasya hṛtaṃ mayā
mṛga|veṣeṇa Kaunteya jijñās"|ârthaṃ tava prabho.»

Vaiśaṃpāyana uvāca:

«Dadān' îty» eva bhagavān uttaraṃ pratyapadyata.
«anyaṃ varaya, bhadraṃ te! varaṃ tvam amar'|ôpama.»

that warrior who can slay them all. I can see that their senses 5
have been sweetly awakened—are you, lord, our friend? Or
are you our father?"

The *yaksha* said:

"My son, so mild in your power, I am your father, the
Law. Know that I have come because I wanted to see you,
bull of the Bharatas. Fame, truth, self-control, purity, hon-
esty, modesty, steadiness, liberality, asceticism, chastity—
these are my bodies. Nonviolence, equanimity, peace, as-
ceticism, purity, lack of envy —know that these are my
doors. You are ever dear to me. It is fortunate that you are
devoted to the five,* it is fortunate that you have conquered
the six states —two early, two between, two at the end, lead-
ing to the next world. Honor be yours. I am the Law, come 10
here to examine you. I am pleased by your compassion: I
shall give you a gift, blameless man. Lord of kings, blameless
man, choose a gift, for I shall give it. Nothing bad happens
after death to those men who are devoted to me."

YUDHI·SHTHIRA said:

"May the fire ritual of the brahmin whose fire sticks the deer carried away not be disrupted. Let that be my first gift."

The LAW said:

"Lord Kauntéya, in the guise of a deer I took the brahmin's fire sticks in order to test you."

VAISHAM·PÁYANA said:

"I give it!" said the lord in reply. "Honor to you! Choose another gift, man like an immortal."

YUDHIṢṬHIRA uvāca:

15 Varṣāṇi dvādaś' āraṇye trayodaśam upasthitam.
tatra no n' âbhijānīyur vasato manujāḥ kva cit.

VAIŚAMPĀYANA uvāca:

«Dadān' îty» eva bhagavān uttaraṃ pratyapadyata.
bhūyaś c' âśvāsayām āsa Kaunteyaṃ satya|vikramam:
«Yady api svena rūpeṇa cariṣyatha mahīm imām
na vo vijñāsyate kaś cit triṣu lokeṣu Bhārata.
Varṣaṃ trayodaśaṃ idaṃ mat|prasādāt Kur'|ûdvahāḥ
Virāṭa|nagare gūḍhā avijñātāś cariṣyatha.
Yad vaḥ saṃkalpitaṃ rūpaṃ manasā yasya yādṛśam
tādṛśaṃ tādṛśaṃ sarve chandato dhārayiṣyatha.
20 Araṇī|sahitaṃ c' êdaṃ brāhmaṇāya prayacchata
jijñās"|ârthaṃ mayā hy etad āhṛtaṃ mṛga|rūpiṇā.
Pravṛṇīṣv' âparaṃ saumya varam, iṣṭaṃ dadāni te.
na tṛpyāmi nara|śreṣṭha prayacchan vai varāṃs; tayā
Tṛtīyaṃ gṛhyatāṃ putra varam apratimaṃ mahat.
tvaṃ hi mat|prabhavo rājan Viduraś ca mam' âṃśajaḥ.»

YUDHIṢṬHIRA uvāca:

«Deva|devo mayā dṛṣṭo bhavān sākṣāt sanātanaḥ
yaṃ dadāsi varaṃ tuṣṭas taṃ grahīṣyāmy ahaṃ pitaḥ.
Jayeyaṃ lobha|mohau ca krodhaṃ c' âhaṃ sadā vibho
dāne tapasi satye ca mano me satataṃ bhavet.»

DHARMA uvāca:

25 «Upapanno guṇaiḥ etaiḥ svabhāven' âsi Pāṇḍava
bhavān dharmaḥ punaś c' âiva yath"|ôktaṃ te bhaviṣyati.»

YUDHI·SHTHIRA said:

We have been twelve years in the forest, and the thirteenth 15
is starting. Wherever we dwell, may men fail to recognize
us there.

VAISHAM·PÁYANA said:

"I give it!" said the lord in reply. And again he reassured
Kauntéya, whose prowess was truth. "Even if you wander
this earth in your own shape, Bhárata, no one in the three
worlds will recognize you. By my grace, offspring of the
Kurus, you shall spend this thirteenth year in Viráta's city,
hidden and unrecognized. Whatever appearance each of
you proposes, that you shall all assume, according to your
desire. And return these fire sticks to the brahmin, for, in 20
order to examine you, they were borne away by me in the
form of a deer. Choose another gift, excellent man—I shall
give you what you desire. I am not yet satisfied, best of men,
with giving gifts to you. Take a third, immeasurably great
gift, my son. For you, king, were born of me, and Vídura
of a portion of me."

YUDHI·SHTHIRA said:

"Eternal lord, god of gods, I have seen you with my own eyes. I am satisfied to take whatever gift you give me, father. Lord, may I conquer greed, delusion and anger forever. May my mind be always on liberality, asceticism and truth."

The LAW said:

"You are endowed with these qualities by your own na- 25
ture, Pándava. You are the Law lord—what you asked for
you shall have."

VAIŚAMPĀYANA uvāca:

Ity uktv" ântardadhe dharmo bhagavāl̐ loka|bhāvanaḥ
sametāḥ Pāṇḍavāś c' âiva sukha|suptā manasvinaḥ.
Upetya c' āśramaṃ vīrāḥ sarva eva gata|klamāḥ
āraṇeyaṃ dadus tasmai brāhmaṇāya tapasvine.
Idaṃ samutthāna|samāgataṃ mahat
pituś ca putrasya ca kīrti|vardhanam
paṭhan naraḥ syād vijit'|êndriyo vaśī
sa|putra|pautraḥ śata|varṣa|bhāg bhavet.
Na c' âpy adharme na suhṛd|vibhedane
para|sva|hāre para|dāra|marśane
kadarya|bhāve na ramen manaḥ sadā
nṛṇāṃ sad|ākhyānam idaṃ vijānatām.

VAIŚAMPĀYANA uvāca:

315.1 Dharmeṇa te 'bhyanujñātāḥ Pāṇḍavāḥ satya|vikramāḥ
ajñāta|vāsaṃ vatsyantaś channā varṣaṃ trayodaśam
Upopaviṣṭā vidvāṃsaḥ sahitāḥ saṃśita|vratāḥ
ye tad|bhaktā vasanti sma vana|vāse tapasvinaḥ.
Tān abruvan mah"|ātmānaḥ sthitāḥ prāñjalayas tadā
abhyanujñāpayiṣyantas taṃ nivāsaṃ dhṛta|vratāḥ:
«Viditaṃ bhavatāṃ sarvaṃ Dhārtarāṣṭrair yathā vayam
chadmanā hṛta|rājyāś c' ânyāś ca bahuśaḥ kṛtāḥ.
5 Uṣitāś ca vane kṛcche vayaṃ dvādaśa vatsarān
ajñāta|vāsa|samayaṃ śeṣaṃ varṣaṃ trayodaśam.

VAISHAM·PÁYANA said:

Having said this, the Law, the blessed lord who promotes the welfare of the worlds, disappeared, and the high-minded Pándavas slept together peacefully. Refreshed, the heroes all returned to the hermitage, and gave the fire sticks to that ascetic brahmin.

The man whose senses are controlled,
Who is master of himself,
Who tells this fame-enhancing story of the recovery,
and the reunion of father and son,
Shall live for a hundred years with his sons and
grandsons.
And men who know this true story
Shall never take delight in unlawfulness,
Splitting up friends, taking another's property,
Adultery or miserliness.

VAISHAM·PÁYANA said:

Dismissed by the Law, the Pándavas, whose prowess was 315.1
truth, preparing to spend their thirteenth year disguised and unrecognized, seated themselves close to the wise ascetics, whose vows were strict, and who, through devotion, had been living in the forest with them.

Then, sitting with folded hands, the great-spirited men spoke to them, wanting them to assent to the end of the way of life to which they had been vowed:

"How the Dharta·rashtras deprived us of our kingdom through deceit, and did many other things, is all known to
you. We have lived a difficult life in the forest for twelve 5
years: the thirteenth year, which we have to spend unrec-

Tad vatsyāmo vayaṃ channās, tad anujñātum arhatha.
Suyodhanaś ca duṣṭ'|ātmā Karṇaś ca saha|Saubalaḥ
Jānanto viṣamaṃ kuryur asmāsv atyanta|vairiṇaḥ
yukt'|ācārāś ca yuktāś ca paurasya sva|janasya ca.
Api nas tad bhaved bhūyo yad vayaṃ brāhmaṇaiḥ saha
samastāḥ sveṣu rāṣṭreṣu sva|rājya|sthā bhavemahi?»

VAIŚAMPĀYANA uvāca:

Ity uktvā duḥkha|śok'|ārtaḥ śucir dharma|sutas tadā
saṃmūrchito 'bhavad rājā s'|âśru|kaṇṭho Yudhiṣṭhiraḥ.
10 Tam ath' āśvāsayan sarve brāhmaṇā bhrātṛbhiḥ saha.
atha Dhaumyo 'bravīd vākyaṃ mah"|ârthaṃ nṛpatiṃ tadā:
«Rājan vidvān bhavān dāntaḥ satya|saṃdho jit'|êndriyaḥ.
n' âivaṃ|vidhāḥ pramuhyanti narāḥ kasyāṃ cid āpadi.
Devair apy āpadaḥ prāptāś channaiś ca bahuśas tathā
tatra tatra sapatnānāṃ nigrah'|ârthaṃ mah"|ātmabhiḥ.
Indreṇa Niṣadhān prāpya giri|prasth'|āśrame tadā
channen' ôṣya kṛtaṃ karma dviṣatāṃ ca vinigrahe.
Viṣṇun" âśva|śiraḥ prāpya tath" Adityāṃ nivatsyatā
garbhe vadh'|ârthaṃ daityānām ajñāten' ôṣitaṃ ciram.
15 Prāpya vāmana|rūpeṇa pracchannaṃ Brahma|rūpiṇā
Baler yathā hṛtaṃ rājyaṃ vikramais tac ca te śrutam.
Hut'|âśanena yac c' āpaḥ praviśya channam āsatā
vibudhānāṃ kṛtaṃ karma tac ca sarvaṃ śrutaṃ tvayā.
Pracchannaṃ c' âpi dharma|jña Hariṇ" âri|vinigrahe
vajraṃ praviśya Śakrasya yat kṛtaṃ tac ca te śrutam.
Aurveṇa vasatā channam ūrau Brahma'|rṣiṇā tadā

ognized, remains. Give us permission to live hidden in that way. Should evil-spirited Suyódhana, and Karna, together with Sáubala, discover us, they will make very bad trouble for our relatives and townsfolk; they are committed and dedicated to that kind of action. Can it be that, once again, we shall be established in our sovereignty, united, alongside brahmins, in our kingdoms?"

VAISHAM·PÁYANA said:

Saying this, his voice full of tears, pure King Yudhi·sh·thira, the Law's son, overcome by sorrow and grief, passed out. All the brahmins, and his brothers, revived him. Then Dhaumya made a speech of great moment to the king:

"You are wise, king, mild—a promise-keeper who has controlled his senses. Such men are not discomfited, whatever the emergency. In an emergency, even the great-spirited gods have often hidden themselves in various places so as to overcome their rivals. After going to the Níshadhas, Indra lived in hiding in a refuge on a table-top mountain and did the job of subduing his enemies. Before lying in Áditi's womb, Vishnu, wearing a horse's head, lived for a long time unrecognized in order to kill the *daityas*. You have heard how he whose form is Brahman* hid in the shape of a dwarf, and with his strides took the kingdom from Bali. You have heard everything that Fire did for the gods, once he had entered the waters and hidden himself. And you have heard, Law-knower, what Hari did to subdue his enemies, having entered Shakra's thunderbolt and hidden himself there. You have heard, sinless son, what the brahmin seer Aurva did for the gods, lying hidden in his mother's* thigh.

yat kṛtaṃ tāta deveṣu karma tat te 'nagha śrutaṃ.
Evaṃ Vivasvatā tāta channen' ôttama|tejasā
nirdagdhāḥ śatravāḥ sarve vasatā bhuvi sarvaśaḥ.
20 Viṣṇunā vasatā c" âpi gṛhe Daśarathasya vai
daśa|grīvo hataś channaṃ saṃyuge bhīma|karmaṇā.
Evam ete mah"|ātmānaḥ pracchannās tatra tatra ha
ajayañ śātravān yuddhe; tathā tvam api jeṣyasi.»

Tathā Dhaumyena dharma|jño vākyaiḥ saṃparitoṣitaḥ
śāstra|buddhyā sva|buddhyā ca na cacāla Yudhiṣṭhiraḥ.
Ath' âbravīn mahā|bāhur Bhīmaseno mahā|balaḥ
rājānaṃ balināṃ śreṣṭho girā saṃpariharṣayan:

«Avekṣayā mahā|rāja tava Gāṇḍīva|dhanvanā
dharm'|ânugatayā buddhyā na kiṃ cit sāhasaṃ kṛtam.
25 Sahadevo mayā nityaṃ Nakulaś ca nivāritau
śaktau vidhvaṃsane teṣāṃ śatrūṇāṃ bhīma|vikramau.
Na vayaṃ tat prahāsyāmo yasmin yokṣyati* no bhavān.
bhavān vidhattāṃ tat sarvaṃ; kṣipraṃ jeṣyāmahe ripūn.»

Ity ukte Bhīmasenena brāhmaṇāḥ param'|āśiṣā
uktvā c' āpṛcchya Bharatān yathā svān svān yayur gṛhān.
Sarve veda|vido mukhyā yatayo munayas tathā
asedus te yathā|nyāyaṃ punar darśana|kāṅkṣiṇaḥ
Saha Dhaumyena vidvāṃsas tathā pañca ca Pāṇḍavāḥ
utthāya prayayur vīrāḥ Kṛṣṇām ādāya dhanvinaḥ.
30 Krośa|mātram upagamya tasmād deśān nimittataḥ
śvo|bhūte manuja|vyāghrāś channa|vās'|ârtham udyatāḥ
Pṛthak|śāstra|vidaḥ sarve sarve mantra|viśāradāḥ
saṃdhi|vigraha|kāla|jñā mantrāya samupāviśan.

So too Vivásvat, my boy, whose luster is supreme, who lived
hidden on earth, and entirely incinerated all his enemies.
Living disguised in Dasha·ratha's house,* Vishnu, whose 20
deeds are terrible, killed the ten-headed one in combat. So
these great souls, hiding in various places, defeated their
enemies in battle. In that way, you too shall be victorious."

Thus the Law-knower was comforted by Dhaumya's
words; because of his inherent knowledge, and because he
knew the texts, Yudhi·shthira did not falter. Then the fore-
most of the strong, supremely strong, great-armed Bhima·
sena spoke encouraging words to the king:

"Out of respect for you, great king, the Gandíva bowman,
with an intelligence in line with the Law, has not done
anything violent. Saha·deva and Nákula, whose prowess is 25
terrible, and who have the power to crush their enemies, are
constantly restrained by me. We shall not give up what you
employ us to do. You direct everything—we shall quickly
conquer our enemies."

So spoke Bhima·sena. Then the brahmins, having pro-
nounced the greatest blessings, took leave of the Bharatas,
and went each to his own home. Then all the preeminent,
Veda-knowing ascetics and hermits departed, in the hope
that they would see them again. Along with Dhaumya, the
five wise Pándavas rose up, and, taking Krishná, the archer
heroes set out.

Having gone, for a reason, only within shouting distance 30
of that place, on the next day those tigerish men, ready for
their life in disguise, all familiar with different techniques,
all experienced in conference, knowing the time for peace
and the time for war, sat down together in council.

NOTES

Bold *references are to the English text;* ***bold italic*** *references are to the Sanskrit text. An asterisk (*) in the body of the text marks the word or passage being annotated.*

273.1 The special accenting of **Krishná** on the final syllable is in order to properly differentiate her name, *Kṛṣṇā* (with a Sanskrit feminine ending), from that of the well-known, male, Krishna, *Kṛṣṇa*. **Krishná's abduction**: i.e. the abduction of Dráupadi, the Pándavas' wife.

273.6 KINJAWADEKAR's *bhagavān* emended to ***balavān***.

273.12 KINJAWADEKAR's *iyam* emended to ***ayam***.

275.40 **Because he made the worlds cry out:** a play on *rāvayām*, "causing to cry out," so deriving an etymology of Rávana's name from the verbal root *ru*, "to cry out."

276.6 **The grandfather:** Brahma.

277.26 **Rághava:** Rama.

277.39 **His sandals:** i.e., Rama's sandals, demonstrating the latter's superiority.

277.43 **Rághava:** Rama.

277.55 **Trident-bearer:** Shiva.

278.13 **Kákutstha:** Rama.

278.14 **Performed the water offering for himself:** in anticipation of his death.

278.17 **The princess of Vidéha:** Sita.

278.19 **Rudra after the stellar deer:** in a well-known myth, Rudra (Shiva) disrupts the gods' sacrifice, which then flees to the sky in the form of a deer.

278.28 **Rághava:** Rama.

278.38 **The delight of Raghu:** Rama.

278.40 KINJAWADEKAR's *smaret* emended to ***smare***.

279.11 **He:** i.e., Rávana.

279.16 KINJAWADEKAR's *Vaidehīm iti* emended to ***Vaidehī neti***.

279.38 **His right arm:** i.e., the demon's.

280.38 Kinjawadekar's *tārāpatisamaujasam* emended to ***tārāpatim iva cyutam***.

280.41 **Nándana:** Indra's celestial pleasure garden.

280.42 **Ashóka:** a type of tree.

280.53 Kinjawadekar's *ādṛtāḥ* emended to ***āditaḥ***.

281.3 **Ashóka:** a type of tree.

281.5 Kinjawadekar's *na* emended to ***sa***.

281.21 Kinjawadekar's *opayikī* emended to ***aupayikī***.

281.27 **Mákara-bannered god:** the Mákara is a mythical crocodile-like animal; one is represented on the banner of Kama, the god of love.

282.27 **The son of the Wind:** Hanúmat.

282.30 **The princess of Míthila:** Sita.

282.39 **Yójanas:** according to some calculations, a *yójana* is a distance of about nine miles.

282.47 **Son of Vínata:** Gáruda.

282.59 **My father:** the Wind.

282.70 **The arrow thrown at the crow on Chitra·kuta peak:** an incident in which Rama had saved Sita from a pestering crow.

283.5 Kinjawadekar's *śatasasrāṇi* (misprint?) emended to ***śatasahasrāṇi***.

283.32 **Kusha grass:** sacred grass used in Vedic ritual.

283.38 **Váruna's resort:** the sea.

284.3 **Khádira wood:** wood used for making sacrificial posts.

284.23 **The joy of Raghu:** Rama.

284.28 **Shirísha:** a delicate flower similar to the mimosa.

284.40 **Sumítra's son:** Lákshmana.

285.6 **Úshanas:** the preceptor of the demons.

285.7 **Brihas·pati:** the preceptor of the gods.

288.3 **Husband of Shachi:** Indra.

288.17 KINJAWADEKAR's *pāśva* (misprint?) emended to ***pārśve***.

289.17 **Before he had performed his daily rites:** since, according to Vibhíshana (in the RAMÁYANA), he will be invincible if allowed to complete them.

289.27 **Ashóka:** a type of tree.

291.4 **Imperishable one:** Yudhi·shthira.

291.17 **Pure-spirited god:** Brahma.

291.61 **He returned again:** i.e., Rama returned again.

292.4 **The thunderbolt-wielder:** Indra.

293.9 **Sávitri mantra:** a famous and powerful mantra (also known as Gáyatri) addressed to the Sun. Taken from Ṛg Veda 3.62.10, it is supposed to be recited by every male who has been initiated into Vedic ritual at his morning and evening rites.

293.10 **Sávitri:** the personification of the mantra as a goddess.

293.11 **Agni·hotra:** the daily oblation made to the fire, and the ritual named after it. The Savítri mantra is recited as part of this ritual.

293.14 KINJAWADEKAR's *apatyāthaḥ* emended to ***apatyārthaḥ***.

293.15 **Twice-born:** those initiated into Vedic ritual, especially brahmins.

293.16 **The Grandsire:** Brahma.

293.17 **The Self-existent:** Brahma.

294.12 **"Sátyavat":** literally "possessing the truth" *(satya/vat)*.

294.13 **"Chitráshva":** literally 'has painted horses' *(citr'/âśva)*.

295.4 **Kusha:** species of grass, regarded as sacred, and so a suitable seat for a king.

295.12 KINJAWADEKAR's *sutaḥ* emended to ***sutām***.

295.23 For KINJAWADEKAR's *sāvitryā glāyamāmāyās tiṣṭhantyās tu* read ***sāvitryās tu śayānāyās tiṣṭhantyāś ca***.

297.19 **The south:** the direction of death. Yama is Dákshina·pati, "the lord of the south."

297.23 KINJAWADEKAR's *tatvārthadarśinaḥ* emended to ***tattvārthadarśinaḥ***.

297.36 KINJAWADEKAR's *eyaṃ* (misprint?) emended to ***evaṃ***.

297.34 Status as Yama: "Constrainer"; he constrains creatures and leads them off, but he does so under the constraint of natural law, not because he wants to.

297.49 **The Nobles:** lit. the Aryans, the self-designation of those who brought Vedic culture into the subcontinent.

297.51 KINJAWADEKAR's *manonukulaṃ* emended to ***manonukūlaṃ***.

297.70 **Asmi iti:** with hiatus.

297.110 KINJAWADEKAR's *uttareṇaḥ* (misprint?) emended to ***uttareṇa***.

299.16 **Kámyaka:** one of the areas in which the Pándavas were living in exile in the forest.

300.9 KINJAWADEKAR's *yogardhirūpavān* (misprint?) emended to ***yogarddhirūpavān***.

300.38 KINJAWADEKAR's *vīddhi* (misprint?) emended to ***viddhi***.

301.16 **Left-handed archer:** Árjuna.

304.9 **Chyávana. . . Sukánya:** see "The Forest" 3.122f. (Crit. Ed. 3.121f.) for an account of this episode.

304.14 KINJAWADEKAR's *yatā* (misprint?) emended to ***yat***.

304.17 KINJAWADEKAR's *ukta* emended to ***ukte***.

304.17 KINJAWADEKAR's *asmat* emended to ***asya***.

307.13 The verbal root *kan* means "to desire"; *kanyā* is a noun, derived from the root, meaning "young girl" or "virgin."

308.26 **The *suta:*** Ádhiratha (see 3.309); the designation *suta* shows that he is of mixed caste.

309.13 **Vasu·shena:** derived here from the word meaning "valuable" *(vasu)*.

309.16 **The city named after the elephant:** Hástina·pura.

310.18 KINJAWADEKAR's *āyān* emended to ***āyann***.

310.27 **The very one you want:** Árjuna.

310.38 **He is "Karna":** *karṇa* means "ear."

310.42 KINJAWADEKAR's *Kāmyāśu?* emended to ***Kāmyakād***.

310.43 Verse omitted from KINJAWADEKAR's ed. (in error?), supplied from Critical Edition.

310.43 **Dvaita·vana:** another part of the forest.

311.10 **agni·hotra:** the daily oblation made to the fire, and the ritual named after it.

312.3 **The Suta's son:** Karna.

312.40 KINJAWADEKAR's *anuktaiva tu* emended to ***avijñāyaiva***.

312.45 KINJAWADEKAR's *sindhuvāraiḥ sacetasaiḥ* emended to ***sindhuvārais ca vetasaiḥ***.

313.23 **Gandhára king:** Duryódhana.

313.32 **Himálaya, Pariyátra, Vindhya and Málaya:** mountain ranges, here compared to the four stricken Pándavas.

313.44 KINJAWADEKAR's *praśaṃse puruṣarṣabha* emended to ***praśaṃset puruṣaḥ prabho***.

313.86 **A brahmin is the time for the ritual for the dead:** i.e., whenever a brahmin is available there is an opportunity to perform the ritual.

313.89 KINJAWADEKAR's *ārjam* (misprint?) emended to ***ārjavam***.

313.98 **A stupid person. . . :** in the Sanskrit a single answer is provided to both questions, which can be read in either of the ways indicated in the translation.

313.111 **A servant:** i.e., someone belonging to the *śūdra* class or estate, which is not allowed access to the Veda.

314.3 **The thunderbolt-wielder:** Indra.

314.9 **The five:** according to the commentator Nila·kantha, freedom from passions, restraint, indifference, endurance and meditation. **The six states:** according to Nila·kantha, hunger and thirst, grief and delusion, decrepitude and death.

315.15 **He whose form is Brahman:** Vishnu.

315.18 "His mother's" supplied.

315.20 **Disguised in Dasha·ratha's house:** as Rama. **The ten-headed one:** Rávana.

315.26 KINJAWADEKAR's *yokṣyati* emended to ***mokṣyati***.

PROPER NAMES AND EPITHETS

Áchyuta Yudhi·shthira

Ádhiratha Karna's foster father

Áditi Vedic goddess of space; mother of the gods

Ádityas a collection of gods

Agni fire, and the fire god

Aja a king of the Ikshváku dynasty; father of Dasha·ratha; grandfather of Rama, Lákshmana, Shatru·ghna and Bharata

Ajáta·shatru Yudhi·shthira

Ángada a commander in Sugríva's monkey-army; son of Valin and Tará; nephew of Sugríva

Āpa·stamba ancient seer and priest

Ápsaras celestial "nymphs"; companions of the *gandhárvas*

Árjuna third of the five Pándava brothers; = Dhanam·jaya = Partha Dhanam·jaya

Áruna the god of the dawn; Jatáyu's father

Áruja one of the Pishácha and demon warriors

Ashva·pati king of the Madras; father of Savítri

Ashvins twin gods; fathers of the Pándava twins, Nákula and Saha·deva, by Madri

Athárva·shiras name of an Upanishad

Aurva brahmin seer miraculously born from his mother's thigh

Avíndhya a minister of Rávana

Bala one of the monkey-army

Bali a king tricked by Vishnu, in the shape of a dwarf, into giving his kingdom to the brahmins

Bhima second of the five Pándava brothers; = Bhima·sena = Vrikódara

Bhima·sena Bhima

Bharad·vaja an ancient seer

Bharata (1) son of Dasha·ratha and Kaikéyi; younger brother of Rama

BHARATA (2) prototypical ruler of northern India; ancestor of most of the characters in the MAHA·BHÁRATA

BHÁRATA descendant of Bharata; Yudhi·shthira

BRAHMA creator god; = the Grandsire; = the Self-existent

BRAHMAN the Absolute, equated at 315.15 with Vishnu

BRIHAS·PATI the priest or preceptor of the gods

CHANDA·BALA one of the monkey-army

CHÁRANAS celestial beings

CHITRÁSHVA "having painted horses"; = Sátyavat

CHYÁVANA an ancient seer; husband of Sukánya

DADHI·MUKHA a monkey general; Sugríva's uncle

DAITYA one of a group of anti-gods

DALBHYA an ancient seer

DÁNAVA one of a group of anti-gods

DASHA·RATHA father of Rama, Lákshmana, Shatru·ghna and Bharata; king of Ayódhya

DÚSHANA a demon general

DHRITA·RASHTRA the blind Kuru king; father of the hundred Káuravas, including Duryódhana

DHANAM·JAYA Árjuna

DHARMA the personification of the Law (dharma); a god, and Yudhi·shthira's father

DHARTA·RSHTRAS the Káuravas

DHAUMYA (1) an ancient seer

DHAUMYA (2) family priest of the Pándavas

DHUMRÁKSHA a demon general

DIRGHA·JIHVA a demoness at Rávana's palace

DRÁUPADI wife of the five Pándava brothers; Drúpada's daughter; = Krishná

DRONA brahmin warrior; teacher of the Káuravas and Pándavas; father of Ashva·tthaman

DRÚPADA king of the Panchálas; father of Dráupadi

DÚNDUBHI a *gandhárvi* who descends into the world of men as the hunchback Mánthara

DURYÓDHANA eldest son of Dhrita·rashtra; king of the Káuravas

DVI·VIDA one of Sugríva's counsellors, and a general in the monkey-army

DYUMAT·SENA king of the Shalvas; husband of Shaibya; father of Sátyavat

GAJA a monkey general

GANDHA·MÁDANA (1) a monkey general

GANDHA·MÁDANA (2) a mountain in the Himálayas

GANDHÁRA (king) Duryódhana

GANDHÁRVI a female *gandhárva*

GANDHÁRVA celestial beings; companions of the *ápsaras*

GANDÍVA (bowman) Árjuna

GÁRUDA a bird deity; Vishnu-Krishna's "vehicle," or mount; son of Vínata

GÁUTAMA an ancient seer

GAVÁKSHA a monkey general

GÁVAYA a monkey general

GUDA·KESHA Árjuna

GÚHYAKA a celestial being associated with Kubéra

HANÚMAT popularly known as Hanúman; one of Sugríva's counsellors, and a general in the monkey-army; son of Vayu (the Wind)

HARI (1) one of the Pishácha and demon warriors

HARI (2) Vishnu

IKSHVÁKU the first king of Ayódhya; dynasty named after him

INDRA king of the gods; father of Árjuna; = Shakra = Vásava

INDRA·JIT eldest son of Rávana; = Megha·nada; known by the epithet "Indra·jit" – "Conqueror of Indra" – because he once overcame the god Indra in battle

ISHÁNA = a form of Shiva, one of the two great Hindu gods (cf. Vishnu)

JATÁYU king of the vultures

JAMAD·AGNYA brahmin with warrior tendencies

JÁMBAVAT the king of the bears; one of Sugríva's counsellors

JAMBHA one of the *pishácha* and demon warriors

JÁNAKI = Sita

JÁNAKA king of Vidéha; Sita's father

JANAM·EJAYA a king; direct descendant of the Pándavas; the Maha·bhárata is recited to him by Vaishaṃ·páyana

JAYAD·RATHA king of Sindh; brother-in-law of Duryódhana; during their exile in the forest, abducts the Pándavas' wife, Dráupadi (= Krishná)

JISHNU Árjuna

KABÁNDHA a monster; takes its name from a round-bellied water pot, or cask, which it resembles

KAIKÉYI one of Dasha·ratha's wives; Bharata's mother

KÁKUTSTHA "descendant of Kakútstha"; = Rama; = (less frequently) Lákshmana

KARNA ally of Duryódhana; the Pándavas' older half brother; son of Kuntí and the Sun; foster son of Ádhiratha and Radha; = Radhéya = Vrisha = Vasu·shena

KÁUNTEYA Yudhi·shthira

KÁUSALYA wife of Dasha·ratha; mother of Rama; princess of Kósala

KÉTAKAS a kind of tree or bush

KHARA (1) one of the *pishácha* and demon warriors

KHARA (2) Rávana's younger brother

KIM·NARA "quasi-man"; similar to *yaksha*, but resembling a man; = Kim·púrusha

KIM·PÚRUSHA = *kim·nara*

KÓSALA country of which Ayódhya is the capital

KRATHA a commander in Sugríva's monkey-army

KRODHA·VASHA one of the *pishácha* and demon warriors

KRISHNÁ = Dráupadi

KRISHNA descent *(avatár)* of the god Vishnu; allied to the Pándavas

KUBÉRA lord of riches; leader of the *yaksha*s and demons; = Vaishrávana

KUMBHA·KARNA "pot-eared"; Rávana's giant brother

KÚMUDA one of Sugríva's monkey followers

KUNTÍ adopted daughter of King Kunti·bhoja; wife of Pandu; mother of the three eldest Pándava brothers, and, by the Sun, of Karna; = Pritha

KUNTI = Kunti·bhoja

KUNTI·BHOJA foster father of Kuntí

KURUS (best of the) Yudhi·shthira

KURUS descendants of Kuru; the Káuravas and Pándavas; sometimes just the sons of Dhrita·rashtra and their followers

LÁKSHMANA younger half brother of Rama; elder twin brother of Shatru·ghna; son of Dasha·ratha and Sumítra

LANKA name of an island; Rávana's capital city on that island

LÓMASHA seer accompanying the Pándavas and Dráupadi

MADRAS people of the North; ruled over by Ashva·pati

MÁDREYA "son of Madri" (Nákula)

MADRI Pandu's second wife; mother of the Pándava twins Nákula and Saha·deva

MÁGHAVAT Indra

MAINDA one of Sugríva's counsellors, and a general in the monkey-army

MÁLAVI wife to Ashva·pati

MÁLAVA descendants of Málavi

MÁLINI a demoness; mother of Vibhíshana

MANDÓDARI Rávana's favorite wife; mother of Indra·jit

MÁNTHARA Kaikéyi's maidservant; incarnation of Dúndubhi

MANU first man, and progenitor of the human race; archetypal sage

MARÍCHA demon; once a minister of Rávana

MARKANDÉYA ancient brahmin sage; narrator of the stories of Rama and Sávitri

MARUTS storm gods, forming Indra's entourage

MÁTALI Indra's charioteer

MAYA architect of the *daityas*; earthly counterpoint of Vishva·karman

MÍTHILA capital city of Vidéha; ruled by Jánaka

NÁKULA one of the Pándava twins (brother of Saha·deva); son of Madri and the Ashvins

NALA a monkey general

NALA·KÚBARA son of Kubéra (= Vaishrávana); nephew of Rávana; husband of Rambha

NÁNDANA Indra's garden

NANDI·GRAMA a village

NÁRADA an ancient seer

NARÁYANA name of Vishnu; = Krishna

NIKHÁRVATA a demon

NOLA a monkey general

NÍRRITI goddess of death, evil and dissolution; mother of demons

NÍSHADHAS name of a people

PAKA a *daitya* killed by Indra

PÁNASA a monkey general

PÁNDAVAS the five sons of Pandu, viz. Yudhi·shthira, Bhima, Árjuna, Nákula, Saha·deva; their followers and relatives

PANDU heir to the Lunar Dynasty; brother of Dhrita·rashtra; legal father of the Pándavas; husband of Kuntí and Madri

PANDU'S SON Yudhi·shthira

PANDUS Pándavas

PARTHA DHANAM·JAYA Árjuna

PARTHA "son of Pritha (Kuntí)": Yudhi·shthira

PARTHAS the three Pándava sons of Pritha (Kuntí)

PÁRVANA one of the Pishácha and demon warriors

PÁTANA one of the Pishácha and demon warriors

PÁTUSHA a demon

PÁULASTYA descendant of Pulástya

PAULÓMI a goddess pesonifying divine power; daughter of Pulóman; wife of Indra; = Shachi

PHÁLGUNA Árjuna

PISHÁCHA low, flesh-eating demon

PRABHÁVATI a female ascetic

PRÁGHASA one of the Pishácha and demon warriors

PRAHÁSTA Rávana's chief counsellor

PRAHLÁDA a *daitya* who, inter alia, tried to claim Indra's throne

PRAJA·PATI the secondary creator or demiurge

PRAMÁTHIN a demon

PRÁRUJA one of the Pishácha and demon warriors

PRITHA Kuntí

PURAN·DARA "destroyer of strongholds"; = Indra

PULÁSTYA the father of Vaishrávana (= Kubéra) and (as Víshravas) of Rávana, Vibhíshana and others

PÚSHPAKA a sky-going chariot belonging to Kubéra; taken by Rávana, but retaken by Rama, and returned to Kubéra

PUSHPÓTKATA a demoness; mother of Rávana and Kumbha·karna

PUSHYA name of an asterism

RADHA foster mother of Karna

RADHÉYA Karna

RÁGHAVA "descendant of Raghu"; = Rama

RAGHU Rama's great-grandfather

RAKA a demoness

RAMA son of Dasha·ratha and Kausályа; husband of Sita; half brother of Lákshmana; eventual ruler of Ayódhya; either associated with Vishnu or his incarnation

RAMBHA an *ápsaras*; wife of Nala·kúbara

RANTI·DEVA Sánkriti a king of the Lunar dynasty who spent his wealth on sacrifices (and so on giving to priests)

RÁVANA ten-headed demon-king; ruler of Lanka; son of Víshravas and Pushpótkata

RÓHINI a lunar asterism

RUDRA Vedic storm god; later = Shiva

SHACHI (husband of) Indra

SADHYA celestial being

SAHA·DEVA one of the Pándava twins (brother of Nákula); son of Madri and the Ashvins

SHAIBYA wife of Dyumat·sena; mother of Sátyavat

SÁINDHAVA "coming from the country of Sindh (Sindhu)"; Jayad·ratha

SHAKRA Indra

SHÁKUNI king of Gandhára; uncle of Duryódhana, for whom he wins the rigged dicing match against Yudhi·shthira

SHALVA people ruled over by Dyumat·sena

SAMPÁTI vulture king; son of Áruna; brother of Jatáyu

SHARA·BHANGA a seer

SÁRANA demon; one of Rávana's counsellors

SHATRU·GHNA son of Dasha·ratha and Sumítra; younger twin brother of Lákshmana; half brother of Rama and Bharata

SÁTYAVAT son of Dyumat·sena and Shaibya; husband of Savítri

SAUBALA Shákuni

SAVÍTRI (1) daughter of Ashva·pati; wife of Sátyavat

SAVÍTRI (2) name of a mantra, personified as a goddess; = Gayátri

SHIBI AUSHÍNARA (1) an ancient seer

SHIBI AUSHÍNARA (2) a king renowned for his liberality and unselfishness

SIDDHAS ascetics who have acquired great powers; equivalent celestial beings

SITA wife of Rama; daughter of Jánaka; princess of Vidéha; = Jánaki

SHIVA one of the two great Hindu gods (cf. Vishnu)

SHRI goddess of prosperity

SUGRÍVA the monkey-king; younger brother of Valin

SHUKA one of Rávana's counsellors

SUKÁNYA young wife of the ancient seer Chyávana

SUMÍTRA wife of Dasha·ratha; mother of Lákshmana and Shatru·ghna

SHURA a Yádava; father of Vasu·deva and Pritha (Kuntí)

SHURPA·NAKHA demoness; Rávana's younger half sister

SURYA (god of) the sun

SUSHÉNA a monkey-general

SUVARCHAS Agni

SUYÓDHANA Duryódhana

SVAR·BHANU demon associated with darkness and eclipses

TALA·JANGHA an anti-god

TARA a monkey-general

TARÁ female monkey; daughter of Sushéna; wife of Valin (then of Sugríva); mother of Ángada

TRI·JATA a demoness

TUNDA a demon

ÚSHANAS the priest or preceptor of the demons

VÁISHNAVA constellation governed by Vishnu

VAISHAM·PÁYANA pupil of Vyasa (seer and "author" of the epic); recites the MAHA·BHÁRATA to Janam·ejaya

VAISHRÁVANA = Kubéra

VAIVÁSVATA descendant of Vivásvat; Yama

VAJRA·BAHU a monkey warrior

VAJRA·VEGA a demon

VALA demonic being defeated by Indra

VALIN a monkey-king; ruler of Kishkíndha; elder brother of Sugríva; husband of Tara; father of Ángada

VAMA·DEVA seer; one of Dasha·ratha's ministers

VÁRUNA major god of the Vedic pantheon; in later mythology god of the ocean

VÁSAVA Indra

VASÍSHTHA Vedic seer and priest of the Ikshváku dynasty

VASU·SHENA Karna

VASU·DEVA brother of Pritha (Kuntí)

VASU a class of gods

VATÁPI an anti-god

VAYU god of the wind

VISHNU one of the two great Hindu gods (cf. Shiva); from time to time equated in the MAHA·BHÁRATA with Rama and, in particular, with Krishna

VIBHÍSHANA demon; son of Víshravas and Málini; younger half brother of Rávana

VIDÉHA country ruled by Jánaka

VÍDURA uncle of both sets of cousins (the Kurus and the Pándavas)

VÍJAYA Árjuna

VÍNATA mother of Gáruda

VIRÁTA king of the Matsyas

VIRUPÁKSHA a demon

VISHÁKHA a constellation

VÍSHRAVAS father of Rávana, Vibhíshana and other demons; cf. Pulástya

VISHVA·KARMAN architect of the gods

VISHVA·VASU a *gandhárva*; emerges from Kabándha's body

VIVÁSVAT "the brilliant one" = the Sun

VRIKÓDARA "wolf belly" = Bhima

VRISHA Karna

VRISHNIS Krishna's "race," and under his protection

VRITRA Vedic demon, the instigator of a universal drought; killed by Indra

YAKSHAS tree spirits, able to assume any shape

YAMA the god of death

YAYÁTI an ancient king

YUDHI·SHTHIRA first of the five Pándava brothers; = Bhárata; = Partha; = "best of the Kurus"

INDEX

Sanskrit words are given according to the accented CSL pronuncuation aid in the English alphabetical order. They are followed by the conventional diacritics in brackets.

Permitted finals:

k	ṭ	t	p	ṅ	n	m	(*Except* āḥ/aḥ) ḥ/r	āḥ	aḥ	*Initial letters:*
k	ṭ	t	p	ṅ	n	ṃ	ḥ	āḥ	aḥ	k/kh
g	ḍ	d	b	ṅ	n	ṃ	r	ā	o	g/gh
k	ṭ	c	p	ṅ	ṃś	ṃ	ś	āś	aś	c/ch
g	ḍ	j	b	ṅ	ñ	ṃ	r	ā	o	j/jh
k	ṭ	ṭ	p	ṅ	ṃṣ	ṃ	ṣ	āṣ	aṣ	ṭ/ṭh
g	ḍ	ḍ	b	ṅ	ṇ	ṃ	r	ā	o	ḍ/ḍh
k	ṭ	t	p	ṅ	ṃs	ṃ	s	ās	as	t/th
g	ḍ	d	b	ṅ	n	ṃ	r	ā	o	d/dh
k	ṭ	t	p	ṅ	n	ṃ	ḥ	āḥ	aḥ	p/ph
g	ḍ	d	b	ṅ	n	ṃ	r	ā	o	b/bh
ṅ	ṇ	n	m	ṅ	n	ṃ	r	ā	o	*nasals* (n/m)
g	ḍ	d	b	ṅ	n	ṃ	r	ā	o	y/v
g	ḍ	d	b	ṅ	n	ṃ	*zero*[1]	ā	o	r
g	ḍ	l	b	ṅ	l̃[2]	ṃ	r	ā	o	l
k	ṭ	c ch	p	ṅ	ñ ś/ch	ṃ	ḥ	āḥ	aḥ	ś
k	ṭ	t	p	ṅ	n	ṃ	ḥ	āḥ	aḥ	ṣ/s
gg h	ḍḍ h	dd h	bb h	ṅ	n	ṃ	r	ā	o	h
g	ḍ	d	b	ṅ/ṅṅ[3]	n/nn[3]	m	r	ā	a[4]	*vowels*
k	ṭ	t	p	ṅ	n	m	ḥ	āḥ	aḥ	*zero*

[1]ḥ or r disappears, and if a/i/u precedes, this lengthens to ā/ī/ū. [2]e.g. tān+lokān=tāl̃ lokān.
[3]The doubling occurs if the preceding vowel is short. [4]Except: aḥ+a=o '.